On Trial:
American History Through Court Proceedings and Hearings

On Trial:

American History Through Court Proceedings and Hearings

Volume II

Edited by

Robert D. Marcus and Anthony Marcus

BRANDYWINE PRESS • St. James, New York

Cover design by Jill Gussow

Table of Contents

To

Abigail, Benjamin, Elizabeth, and Zora

PREFACE

Both historians and the general public have long shared a fascination with judicial proceedings. Newspapers give extensive coverage to trials, both those that command national attention and the many that appeal to local interest. Fictional trials are a steady theme of television and film. Since the Civil War, legislative hearings and similar quasi-judicial public investigations have periodically fixed public attention on a wide variety of phenomena, among them the Ku Klux Klan; the insurance, armaments, and tobacco industries; Brooklyn's Murder Incorporated; Communists in government; the assassination of John F. Kennedy; the Watergate affair; and sexual harassment. Historians study these trials and hearings not only to gain an understanding of the case or issue under examination, but also to deepen understanding of the society in which they occurred. As the distinguished historian Natalie Zemon Davis writes, "a remarkable dispute can sometimes uncover motivations and values that are lost in the welter of the everyday."

On Trial is the first anthology based on edited transcripts of American trials and hearings for use in American history survey classrooms. Selections are of appropriate length for student assignment and for insight into the cases and their circumstances without weighting the reader down in technicalities of legal procedure. This volume presents through unusually rich and engaging historical material many of the standard subjects taught in the second half of American history surveys. Students will encounter the Reconstruction era through one of the South Carolina Ku Klux Klan trials, women's rights in Susan B. Anthony's trial for registering and voting in the 1872 elections; Western history in the trial of Frank James for train robbery and murder; a snapshot of American labor in the Haymarket trials; the contest between urban progressives and city bosses in Edward Butler's trial, and the beginnings of protective labor legislation in the progressive era through briefs from *Muller v. Oregon*. In the trial of Kate O'Hare under the Sedition Act, the domestic impact of World War I reveals itself. The Scopes trial captures the cultural tension of the 1920s, the Scottsboro case, the tortured path toward civil rights in the 1930s, the Army-McCarthy

Hearings, domestic effects of the Cold War. Complex dilemmas the Supreme Court has faced in dealing with its most controversial cases since World War II are articulated through oral arguments in one of the school segregation cases that culminate in *Brown v. Board of Education* and in the abortion case *Roe v. Wade*. The Karen Ann Quinlan case dramatizes new issues of life and death created by modern medical technology. The volume ends with the hearings involving Ms. Anita Hill before the Senate Judiciary Committee over the nomination of Clarence Thomas to the Supreme Court.

We would like to thank the many people who helped us with this book, especially Jill Gussow, who designed the cover, Tom West and David Burner, who edited the manuscript, and Charles A. Peach, who produced the books.

Robert D. Marcus
Anthony Marcus

1
Reconstruction in the South
The Lynching of Jim Williams
1871

The original Ku Klux Klan, founded as a fraternity in Pulaski, Tennessee, in 1866, quickly turned into a terrorist organization. Its actions were sporadic and never widely coordinated, but in many rural counties the Klan, enrolling much of the white male population, intimidated, assaulted, and murdered blacks and their Republican allies to prevent African Americans from exercising their newly acquired right to vote. In 1871, when these night riders rampaged unhindered through an entire section of South Carolina, their outrages provoked the Republican Congress to pass the Ku Klux Klan Act giving the President extraordinary temporary powers to use the United States Army to make arrests when the local authorities dominated by the Klan refused to do so. After a large posse of Klansmen, led by some of the first citizens of Yorkville, South Carolina, seized and hanged Jim Williams, a leader of black opposition to the Klan, on the night of March 6, 1871, President Ulysses S. Grant ordered the army into action. Arrests of hundreds of Klansmen led to numerous prosecutions in federal courts. Government attorneys, questioning many witnesses and citing numerous documents, revealed the conspiratorial and terrorist nature of the Klan, sent a few Klansmen to jail, and effectively ended the Reconstruction Klan's activities. Robert Hayes Mitchell, whose trial is presented here, was tried for participating in the raid that led to Jim Williams's hanging, but not for the murder itself.

The Trial of Robert Hayes Mitchell for Conspiracy, _In the United States Circuit Court, Columbia, South Carolina, December, 1871._
HON. HUGH L. BOND, and HON. GEORGE L. BRYAN, _Judges_

The prisoner, _Robert Hayes Mitchell,_ had been indicted by the grand jury for conspiracy: 1st, to prevent colored voters of that county from exercising the right to vote; 2nd, to oppress, threaten and intimidate one Jim Williams, a negro, because he had exercised the right to vote at an election in October, 1870.

SUGGESTIONS FOR FURTHER READING: Allan W. Trelease, _White Terror: The Ku Klux Klan Conspiracy and Southern Reconstruction_, New York: Harper & Row, 1971; Eric Foner, _Reconstruction: America's Unfinished Revolution_, New York: Harper & Row, 1988.

D. T. Corbin and *D. H. Chamberlain* for the United States.
Henry Stanbery and *Revedy Johnson* for the Prisoner.

Mr. Corbin. May it please the Court and gentlemen of the jury [all the jurors but two were African Americans], the case now to be presented to you is one of an unusual importance. It is one of a somewhat startling character in this country. The defendant, who is now called before you, is charged with having entered into a conspiracy for the purpose of preventing and restraining various male citizens of the United States, of African descent, and qualified to vote, from exercising the right of voting.

We shall first show you that he entered into a general conspiracy, existing in the County of York, for the purpose of preventing colored voters of that county from exercising the right to vote.

We shall prove the existence of an organization [the Ku Klux Klan], perfect in all its details, armed and disguised; that this organization was bound together by a terrible oath, the penalty for breaking of which was declared to be the doom of a traitor—death! death!! death!!! We shall show that this organization had a constitution and by-laws, regulating, in detail, all the duties of its members; that it pervaded the whole county, or a large portion of it; that it was inaugurated in 1868; that its active operations were somewhat suspended during the years 1869 and 1870, but that in 1871, particularly, it became very active; that great numbers of colored citizens, who were entitled, by law, to vote, in that county, were visited by the Klan, and whipped, and many of them murdered. In this case, we shall show to you that this organization deliberately planned and executed the murder of Jim Williams, whose name you will find in this indictment, in pursuance of the purpose of the organization. We shall prove to you, gentlemen, that the defendant was present, aided and assisted in carrying out the purpose of the organization; and was present at the execution of Jim Williams.

The details will all come out in proof. The raid—as it was called in that county—that killed Jim Williams, consisted of some forty, fifty or sixty persons. It met at what is called, in the County of York, the "Briar Patch," an old "muster" field, armed, disguised and mounted; that, under the command of a leader, J. W. Avery, this organization proceeded to the house of Jim Williams, broke in his door, took him out, fastened a rope about his neck, took him to the woods nearby, and hung him till he was dead. That they left a card upon him, which was found on the morning following the execution, containing the words "Jim Williams on his big muster." That, on the same night, they visited various other houses of colored people, threatened them, took them out, robbed them of their arms, and informed them that, if they should vote again, they would be killed. . . .

The Witnesses for the Government.

Lieutenant Godfrey. Am an officer of the U.S. army; was ordered on 20th of October to go to the house of Samuel G. Brown and obtain the constitution and by-laws of the Ku Klux Klan. Mr. Brown gave me an order to his daughter who took the paper, produced from his desk and gave it to me. This is the paper.

Obligation.

I, (name) before the immaculate Judge of Heaven and Earth, and upon the Holy Evangelists of Almighty God, do, of my own free will and accord, subscribe to the following sacredly binding obligation:

1. We are on the side of justice, humanity and constitutional liberty, as bequeathed to us in its purity by our forefathers.
2. We oppose and reject the principles of the Radical party.
3. We pledge mutual aid to each other in sickness, distress and pecuniary embarrassment.
4. Female friends, widows and their households shall ever be special objects of our regard and protection.

Any member divulging, or causing to be divulged, any of the foregoing obligation, shall meet the fearful penalty and traitor's doom, which is Death! Death! Death!

Albertus Hope. Was a member of the Ku Klux; went to a meeting at which I was elected chief. The condition of the up-country demanded something at that time. They had been burning and making threats in the country. Word was left at my house to go to that meeting; came very near not going; when I did go, I asked the object of the meeting and was told that as there had been so much burning and threats round our county, that it was necessary we should know where to get assistance.

Kirkland L. Gunn. During my residence in Yorkville was a member of the Ku Klux Klan. The obligation I took was I should not divulge any part of the secrets of the Klan; and it was for the purpose of putting down Radical rule and negro suffrage. Heard the constitution and by-laws of the order read when I was initiated. I was knelt down and the oath and constitution and by-laws were read to me. This paper the same that I heard read.

Now those purposes were to be carried into effect by killing off the white Radicals, and by whipping and intimidating the negroes, so as to keep them from voting for any men who held Radical offices. They did this at night time. The organization was armed, pistols, sometimes shot guns, muskets, &c. The Ku Klux gown referred to in the by-laws is a large gown made of some solid colored goods; don't know what the color was; never saw a gown in daylight. These gowns are worn to disguise the person. Have been on two raids; the order for a raid is given by the Chief; the officers are known as Night Hawks. . . . Members of the order could be called upon from one Klan by the other. On Charley Byers' raid on Roland Thompson's plantation I met Byers, Wesley Smith, Joe Smith and others; did not go on that raid, because I had no saddle to ride. The object of the raid, I was told, was that they wanted to drive this negro woman from Dr. John Good's premises; that she was a nuisance to his wife, and they thought it a duty of the order to drive her away from there. The password was, if you met any one in the night, you should spell the word I-s-a-y, and not pronounce it; if it was a member of the order whom you met, he would spell N-o-t-h-i-n-g, and not pronounce it. That signal whistle spoken of in the by-laws was a shrill, gurgling noise. Each member was required to have a whistle to give signals with. If the Chief sounded his whistle, and they were marching, they were to stop, and if they were standing the sound of his whistle meant to march on. Know Squire Samuel G. Brown, of York county. He told me he was Chief of his Klan, or told it to Wesley Smith in my presence, sir. He and Wesley Smith were in conversation, and I stepped up, and he gave me the sign, which I returned. He said, "I can kill and whip more damned niggers with my Klan than all the rest of York county." Cannot give any correct idea about the number of Klans, but I think the majority of the white people of York county belong to the order. . . .

Charles W. Foster. Was born and reside in York county; have lived there since the surrender; joined the Ku Klux about the 15th of December last; Aleck Smith's Klan first, and was transferred to John W. Mitchell's. Remember the oath I took; the first was to protect women and children, put down Radicalism—put down Union Leagues, &c. The penalty was if a man divulged any secret of the society, he was to suffer death! death!! death!!! . . . The purposes of the order were to be carried out by whipping the men who belonged to the Union League—both white and black. The understanding was, they never were to go in disguise only of a night; show no signs in the day time. . . .

The understanding of the persons who signed the paper was not to divulge any secrets; to attend all meetings; to go on all raids that was ordered. They were to be fined a certain fee, whatever the Klan pleased to put on them, if they did not. The raids were to put down Radicalism. Was at one regular meeting; that was when the Klan was organized; was on two other meetings after that to go on raids. We were ordered to meet at Howell's Ferry, and went and whipped five colored men. The men on these raids were more than twenty; they had red gowns, and had white covers over their horses. Some had pistols and some had guns. The object in whipping Presley Holmes was for some threats he had made about going to be buried in Salem graveyard. They dragged him out, and led him off, stripped his shirt and whipped him. They whipped Jerry Thompson at the next place about some threats he had made about an old soldier. He said he would kick the old soldier's hind parts; told him never to go to any more meetings; to stay at home and attend to his own business. At the next place they whipped Charley Good; he was supposed to be an officer in the League. They whipped him very severe; they beat him with a pole and kicked him down on the ground; told him to let Radicalism alone; not to go to any more League meetings; if he did, his doom would be fatal. They went then to Charley Leach's, at Mathew Smarr's house. They whipped him. The second raid we were ordered to meet in an old field, below Dr. Whiteside's. Julius Howe was leading the Klan that night. The first place they stopped was at Mrs. Watson's; called for a nigger there, but he was sick and they didn't disturb him; went on then to Mr. Moore's quarter, and there they got a double-barrelled shot gun; didn't whip anybody though; went on down to Theo. Byers'; they didn't do anything there; and then they went to Chancellor Chambers', and got a gun there. Went on down to Ed. Byers' or Theo. Byers' place, I don't know which; they whipped a couple of niggers there; one pretty severe; he was named Adolphus Moore; think that the impression was that they had been concerned in some burning, probably. These parties had no trial; if they had it was unbeknown to me. Most of the members of the Klan had been soldiers. Some were young boys. Captain Mitchell was a captain in the war. . . . The whipping of Pressly Thompson was because he says he wanted to be buried in a white person's graveyard. Jerry Thompson had said he would kick an old soldier's hind parts.

Andy Tims. Knew Jim Williams before he died; had been knowing him for fifteen or twenty years; he was a resident and voter in York county; he voted a Republican ticket. That night, I think something after 2 o'clock there were three disguised men came to my house, cussing and swearing. They said: "Here we come—we are the Ku Klux. Here we come right from hell," and two rode up on one side of my house, and one to the other. They commenced with their guns and beat at the doors, and hollering "G—d d—n you, open, open the doors." Before I got to the door they bursted the latch off, and two came in, and one got me by the arms and says, "we want your guns." Told them I didn't have any guns; there was one there, but not mine; they asked for a pistol; told them I didn't have any pistol at that time; they asked if I knew where Captain Williams lived; told them about two miles; says he, "we want to see your captain to-night; we don't want any more of you to-night." Asked me if I knew any of them; told them I did not know them; they got on their horses and bid me good night; about 50 yards from my house they stopped, talking very low to each other; I jumped out and started down across to the other house, and met Henry Haynes and Andrew Bratton, colored; they heard them and left their houses. We went down to Captain Williams'; Williams was not there; passed where Mr. Williams' company were—the militia; we followed the course the Ku Klux had went; we tracked them then, by bayonets and accoutrements, &c.; concluded to hunt for Williams; we went across the country to Williams', and before we got to the house we saw the tracks, where they had come out of the field; we pursued on until we came to where the horses were hitched; we saw Williams hanging on a tree, dead. There was a paper on his breast; the foreman of the jury said it said "Jim Williams on his big muster." I went from there to York, after the coroner; he hung there till we came back, and the jury all met.

Mrs. Rosy Williams. Am wife of Jim Williams. Some disguised men came to my house about 2 o'clock in the night and called on my husband. He went under the house before they came, and after they came in he came up in the house and gave them the guns. There were but two in the house, and they asked him for the others, and cussed, and told him to come out. He went with them, and after they had took him out doors they came in the house after me, and said there were some guns hid. After they had went out there, I heard my husband make a fuss like he was strangling. I looked out of the crack after them until they got under the shadows of the tree. I couldn't see them then. Next morning I went and looked for him, but I didn't find him. I met an old man who told me they had found him, and said he was dead. Saw him next morning hung on a pine tree with a rope around his neck, dead.

The Witnesses for the Defense.

Julia Rainey. Reside in York County; know Jim Rainey [a companion of Jim Williams]; he was a servant in my family, my former slave; he was captain of a militia company; that company caused a great deal of disturbance and uneasiness generally; they were under his control entirely, and they were not very orderly managed; he had been absent one year with Sherman's army; their conduct was disturbing, indeed; they had begun to alarm the whole country; my husband treated him very kindly, retaining all the old family; he always felt at liberty to enter my kitchen at any time to see the old family servants; his threats became very dangerous, indeed, and seemed to be disturbing the neighborhood, generally; his threats were very common to me—through the servants; never heard him myself. There were fires in our neighborhood previous to his death, committed by incendiaries. There was alarm in the neighborhood, fearing an attack by the negroes.

John A. Moroso. Live in Charleston. In the fall of 1870 was editor of the Charleston Courier; visited various parts of the country and precincts to report the progress of the canvass; was present at Yorkville three days, there was a great deal of excitement, caused by reports of the negro militia coming into town; I saw five militia-men, armed with Winchester rifles; they were State Constables; they came galloping into town before the meeting was called; they proceeded down the street to a place called the militia headquarters; at this place there was a kettle and a bass drum, and two men were employed to keep these drums going. I heard white people expressing much anger at the attempted interruption. When I passed through the county, they were in great alarm about the militia who were armed, and parading about the country at that time; that was the impression on all sides, and they were in a great state of alarm.

Richard B. Carpenter. Was a candidate at the last fall election for Governor of the State. Visited the country about Yorkville and Chester in August or September of 1870. There was anxiety and alarm on the part of the people in consequence of the armed militia. I do not think the white people were, as a general thing, alarmed; it seemed to have more terror to the colored people than the whites, in that country, because some were armed and some were not. The Conservative colored people were very much alarmed. Those who were armed all belonged to one party. The party supporting the then and present State dynasty is the Radical or Republican party; the party with which I was connected was called the Reform party. It was a party for the reform of the State government; men of all political parties belonged to it; and its object was the reform of the State government. The party in power in the State government was the Radical party.

Bill Lindsay (colored). Had a conversation with Jim Williams about getting ammunition for his company. He told me he was going to get ammunition from York. That he was going to kill from the cradle up. That was Friday before March. Know that such threats were made by Williams to others; heard other people speak of it in this neighborhood; people generally understood that Williams had made that threat. Up to that time there had been no violence or raids of Ku Klux or anybody else; was at home on the night Jim Williams was hung. They asked me if there were any guns there. I said no. Take it down, said they, and hand it to the men outside. The man outside hallooed: It's a double-barrel gun; give it back to him again. A militia party came there; about fifteen or twenty. The head man hallooed out to come out, quick. They asked me if there had been any Ku Klux there; then they asked which way they went. One of them took my gun away; they sent it back to me the next day. They were part of the colored militia; saw some of them at the election, in squads; they had their side arms on, the whole of them.

Speeches to the Jury.

Mr. Chamberlain for the prosecution.

Mr. Chamberlain. Your Honors and Gentlemen of the Jury: You are now approaching the close of a long trial. The issue between the United States and this prisoner [Robert Hayes Mitchell] is now to be submitted to you upon the law and upon the evidence, as developed in this trial. You cannot, gentlemen of the jury, be unaware that this case, in all its features, is a most remarkable and interesting one. You cannot be unaware that, not only the community in this State is interested in this trial, but that the entire country is watching, with unusual interest and anxiety, for the issue of this inquiry. You know, gentlemen of the jury, that not only your individual interests, your safety, your protection, your security as citizens, is involved in this trial, but you know, before I remind you, that broader interests than yours, or those of this defendant, are to be determined by your verdict. . . . This indictment contains two counts against this defendant. The first charges him with conspiring with others to violate the provisions of the first Section of the Act of 1870, by hindering and preventing divers male citizens of African descent from voting at future elections, and names the election to occur in October, 1872, as the time when this prevention and this intimidation was to take effect.

The second count charges him with conspiring with others to injure, oppress and intimidate Jim Williams, because he had voted at a former election for a member of the Congress of the United States. That is the scope of this indictment.

And now, gentlemen of the jury, let me tell you, before I proceed further, what a conspiracy is. A conspiracy is an agreement or combination between two or more persons, by their concerted action, to do an unlawful act. . . .

We come now to the 6th day of March, 1871. We are to see whether Robert H. Mitchell, this prisoner, with the others named in this indictment, did, on the specific occasion, undertake to carry out this general purpose which we have described in the agreement, and by the standards of acknowledged members.

You remember, gentlemen of the jury, the story of the Jim Williams raid; that it was on the night of the 6th of March, 1871. You remember the testimony of members of the Klan present on that occasion. You remember the meeting at the Briar Patch, and the conspirators there assembled, going to the cross-roads, near Squire Wallace's, where they met the four Shearer boys, and where this prisoner, Robert Hayes Mitchell, first appears. You remember that the four Shearer boys were sworn into the order at the cross-roads, near Squire Wallace's, and that then they took up their march. Here, gentlemen of the jury, we have the conspiracy literally and visibly in motion. This general conspiracy of the Ku Klux Klan takes up its line of march for the accomplishment of its purposes.

And now comes the evidence which points to this defendant as guilty upon this indictment. Now mark, near Squire Wallace's, their ranks are recruited by this defendant, and they take up their line of march, disguised, marching two by two, under the lead of Dr. James Rufus Bratton, upon an innocent undertaking, upon a charitable errand! No harm intended to any one, but simply protection against those horrible outrages of the negro militia! And here is James Rufus Bratton, the leader of that moving conspiracy. They come to McConnellsville; they arrive at the plantation of James Moore; they knocked at the door of Gadsden Steele, a colored man; and now remember, gentlemen of the jury, that every act and every word of any one member of that marching conspiracy, is the act and word of every other member of that marching conspiracy. If the humblest man who rode in that party did an act, or uttered a word, it is the act and the word of every other man who formed a part of that conspiracy.

They come to the door of Gadsden Steele, on the plantation of James Moore; they bring him forth and question him about his gun, and not being satisfied with his answer, they take him to Mr. Moore himself, and calling him out, they ask him about the guns. He says that Gadsden has no guns.

"Well, what ticket did he vote?" Nothing political! Self-protection! Charity! Mr. Moore says I will not tell a lie for he—"he voted the Radical ticket." And the voice now comes forth from that group of conspirators, "There, God damn you, we'll kill you for that." Not political! Only a search for guns! All because of the panic among the white people! Yet Gadsden Steele's offense, for which he is promised death, is that, by the statement of Mr. Moore, he voted the Radical ticket! Who uttered those words? No matter who uttered them; some one of those disguised men, there in front of Mr. James Moore's house, uttered them, and the voice was the voice of the conspiracy; every man uttered those words; they had but one breath—one utterance. "We will kill you, because you voted the Radical ticket."

What now? Gadsden Steel is told to mount a mule and go with them, and conduct them to Jim Williams' house. He mounts the mule and goes a short distance. He is then put down, and two men, who are riding with them—disguised Ku Klux, on this Jim Williams raid—then turn to him, and point their guns at him, and then, gentlemen of the jury, they declare the whole purpose of that night's raid. They say to him, "We are going to kill Jim Williams, and we are going to kill all you damned niggers who voted the Radical ticket." Whose voice was that? No matter whose voice it was; it was the voice of the conspiracy; and yet we are told this was not a conspiracy to interfere with anybody's voting! But they say, "We are going to kill Jim Williams, and we are going to kill all you niggers that vote the Radical ticket." That is the voice of the conspiracy—not of Rufus Bratton only, but of Robert Hayes Mitchell. That is in evidence before you today as the purpose of every man who rode on that marching conspiracy.

Well, gentlemen of the jury, follow them. They pass on; they turn aside from the public highway, and cross the field; they halt in a piney thicket and dismount; a detail is ordered to go forward; the detail is made up, and they put on a disguise, according to the testimony. From half an hour to an hour, while they are absent, nobody hears anything from them, except Elias Ramsay, who heard what he thought were the cries of a woman in distress. They return, and the order is given, "Mount, mount, and let us be off."

After they have moved away, some of these conspirators learn, for the first time, that Jim Williams has been killed. John Caldwell rides to the head of the column, and asks Dr. Rufus Bratton what they had done with the nigger, or where the nigger was. His reply is, "He is in hell, I expect." He draws out his watch, and looks at it by the light of the moon, and says, with a coolness that I think was never excelled, "Let us make haste; we have got two or three more to visit yet tonight." He has only hung one negro, and he is going to visit two or three more.

You see here, gentlemen of the jury, as you will, perhaps, never see again, the terrible power of organization. Probably no one, no two, no three of that party could have been induced to commit that murder; but, under the cloak and sanction of this vast organization, the responsibility of crime was divided until it was not felt. Murder, violent murder, excited no compunction, because behind Rufus Bratton was a column of seventy men, who were to divide the responsibility with him. This is the terror, gentlemen, of conspiracy. That is why these terrible combinations are made possible, because no man in that seventy felt that he, himself, had murdered Jim Williams. But the deed is done, the secret is safe, and every man says, "We are all sworn to secrecy." "Williams is dead, and the world will never know who hung him." Ah! Gentlemen of the jury, as a more eloquent voice than mine has said, "That was a dreadful mistake. Such a secret can be safe nowhere. The world has no nook or corner where the guilty can bestow it, and say it is safe." And here, today, after months of delay, you stand face to face with one of the men who joined in that conspiracy to kill Jim Willliams. . . .

Gentlemen of the jury, do you believe [Williams] ever made those threats? Do you believe that except, possibly, in view of the raiding of the Klan through the country, and the fact that his own company, himself and his neighbors, were hunted like wild beasts from their homes, do you believe that, except in connection with such events, [Jim Williams] ever uttered any threats against the white people of that County? I can believe, gentlemen of the jury—and I do not blame him for it—I can believe that he said, and that he meant, that, if they did not stop murdering his people, retaliation would commence. But, gentlemen of the jury, who are these witnesses who tell you of these threats? They are exclusively the white people of York County and three Democratic negroes! No negro, who was not a member of the Democratic party—who was not anti-Radical—ever heard Jim Williams make these threats, or ever heard of such threats till after he was killed. There is the evidence, gentlemen, and I leave it with you.

Mr. Stanbery for the prisoner.
Mr. Stanbery. Your Honors and Gentlemen of the Jury:
It is gratifying, gentlemen, not only to my learned friend who has just taken his seat, but to all parties, to witness with what close and undivided attention you have listened to the argument which has just been delivered. You know, gentlemen, those of you, at least, who belong to the colored race, that grave doubts have been entertained whether, in consideration of your previous condition, you have arrived, at this time, at a state of improvement which would justify your receiving the right to sit in judgment upon your fellow men, where you now sit in that jury box. So far, gentlemen, you have shown a disposition to give undivided attention to the case. You have at least shown one qualification for a juryman—you have listened, but as yet, to one side—perhaps to that side to which your sympathies are most drawn. Now, gentlemen, can you hear the other side? Can you give the same undivided attention to the advocate for the defendant, as you have given to the advocate who has stood up for the Government? If you can do that, gentlemen, you have gone one step further, and a great step further, towards vindicating your right to sit in the jury box. But, individual attention is not all that is required of a juryman. The juryman does not hold up his hand before God and swear that he will listen to the argument and the evidence with undivided attention. That is not all; he swears that, after he has heard the testimony and listened to the argument, and the case is committed to his hands, he will truly, justly, and impartially decide between the State and the prisoner.

Now, gentlemen, if you reach that future point and show that you are capable of divesting yourselves of the prejudices of race and color; show that you can act with impartiality, whether the man on trial is black or white, Radical or Democrat; if you can go that other step forward, then, gentlemen jurors, I am ready to say, that you, at least, are entitled to sit in the jury box. If, therefore, you earn a title to exercise that supreme right over the lives, liberty and property of your fellow men, black and white, you have earned the highest title to enjoy all political privileges. Show yourselves fit for that, and you will show yourselves fit for everything. . . .

Now, consider the condition of the people then. Imagine yourselves the white men, and of opposite politics, with a wife and children unprotected in your house, without any organization to protect you, and a man with a character and determination like Williams had threatened that if any outrage was committed upon him and his people, he would lay the whole country waste; that you would see a mighty work done, and that the fires that you had had would be nothing to such as would take place, and that he would lay the country waste and kill from the cradle up. Gentlemen, if I had lived there, in the vicinity of Yorkville, on a plantation, with my wife and children, and such a devil as that was in the country—a man that would make such threats, and with a hundred armed men under his influence, obeying his word of command—if there had been such a man in my neighborhood, I would have joined the first squad that came along to go and disarm them. I would have taken the consequences; I would rather take imprisonment, if necessary, than for one single night allow such a demon as that to be in my neighborhood; and that is what every one of you would do. Why, gentlemen, if you have the same consideration for your wife and children as I have—putting yourself aside entirely—could you sit quietly at your firesides, hear such threats, see these fires, feel that the whole atmosphere was full of panic and alarm—could you sit there quietly and do nothing? Why, you would not deserve to have wives and children. No; your first impulse would be to put down such a threatened danger as that; to disarm such a wild beast as that; and to disarm all those that were ready to follow him.

Why, gentlemen, I have no doubt that there were good and true colored men in that company that Jim couldn't get to go with him. I rather think those two or three colored men that quarreled with him would not have gone with him at the word of command. But some of them would, there is no doubt. You know what an influence over the race of colored people such a man will have, exciting their passions—accustomed to obedience, as they were; do not you know enough about your own race, gentlemen, to know that it wouldn't do to trust them, that it wouldn't do to allow them to follow such a leader! Are you immaculate? Is there no danger, gentlemen? I put it to you, as intelligent men of that race, are there no circumstances under which you would be alarmed? Are there not those in your race that you would fear and dread? That you would not leave in your house without your own protection; that you would not dare to trust the life of your wife, or the sanctity of her person with? Are there no such people in your race? Are there not bad men among you, and men who can be influenced by bad leaders. Now have you heard of any one that has quite as bad a record as Jim Williams, out of his own mouth and confession?

Let us see what this young man, the defendant has done. He is a very young man, scarcely past his majority. Look at him. Does he look like a murderer? Does he look like a dangerous man? What kind of a man have they brought you among all these terrible Ku Klux? Why, gentlemen, it is about the weakest case that they could produce before you. If they must have a Ku Klux, let them get a right sort of Ku Klux—a Ku Klux that has injured somebody; get a Ku Klux that was about a bad business when he was engaged upon a raid. Let us try this man by that standard. Why is he a Ku Klux? He belonged to the society; he was sworn in. What did he know about the Ku Klux at the time? Did he understand that it was a crime to go in that organization? . . . Going into that society, gentlemen, could not make a man guilty, because he could not know, until after he had got in and became advised of the purposes of that organization, that there was any wrong in it. . . . He knew nothing about these Klans, except that they were Ku Klux, and he supposed . . . that they were organized in self-defense. What did he do? He went to one meeting of these Ku Klux, and to one alone, and it was for the simple purpose of electing officers. No pretense that any one told him that the purposes of the Ku Klux were anything other than the protection of the people, he went on this raid of the 6th of March. Now, gentlemen, was there no provocation for going upon that raid? Was there no reason why there should be a raid that night and why such an organization as the Ku Klux should go on it? They were going against armed men and an individual could not go alone, it required an organization to go there and take away those arms. Well, what organization in that county could do that thing except those Ku Klux? They required more people to go with them; they were making Ku Klux that night; what for? To go upon that raid. Now, gentlemen, I have said that the provocation for the people to go there was not absolutely legal, but it was such a duty as no man would shrink from who felt the fears felt in that neighborhood from the danger of leaving those arms in the hands of those men. . . .

Gentlemen, I very much fear that there were some men there who secretly intended to take that man's life, and, perhaps, they had secret appliances with them. That may be; but they took care, gentlemen, to keep that secret from this young man and his companions that night. Why, gentlemen, it is true that this young man was willing to go when it was announced that they were going to take Williams' arms; and there was a strong excuse for his going. Suppose these men had said: "Now we are not going to take Williams' arms away; we are going to take his life away; here are the appliances; we are going to use these ropes." Would this young man have gone with them? At least, gentlemen, can you find that he would have gone, when he has had no opportunity to speak for himself? But this young man supposed he was going for what he considered a proper purpose, and what I would consider a proper purpose if I had lived in that neighborhood. How, in God's name, gentlemen, can you make him responsible for the horrid outrage that followed?

Gentlemen, the right man is not here; you have the proof, but not the offender. When he or they, whoever they may be, shall be arraigned, then will be the time to mete out the just punishment of such a crime; but, gentlemen, I beg of you not to confound the just with the guilty. I pray you, do not allow your feelings to run away with your judgment, but deal fairly with this man, now before you; measure out justice to him. If he is not found guilty of these offenses, gentlemen, acquit him, and you will do honor to yourselves and give a guaranty to the community that a black man knows how to acquit as well as white men, and hold in even poise the scales of justice. But, if you must always have a victim, if, when the right men do not appear, you can get any man with a white face and punish him, vicariously, I do not want to see one of your race on a jury again; but I want to hear better things of you.

The Verdict.

The *Jury* retired, and, on their return, rendered the verdict: "Guilty on the second count; not guilty on the first."

Mr. Stanbery entered a motion for a new trial.

The Sentence.

JUDGE BOND. The Court will overrule the motion for a new trial.

JUDGE BOND. Prisoner, what have you to say for yourself why the Court should be lenient towards you?

The *Prisoner*. Well, sir, I don't know what I ought to say. I might say right smart, and then it mightn't be much benefit. I don't know whether I can say anything to be of any benefit. I never was arrested. I went up to York and gave myself up to Major Merrill, and told him all I knew, except some things he didn't ask me and didn't give me time to tell him, but sent me to jail. I came down here with the intention of pleading guilty, and my lawyer kept me from it, and said not to plead guilty; said it was best for me not to do it. That was the reason I didn't plead guilty. . . . I was guilty of being on the raid; but I didn't do anything. That was proven here, that I didn't do anything to anyone that night. I joined the order in 1868, and I never had been on a raid in my life, and didn't know who else did belong, until the night that we went to McConnellsville. I don't think there was any raiding done, to my knowledge, after I joined, until this last year; a while before this Christmas a year ago, I think, was the first. I didn't know a thing about it until Sunday evening. The man was hung on Monday, and I never heard his name before in my life; I didn't know anything about it at all. I suppose there was men that did know the negro; I didn't, though. Who determined the fact that a negro should have a whipping? I suppose it was the Klan. There was a committee. I am a farmer, have been, the last two years.

JUDGE BRYAN. Mr. Mitchell, it has been your unhappiness to have been connected with a great crime; and if the Court could believe that you were a party to that crime—that you had suspected the terrible deed that was to be done—and had any intimation that you had countenanced it, they would exhaust the full penalty of the law, and then consider that you had been very mercifully dealt with. But you have come in and confessed; your manner has impressed the Court; and, although you were so misguided as to join a body of men to punish people, and punish them without responsibility to the law, yet we feel at liberty to believe that you have dealt candidly with the Court, and that you have told the truth. It is upon that conviction alone, that the Court finds its vindication for accepting your declarations and believing that you were in no way a party to the murder. The sentence of the Court is, that you be imprisoned eighteen months and fined one hundred dollars.

2
Women's Rights
The Susan B. Anthony Trial
1873

When the necessities of Reconstruction politics generated support for extending the franchise to African Americans, the issue of votes for women arose with it. It is hard today to imagine the opposition the idea aroused. In the Congressional debates on women suffrage in 1866, the first in the nation's history, one typical speech in the Senate predicted it would "convert all the now harmonious elements of society into a state of war, and make every home a hell on earth." "Those vestal fires of love and piety" in the home, warned another, would be "put out." Advocates of the vote for women split over whether to support suffrage for black men at the price of acquiescing in its denial to women. Susan B. Anthony, her close associate and friend Elizabeth Cady Stanton, and others organized the National Woman Suffrage Association opposing the Fifteenth Amendment unless it gave the vote to women as well as blacks. Lucy Stone, Elizabeth Blackwell, and others formed the American Woman Suffrage Association supporting the amendment. The rift between the two groups continued for a generation.

In its January 1872 national convention, the National Woman Suffrage Association urged women to assert on the basis of the Fourteenth and Fifteenth amendments the right to vote. Susan B. Anthony was one of about fifty women in the Rochester area who, usually by threatening the registrars with legal action, succeeded in registering to vote. And she was one of fifteen women who voted in the national elections on November 5. With the press urging the arrest of both the women and the inspectors of elections, Anthony's leadership of the national movement made her act of voting into a national issue. She had demanded handcuffing and then refused bail, but the U.S. Marshall would not use his handcuff and her attorney insisted on paying her bail.

At her trial in June, the defendant, as a woman was declared incompetent to testify. After brief testimony, the opposing lawyers' summations consumed five hours. Nevertheless the judge proceeded to pull a paper from his pocket and read a decision written before the trial directing the jury to find Anthony guilty. Then

SUGGESTIONS FOR FURTHER READING: Kathleen Barry, *Susan B. Anthony: A Biography of a Singular Feminist,* New York: New York University Press, 1988; Eleanor Flexner, *Century of Struggle: The Woman's Rights Movement in the United States,* New York: Atheneum, 1968.

he made an error by asking "Has the prisoner anything to say why sentence should not be pronounced?" Anthony had much to say, and said it over the judge's repeated objection. He then fined her $100 and court costs. When she refused to pay, he surprised observers by refusing to commit her to jail. With no penalty exacted, there would be no suffragist in jail, no possibility of further appeal, and no further headlines. Susan B. Anthony was denied the more dramatic martyrdom she sought.

The Trial of Susan B. Anthony for Voting at a Congressional Election, *In the Unites States Circuit Court, Canandaigua, New York 1873.*
HON. WARD HUNT, *Judge*

In the previous month of January the Grand Jury for the Northern District of New York [United States Circuit Court], had returned an indictment against Susan B. Anthony for voting illegally at an election held for members of the Congress of the United States in the city of Rochester, on November 5, 1872. The defendant had pleaded *not guilty* and a jury having been impaneled the trial was begun today.

Richard Crowley, United States District Attorney, for the Government.
Henry R. Selden, and *John Van Voorhis,* for the Defendant.

Mr. Crowley. Gentlemen of the Jury: On the fifth of November, 1872, there was held in this State, as well as in other states of the Union, a general election for different officers, and among those, for candidates to represent several districts of this state in the Congress of the United States. The defendant, Miss Susan B. Anthony, at that time resided in the city of Rochester, in the county of Monroe, Northern District of New York, and upon the fifth day of November, 1872, she voted for a representative in the Congress of the United States to represent the 29th Congressional District of this state, and also for a representative at large for the state of New York, to represent the state in the Congress of the United States. At that time she was a woman. I suppose there will be no question about that. The question in this case, if there be a question of fact about it at all, will, in my judgment, be rather a question of law than one of fact. I suppose that there will be no question of fact, substantially, in the case then all of the evidence is out, and it will be for you to decide under the charge of his Honor, the judge, whether or not the defendant committed the offense of voting for a representative in Congress upon that occasion. We think, on the part of the Government, that there is no question about it either one way or the other, neither a question of fact, nor a question of law, and that whatever Miss Anthony's intentions may have been—whether they were good or otherwise—she did not have a right to vote upon that question, and if she did vote without having a lawful right to vote then there is no question but what she is guilty of violating a law of the United States in that behalf enacted by the Congress of the United States.

Witnesses.

Beverly W. Jones. Resided in Rochester, and was an inspector of elections on November 5, 1872, of the First District. [The other inspectors were Edward T. Marsh and William B. Hall.] Saw Miss Anthony vote the State, Assembly, Congressional and Presidential Election tickets. I received the ballots from her and put them in the separate boxes provided. Nobody challenged her vote at that time.

The voters had been previously registered by myself and the other members of the Board of Registry. Miss Anthony appeared before us, and asked to be registered, but it was objected that as she was not a male citizen she could not register, but we decided in her favor, and registered her name. One of the United States Supervisors of Elections agreed with us, the other did not.

When Miss Anthony was challenged before the Board of Registry, she took the oath that she was a legal voter. She said she did not claim her right under the laws of New York, but under the Fourteenth Amendment to the United States Constitution. The poll list which I have in my hand shows that she voted the Electoral, State, Congressional and Assembly Tickets.

Mr. Selden. Gentlemen of the Jury: This is a case of no ordinary magnitude, although many might regard it as one of little importance. The question whether my client here has done anything to justify her being consigned to a felon's prison or not, is one that interests her very essentially, and that interests the people also essentially. I claim and shall endeavor to establish before you that when she offered to have her name registered as a voter, and when she offered her vote for Member of Congress, she was as much entitled to vote as any man that voted at that election, according to the Constitution and laws of the Government under which she lives. I maintain that proposition, as a matter of course she has committed no offense, and is entitled to be discharged at your hands.

But, beyond that, whether she was a legal voter or not, whether she was entitled to vote or not, if she sincerely believed that she had a right to vote, and offered her ballot in good faith, under that belief, whether right or wrong, by the laws of this country she is guilty of no crime. I apprehend that that proposition, when it is discussed, will be maintained with a clearness and force that shall leave no doubt upon the mind of the Court or upon your minds as the gentlemen of the jury. If I maintain that proposition here, then the further question and the only question which, in my judgment, can come before you to be passed upon by you as a question of fact is whether or not she did vote in good faith, believing that she had a right to vote.

The public prosecutor assumes that, however honestly she may have offered her vote, however sincerely she may have believed that she had a right to vote, if she was mistaken in that judgment, her offering to vote and its being received makes a criminal offense—a proposition to me most abhorrent, as I believe it will be equally abhorrent to your judgment.

Before the registration, and before this election, Miss Anthony called upon me for advice upon the question whether, under the Fourteenth Amendment of the Constitution of the United States, she had a right to vote. I had not examined the question. I told her I would examine it and give her my opinion upon the question of her legal right. She went away and came again after I had made the examination. I advised her that she was as lawful a voter as I am, or as any other man is, and advised her to go and offer her vote. I may have been mistaken in that, and if I was mistaken, I believe she acted in good faith. I believe she acted according to her right as the law and Constitution gave it to her. But whether she did or not, she acted in the most perfect good faith, and if she made a mistake, or if I made one, that is not reason for committing her to a felon's cell.

Mr. Selden. Before the last election, Miss Anthony called upon me for advice, upon the question whether she was or was not a legal voter. I examined the question, and gave her my opinion, unhesitatingly, that the laws and Constitution of the United States, authorized her to vote, as well as they authorize any man to vote; advised her to have her name placed upon the registry and to vote at the election, if the inspectors should receive her vote. I gave the advice in good faith, believing it to be accurate, and I believe it to be accurate still.

John E. Pound. During November and December 1872 and January 1873, I was assistant United States District Attorney for the Northern District of New York. Attended an examination before United States District Attorney Storrs in Rochester, where Miss Anthony was examined as a witness in her own behalf.

Mr. Crowley. Did she, upon that occasion, state that she consulted or talked with Judge Henry R. Selden, of Rochester, in relation to her right to vote? . . . Did she state on that examination, under oath, that she had talked or consulted with Judge Henry R. Selden in relation to her right to vote? Was she asked, upon that examination, if the advice given her by Judge Henry R. Selden would or did make any difference in her action in voting, or in substance that?

Mr. Pound. She stated on the cross-examination, "I should have made the same endeavor to vote that I did had I not consulted Judge Selden. I didn't consult any one before I registered. I was not influenced by his advice in the matter at all; have been resolved to vote, the first time I was at home thirty days, for a number of years."

Mr. Van Voorhis. Was she asked there if she had any doubt about her right to vote, and did she answer "Not a particle"? She stated "Had no doubt as to my right to vote," on the direct examination., There was a stenographic reporter there, was there not? A reporter was there taking notes. Was not this question put to her "Did you have any doubt yourself of your right to vote?" and did she not answer "Not a particle"?

Mr. Selden. I beg leave to state, in regard to my own testimony, Miss Anthony informs me that I was mistaken in the fact that my advice was before her registry. It was my recollection that it was on her way to the registry, but she states to me now that she was registered and came immediately to my office. In that respect I was under a mistake.

The defendant is indicted under the Nineteenth section of the Act of Congress of May 31, 1870, for "voting without having a lawful right to vote."

The words of the Statute, so far as they are material in this case, are as follows: "If at any election for representative or delegate in the Congress of the United States, any person shall knowingly . . . vote without having a lawful right to vote . . . every such person shall be deemed guilty of a crime, . . . and on conviction thereof shall be punished by a fine not exceeding $500, or by imprisonment for a term not exceeding three years, or by both, in the discretion of the Court, and shall pay the costs of prosecution."

The only alleged ground of illegality of the defendant's vote is that she is a woman. If the same act had been done by her brother under the same circumstances, the act would have been not only innocent but honorable and laudable; but having been done by a woman it is said to be a crime. The crime therefore consists not in the act done, but in the simple fact that the person doing it was a woman and not a man. I believe this is the first instance in which a woman has been arraigned in a criminal court, merely on account of her sex.

If the advocates of female suffrage had been allowed to choose the point of attack to be made upon their position, they could not have chosen it more favorably for themselves; and I am disposed to thank those who have been instrumental in this proceeding, for presenting it in the form of a criminal prosecution.

Women have the same interest that men have in the establishment and maintenance of good government; they are to the same extent as men bound to obey the laws; they suffer to the same extent by bad laws, and profit to the same extent by good laws; and upon principles of equal justice, as it would seen, should be allowed equally with men, to express their preference in the choice of law-makers and rulers. But however that may be, no greater absurdity, to use no harsher term, could be presented, than that of rewarding men and punishing women, for the same act, without giving to women any voice in the question which should be rewarded, and which punished.

I am aware, however, that we are here to be governed by the Constitution and laws as they are, and that if the defendant has been guilty of violating the law, she must submit to the penalty, however unjust or absurd the law may be. But courts are not required to so interpret laws or constitutions as to produce either absurdity or injustice, so long as they are open to a more reasonable interpretation. This must be my excuse for what I design to say in regard to the propriety of female suffrage, because with that propriety established there is very little difficulty in finding sufficient warrant in the Constitution for its exercise.

This case, in its legal aspects, presents three questions, which I purpose to discuss.

1. Was the defendant legally entitled to vote at the election in question?
2. If she was not entitled to vote, but believed that she was, and voted in good faith in that belief, did such voting constitute a crime under the statute before referred to?
3. Did the defendant vote in good faith in that belief?

If the first question be decided in accordance with my views, the other questions become immaterial; if the second be decided adversely to my views, the first and third become immaterial. The two first are questions of law to be decided by the Court, the other is a question for the jury. . . .

My first position is that the defendant had the same right to vote as any other citizen who voted at that election.

Before proceeding to the discussion of the purely legal question, I desire, as already intimated, to pay some attention to the propriety and justice of the rule which I claim to have been established by the Constitution.

Miss Anthony, and those united with her in demanding the right of suffrage, claim, and with a strong appearance of justice, that upon the principles upon which our government is founded, and which lie at the basis of all just government, every citizen has a right to take part, upon equal terms with every other citizen, in the formation and administration of government. This claim on the part of the female sex presents a question the magnitude of which is not well appreciated by the writers and speakers who treat it with ridicule. Those engaged in the movement are able, sincere and earnest women, and they will not be silenced by ridicule. On the contrary, they justly place all those things to the account of the wrongs which they think their sex has suffered. They believe, with an intensity of feeling which men who have not associated with them have not yet learned, that their sex has not had, and has not now, its just and true position in the organization of government and society. They may be wrong in their position, but they will not be content until their arguments are fairly, truthfully and candidly answered. . . .

This extension of the suffrage is regarded by many as a source of danger to the stability of free government. I believe it furnishes the greatest security for free government, as it deprives the mass of the people of all motive for revolution; and that government so based is most safe, not because the whole people are less liable to make mistakes in government than a select few, but because they have no interest which can lead them to such mistakes, or to prevent their correction when made. On the contrary, the world has never seen an aristocracy, whether composed of few or many, powerful enough to control a government, who did not honestly believe that their interest was identical with the public interest, and who did not act persistently in accordance with such belief; and, unfortunately, an aristocracy of sex has not proved an exception to the rule. The only method yet discovered of overcoming this tendency to the selfish use of power, whether consciously or unconsciously, by those possessing it, is the distribution of the power among all who are its subjects. Short of this the name free government is a misnomer.

I can discover no ground consistent with the principle on which the franchisee has been given to all men, upon which it can be denied to women. The principal argument against such extension, so far as argument upon that side of the question has fallen under my observation, is based upon the position that women are represented in the government by men, and that their rights and interests are better protected through that indirect representation than they would be by giving them a direct voice in the government. . . .

The state of the law has undergone great changes within the last twenty-five years. The property, real and personal, which a woman possesses before marriage, and such as may be given to her during coverture, remains her own, and is free from the control of the husband. If a married woman is slandered she can prosecute in her own name the slanderer and recover to her own use damages for the injury. The mother now has an equal claim with the father to the custody of their minor children, and in case of controversy on the subject, courts may award the custody to either in their discretion. The husband cannot now by will effectually appoint a guardian for his infant children without the consent of the mother, if living.

These are certainly great ameliorations of the law; but how have they been produced? Mainly as the result of the exertions of a few heroic women, one of the foremost of whom is her who stands arraigned as a criminal before this Court today. For a thousand years the absurdities and cruelties to which I have alluded have been embedded in the common law, and in the statute books, and men have not touched them, and would not until the end of time, had they not been goaded to it by the persistent efforts of the noble women to whom I have alluded.

It is said that women do not desire to vote. Certainly many women do not, but that furnishes no reason for denying the right to those who do desire to vote. Many men decline to vote. Is that a reason for denying the right to those who would vote?

I believe, however, that the public mind is greatly in error in regard to the proportion of female citizens who would vote if their right to do so were recognized. In England there has been to some extent a test of that question, with the following result, as given in the newspapers, the correctness of which, in this respect, I think there is no reason to doubt: "Women suffrage is, to a certain extent, established in England, with the results as detailed in the London Examiner, that in sixty-six municipal elections, out of every thousand women who enjoy equal rights with men on the register, 516 went to the poll, which is but forty-eight less than the proportionate number of men. And out of 27,949 women registered, where a contest occurred, 14,416 voted. Of men there were 166,781 on the register, and 90,080 at the poll." The Examiner thereupon draws this conclusion: "Making allowance for the reluctance of old spinsters to change their inhabits, and the more frequent illness of the sex, it is manifest that women, if they had opportunity, would exercise the franchise as freely as men. There is an end, therefore, of the argument that women would not vote if they had the power."

Another objection is, that the right to hold office must attend the right to vote, and that women are not qualified to discharge the duties of responsible offices.

I beg leave to answer this objection by asking one or more questions. How many of the male bipeds who do our voting are qualified to hold high offices? How many of the large class to whom the right of voting is supposed to have been secured by the Fifteenth Amendment, are qualified to hold office?

Whenever the qualifications of persons to discharge the duties of responsible offices is made the test of their right to vote, and we are to have a competitive examination on that subject open to all claimants, my client will be content to enter the lists, and take her chances among the candidates for such honors.

But the practice of the world, and our own practice, give the lie to this objection. Compare the administration of female sovereigns of great kingdoms, from Semiramis to Victoria, with the average administration of male sovereigns, and which will suffer by the comparison? How often have mothers governed large kingdoms, as regents, during the minority of their sons, and governed them well? Such offices as the "sovereigns" who rule them in this country have allowed women to hold (they having no voice on the subject), they have discharged the duties of with ever increasing satisfaction to the public; and Congress has lately passed an act, making the official bonds of married women valid, so that they could be appointed to the office of postmaster. . . .

Another objection is that women cannot serve as soldiers. To this I answer that capacity for military service has never been made a test of the right to vote. If it were, young men from sixteen to twenty-one would be entitled to vote, and old men from sixty and upwards would not. If that were the test, some women would present much stronger claims than many of the male sex. . . .

I humbly submit to your Honor, therefore, that on the constitutional grounds to which I have referred, Miss Anthony had a lawful right to vote; that her vote was properly received and counted; that the first section of the Fourteenth Amendment secured to her that right, and did not need the aid of any further legislation.

I concede, that if Miss Anthony voted, knowing that as a woman she had no right to vote, she may properly be convicted, and that if she had dressed herself in men's apparel, and assumed a man's name, or resorted to any artifice to deceive the board of inspectors, the jury might properly regard her claim of right, to be merely colorable, and might, in their judgment, pronounce her guilty of the offense charged, in case the Constitution has not secured to her the right she claimed. All I claim is, that if she voted in perfect good faith, believing that it was her right, she has committed no crime. An innocent mistake, whether of law or fact, though a wrongful act may be done in pursuance of it, cannot constitute a crime. . . .

One other matter will close what I have to say. Miss Anthony believed, and was advised that she had a right to vote. She may also have been advised, as was clearly the fact, that the question as to her right could not be brought before the courts for trial, without her voting or offering to vote, and if either was criminal, the one was as much so as the other. Therefore she stands now arraigned as a criminal, for taking the only steps by which it was possible to bring the great constitutional question as to her right, before the tribunals of the country for adjudication. If for thus acting, in the most perfect good faith, with motives as pure and impulses as noble as any which can find place in your Honor's breast in the administration of justice, she is by the laws of her country to be condemned as a criminal, she must abide the consequences. Her condemnation, however, under such circumstances, would only add another most weighty reason to those which I have already advanced, to show that women need the aid of the ballot for their protection.

Upon the remaining question, of the good faith of the defendant, it is not necessary for me to speak. That she acted in the most perfect good faith stands conceded.

Thanking your Honor for the great patience with which you have listened to my too extended remarks, I submit the legal questions which the case involves for your Honor's consideration.

Mr. Justice HUNT. Gentlemen of the Jury: I have given this case such consideration as I have been able to, and, that there might be no misapprehension about my views, I have made a brief statement in writing.

The defendant is indicted under the Act of Congress of 1870, for having voted for Representatives in Congress in November, 1872. Among other things, that Act makes it an offense for any person knowingly to vote for such Representatives without having a right to vote. It is charged that the defendant thus voted, she not having a right to vote because she is a woman. The defendant insists that she has a right to vote; that the provisions of the Constitution of this state limiting the right to vote to persons of the male sex is in violation of the Fourteenth Amendment of the Constitution of the United States, and is void. The Thirteenth, Fourteenth and Fifteenth Amendments were designed mainly for the protection of the newly emancipated negroes, but full effect must nevertheless be given to the language employed. The Thirteenth Amendment provided that neither slavery nor involuntary servitude should longer exist in the United States. If honestly received and fairly applied, this provision would have been enough to guard the rights of the colored race. In some states it was attempted to be evaded by enactments cruel and oppressive in their nature, as that colored persons were forbidden to appear in the towns except in a menial capacity; that they should reside on and cultivate the soil without being allowed to own it; that they were nor permitted to give testimony in cases where a white man was a party. They were excluded from performing particular kinds of business, profitable and reputable, and they were denied the right of suffrage. To meet the difficulties arising from this state of things, the Fourteenth and Fifteenth Amendments were enacted.

The Fourteenth Amendment created and defined citizenship of the United States. It had long been contended, and had been held by many learned authorities, and had never been judicially decided to the contrary, that there was no such thing as a citizen of the United States, except as that condition arose from citizenship of some state. No mode existed, it was said, of obtaining a citizenship of the United States except by first becoming a citizen of some state. This question is now at rest. The Fourteenth Amendment defines and declares who should be citizens of the United States, to wit: "All persons born or naturalized in the United States and subject to the jurisdiction thereof." The latter qualification was intended to exclude the children of foreign representatives and the like. With this qualification every person born in the United States or naturalized is declared to be a citizen of the United States, and of the state wherein he resides. After creating and defining citizenship of the United States, the Amendment provides that no state shall make or enforce any law which shall abridge the privileges or immunities of a citizen of the United States. This clause is intended to be a protection, not to all our rights, but to our rights as citizens of the United States only; that is, the rights existing or belonging to that condition or capacity. . . .

If the state of New York should provide that no person shall vote until he had reached the age of thirty-one years, or after he had reached the age of fifty, or that no person having gray hair, or who had not the use of all his limbs should be entitled to vote, I do not see how it could be held to be a violation of any right derived or held under the Constitution of the United States. We might say that such regulations were unjust, tyrannical, unfit for the regulation of an intelligent state; but if rights of a citizen are thereby violated, they are of that fundamental class derived from his position as a citizen of the state, and not those limited rights belonging to him as a citizen of the United States. . . .

If the Fifteenth Amendment had contained the word "sex," the argument of the defendant would have been potent. She would have said, an attempt by a state to deny the right to vote because one is of a particular sex, is expressly prohibited by that amendment. The amendment, however, does not contain that word. It is limited to race, color, or previous condition of servitude. The Legislature of the state of New York has seen fit to say, that the franchise of voting shall be limited to the male sex. In saying this, there is, in my judgment, no violation of the letter or of the spirit of the Fourteenth or of the Fifteenth Amendment.

The Fourteenth Amendment gives no right to a woman to vote, and the voting by Miss Anthony was in violation of the law.

If she believed she had a right to vote, and voted in reliance upon that belief, does that relieve her from the penalty? It is argued that the knowledge referred to in the act relates to her knowledge of the illegality of the act, and not to the act of voting; for it is said that she must know that she voted. Two principles apply here: First, ignorance of the law excuses no one; second, every person is presumed to understand and to intend the necessary effects of his own acts. Miss Anthony knew that she was a woman, and that the Constitution of this state prohibits her from voting. She intended to violate that provision—intended to test it, perhaps, but certainly intended to violate it. The necessary effect of her act was to violate it, and this she is presumed to have intended. There was no ignorance of any fact, but all the facts being known, she undertook to settle a principle in her own person. She takes the risk, and she cannot escape the consequences. . . .

Upon this evidence I suppose there is no question for the jury and that the jury should be directed to find a verdict of guilty.

Mr. Selden. I submit that on the view which your Honor has taken, that the right to vote and the regulation of it is solely a state matter; that this whole law is out of the jurisdiction of the United States Courts and of Congress. The whole law upon that basis, as I understand it, is not within the constitutional power of the general government, but is one which applies to the states. I suppose that it is for the jury to determine whether the defendant is guilty of a crime or not. And I therefore ask your Honor to submit to the jury these propositions: First—If the defendant, at the time of voting, believed that she had a right to vote and voted in good faith in that belief, she is not guilty of the offense charged. Second—In determining the question whether she did or did not believe that she had a right to vote, the jury may take into consideration, as bearing upon that question, the advice which she received from the counsel to whom she applied. Third—That they may also take into consideration, as bearing upon the same question, the fact that the inspectors considered the question and came to the conclusion that she had a right to vote. Fourth—That the jury have a right to find a general verdict of guilty or not guilty as they shall believe that she has or has not committed the offense described in the Statute.

A professional friend sitting by has made this suggestion which I take leave to avail myself of as bearing upon this question: The Court has listened for many hours to an argument in order to decide whether the defendant has a right to vote. The arguments show the same question has engaged the best minds of the country as an open question. Can it be possible that the defendant is to be convicted for acting upon such advice as she could obtain while the question is an open and undecided one? . . .

Mr. Selden. As long as it is an open question I submit that she has not been guilty of an offense. At all events it is for the jury.

The COURT. The question, gentlemen of the jury, in the form it finally takes, is wholly a question or questions of law, and I have decided as a question of law, in the first place, that under the Fourteenth Amendment, which Miss Anthony claims protects her, she was not protected in a right to vote. And I have decided also that her belief and the advice which she took does not protect her in the act which she committed. If I am right in this, the result must be a verdict on your part of guilty, and I therefore direct that you find a verdict of guilty.

Mr. Selden. That is a direction no Court has power to make in a criminal case.

The COURT. Take the verdict, Mr. Clerk.

The *Clerk.* Gentlemen of the jury, hearken to your verdict as the Court has recorded it. You say you find the defendant guilty of the offense whereof she stands indicted, and so say you all.

Mr. Selden. I don't know whether an exception is available, but I certainly must except to the refusal of the Court to submit those propositions, and especially to the direction of the Court that the jury should find a verdict of guilty. I claim that it is a power that is not given to any Court in a criminal case. Will the Clerk poll the jury?

The COURT. No. Gentlemen of the jury, you are discharged. . . .

Mr. Justice HUNT. The prisoner will stand up. Has the prisoner anything to say why sentence shall not be pronounced?

Miss Anthony. Yes, your Honor, I have many things to say; for in your ordered verdict of guilty, you have trampled under foot every vital principle of our government. My natural rights, my civil rights, my political rights, my judicial rights, are all alike ignored. Robbed of the fundamental privilege of citizenship, I am degraded from the status of a citizen to that of a subject; and not only myself individually, but all of my sex are, by your Honor's verdict, doomed to political subjection under this, so-called, form of government.

Mr. Justice HUNT. The Court cannot listen to a rehearsal of arguments the prisoner's counsel has already consumed three hours in presenting.

Miss Anthony. May it please your Honor, I am not arguing the question, but simply stating the reasons why sentence cannot in justice be pronounced against me. Your denial of my citizen's right to vote, is the denial of my right of consent as one of the governed, the denial of my right of representation as one of the taxed, the denial of my right to a trial by a jury of my peers as an offender against law, therefore the denial of my sacred rights to life, liberty, property and—

Mr. Justice HUNT. The Court cannot allow the prisoner to go on.

Miss Anthony. But your Honor will not deny me this one and only poor privilege of protest against this high-handed outrage upon my citizen's rights. May it please the Court to remember that since the day of my arrest last November, this is the first time that either myself or any person of my disfranchised class has been allowed a word of defense before judge or jury.

Mr. Justice HUNT. The prisoner must sit down—the Court cannot allow it.

Miss Anthony. All my prosecutors, from the Eighth ward corner grocery politician, who entered the complaint, to the United States Marshal, Commissioner, District Attorney, District Judge, your Honor on the bench, not one is my peer, but each and all are my political sovereigns; and had your Honor submitted my case to the jury, as was clearly your duty, even then I should have had just cause of protest, for not one of those men was my peer; but, native or foreign born, white or black, rich or poor, educated or ignorant, awake or asleep, sober or drunk, each and every man of them was my political superior; hence, in no sense, my peer. Even, under such circumstances, a commoner of England, tried before a jury of Lords, would have far less cause to complain than should I, a woman, tried before a jury of men. Even my counsel, the Hon. Henry B. Selden, who has argued my cause so ably, so earnestly, so unanswerably before your Honor, is my political sovereign. Precisely as no disfranchised person is entitled to sit upon a jury, and no woman is entitled to the franchise, so, none but a regularly admitted lawyer is allowed to practice in the courts, and no woman can gain admission to the bar—hence, jury, judge, counsel, must all be of the superior class.

Mr. Justice HUNT. The court must insist—the prisoner has been tried according to the established forms of law.

Miss Anthony. Yes, your Honor, but by forms of law all made by men, interpreted by men, administered by men, in favor of men, and against women; and hence, your Honor's ordered verdict of guilty, against a United States citizen for the exercise of that citizen's right to vote simply because that citizen was a woman and not a man. But, yesterday, the same man made forms of law, declared it a crime punishable with $1,000 fine and six months' imprisonment, for you, or me, or any of us, to give a cup of cold water, a crust of bread, or a night's shelter to a panting fugitive as he was tracking his way to Canada. And every man or woman in whose veins coursed a drop of human sympathy violated that wicked law, reckless of consequences, and was justified in so doing. As then, the slaves who got their freedom must take it over, or under, or through the unjust forms of law, precisely so, now, must women, to get their right to a voice in this government, take it; and I have taken mine, and mean to take it at every possible opportunity.

Mr. Justice HUNT. The Court orders the prisoner to sit down. It will not allow another word.

Miss Anthony. When I was brought before your Honor for trial, I hoped for a broad and liberal interpretation of the Constitution and its recent amendments, that should declare all United States citizens under its protecting ægis—that should declare equality of rights the national guaranty to all persons born or naturalized in the United States. But failing to get this justice—failing, even, to get a trial by a jury not of my peers—I ask not leniency at your hands—but rather the full rigors of the law.

Mr. Justice HUNT. The Court must insist—
[Here Miss Anthony sat down.]

Mr. Justice HUNT. The prisoner will stand up. [Here Miss Anthony arose again.] The sentence of the Court is that you pay a fine of one hundred dollars and the costs of the prosecution.

Miss Anthony. May it please your Honor, I shall never pay a dollar of your unjust penalty. All the stock in trade I possess is a $10,000 debt, incurred by publishing my paper—The Revolution—four years ago, the sole object of which was to educate all women to do precisely as I have done, rebel against your man-made, unjust, unconstitutional forms of law, that tax, fine, imprison and hang women, while they deny them the right of representation in the government; and I shall work on with might and main to pay every dollar of that honest debt, but not a penny shall go to this unjust claim. And I shall earnestly and persistently continue to urge all women to the practical recognition of the old revolutionary maxim, that resistance to tyranny is obedience to God.

Mr. Justice HUNT. Madam, the Court will not order you committed until the fine is paid.

3
The West
The Trial of Frank James for Train Robbery and Murder
1883

Jesse and Frank James, bandit heroes of hundreds of dime novels and at least twenty-five feature length films, largely created their own legend. Their lives literally depended on the task: without some loyalty and protection from gullible folk who believed they were romantic heroes rather than ruthless thieves and murderers, the James gang would not have survived from 1866 to 1882.

During the Civil War the James boys developed their characteristic style of romanticizing robbery and murder as members of Quantrell's Raiders, Confederate guerrillas loosely led by William Clarke Quantrell, who like their Unionist counterparts in Missouri mixed military action and crime in the guerrilla warfare that wracked that officially Unionist state throughout the conflict. Frank, the elder brother, born in 1843, followed a Quantrell lieutenant who came recruiting under the slogan "Join Quantrell and rob the banks." Jesse joined in 1863 at the age of sixteen. He saw much action and was wounded three times, later blaming his criminal career on the persecution his parents suffered for their Confederate sympathies, the wounds he suffered during the war, and his fear of retribution from Unionists after the war.

Whatever their motives, by February 1886 the brothers were part of a gang applying to robbing banks the tactics they had learned during the war: shooting at bystanders and giving the rebel yell as they made their escape on horseback. Within a few years, as their exploits became well known, the publicity machine began. They wrote letters (under pseudonyms) to newspapers boasting of their crimes and actually began their identification with Robin Hood by claiming "we rob the rich and give it to the poor." While there is no evidence whatever for this distributive justice, folklore expanded the boast into undocumented accounts of paying widows' mortgages and demonstrably false tales that they never robbed from preachers, widows, or ex-Confederates. Their supporters, particularly John N. Edwards, a die-hard Missouri rebel who had fled to Mexico rather than surrender in 1865, began spreading their legend, comparing them in print to King Arthur and Sir Lancelot. The gang was particularly proud of its pioneering role

Suggestions for Further Reading: William A. Settle, Jr., *Jesse James Was His Name, or, Fact and Fiction Concerning the Careers of the Notorious James Brothers of Missouri*, University of Missouri Press, 1966; Kent Ladd Steckmesser, *Western Outlaws, The "Good Badman" in Fact, Film, and Folklore*, Regina Books, Claremont, CA, 1983.

*in robbing trains and once handed a conductor a press release with the head-
line THE MOST DARING TRAIN ROBBERY ON RECORD exactly describing the
holdup they had just perpetrated. They enjoyed jokes, puns, and dares as part of
their escape routine, such as posing as law officers chasing the James Boys or
leaving scraps of paper behind them with the taunt "Married Men Turn Around
and Go Home. Single Men Follow." These early masters of spin had positioned
themselves as romantics battling the encroaching railroads and Eastern banks,
ex-rebels persecuted by ex-Unionists, Democrats belabored by Radical Republicans, poor men persecuted by rich corporations and their political minions,
country boys assailed by city slickers—every theme that might resonate with the
Southern-bred backcountry folk who could hide them or give them support were
they captured. These images, which formed an enduring American legend, were
also the critical background of the trial of Frank James in 1883.*

*Missouri officials, goaded by a national press that described Missouri as the
"robber state," broke up the James gang in the early 1880s, arresting members
and securing confessions from them as well as raising among railroad and express companies the reward that led to Jesse's assassination in 1882 by gang
member Robert Ford—the dirty little coward of the famous ballad who shot Mr.
Howard in the back. Frank, hoping to make a deal and fearful of indictments for
crimes in other states where he would not find popular support, surrendered to
Missouri authorities and stood trial in August 1883 for his part in the last exploit
of the James gang, a train robbery at Winston, Missouri on the night of July 5,
1881, in which two people were shot to death. With no witnesses able to make a
positive identification, the oddly—and many charged improperly—selected jury of
twelve Democratic farmers considered sympathetic to former rebels and hostile
to railroad companies, found the defendant not guilty. Frank quit the life of
crime, but not the life of legend-maker, selling postcard photographs of himself,
appearing in some Wild West shows, and eking out a modest living until his
death in 1915.*

The Trial of Frank James for Train Robbery and Murder, *Gallatin, Miss-
ouri, 1883.*
HON. JOHN F. PHILIPS and HON. CHARLES GOODMAN, *Judges*

An indictment had been returned by the grand jury against Frank James for
the murder of Frank McMillan. The prisoner had pleaded Not Guilty.

[JUDGE GOODMAN made a short but pointed address to the crowded room in
which he told the audience what was expected of them during their attendance
upon the trial; that order would be preserved at all hazard. He said the court was
fully able to protect its dignity and the persons of its audience, and therefore any
person detected in the court room with weapons on, will surely, swiftly and to the
full extent of the law be punished. He further stated that for the accommodation of
the populace the trial would be conducted in the opera house, and that to prevent

inconvenience and provide for the safety of the audience the sheriff would issue tickets of admission not to exceed the seating capacity of the house.]

Mr. Wallace for the prosecution.

Mr. Wallace. While criminal practice allows me to make a statement of the magnitude of the crime, and set forth facts that would even augment the heinousness of the crime charged against the defendant, I will not pursue this course, but merely put forth the facts that will corroborate the facts alleged in the indictment. Perhaps this may be a mistaken course on my part. However, I have thought it sufficient to refer only to the irrefutable and overwhelming testimony that will be produced against the defendant. There may be some of the jury who admire the exploits of the accused, his chivalric deeds, his expertness, and other characteristics that have made him famous, and such will regard it as a privilege for such a poor and obscure person as McMillan to be shot down by an individual of such great fame as the accused, but I shall not tax the intelligence of the jury with such a suspicion, nor would it be right to attribute such a sentiment to any other intelligent and law-abiding citizen. A reader of yellow-covered literature might get into a morbid state of mind that would permit such attributes to be attached to the defendant.

[*Mr. Wallace* read the indictment, charging Frank James with complicity in the Winston robbery and the murder of McMillan. He then, in turn, described how the train was signaled and stopped; how, in turn, each step of the robbery and the tragedy of Winston was enacted. The particulars were given in detail, every point minutely mentioned, and it was avowed that each in turn would be proved beyond the possibility of a doubt by the prosecution.]

Mr. Wallace said that five men were engaged in the crime. Evidence would be adduced to show that Frank James, Jesse James, Wood Hite, Clarence Hite and Dick Liddil were the parties. Frank and Jesse James and Wood Hite entered the cars, and Dick Liddil and Clarence Hite had charge of the engine. With this assertion it was proper to refer to the James band, its organization and the purpose of its organization. The band was organized in Tennessee for the purposes of robbery. In 1877, Frank and Jesse James, with their families, moved to northern Tennessee, and subsequently went to living in Nashville. There the band was organized. It consisted of seven, Frank James was the oldest member. Next was Jesse James. Frank went under the name of B. J. Woodson and Jesse as J. D. Howard. Wood Hite, Dick Liddil, Bill Ryan, Jim Cummings and Ed Miller were members of the gang. The three last were not members of the band when the Winston robbery took place. . . .

Mr. Wallace told how the band came to leave Nashville or that vicinity. Bill Ryan left Nashville, where he went under the name of Tom Hill, to visit the Hites near Adairville. En route he got drunk, threatened the life of a justice of the peace, was arrested, and the plunder on his person aroused suspicion. News of Ryan's arrest alarmed Frank, alias B. J. Woodson, Jesse James, alias J. D. Howard, and Dick Liddil, alias Smith, and they left.

Mr. Wallace told how Clarence Hite joined the gang. A box of guns was shipped from Nashville to John Ford at Lexington, Missouri, and thence reshipped to Richmond. John Ford was a brother of Bob and Charlie Ford, and is now dead. The James boys' families left Tennessee just after their husbands, and among their traps was a sewing machine belonging to Mrs. Frank James, which was shipped to Pope City, it being her intention to meet General Shelby.

The gang rendezvous was at Mrs. Samuels' residence near Kearney and at Mrs. Bolton's in Ray county, she being the sister of the Ford boys.

Dick Liddil would be a witness to these facts. A conspiracy, or such a band could only be discovered or broken up by one of its members. Liddil's surrender under promises of exemption from the consequences of his crimes, has accomplished this.

However, there would be testimony introduced, the testimony of respectable citizens of Daviess county, who had seen Frank in this county about the time of the Winston robbery. He was seen, known and recognized by them, and though he wore burnside whiskers at the time, they would swear to his identity now. All this formed circumstantial evidence, but an unbroken chain strong enough to award the punishment due the defendant for the outrage and crime against law and life at Winston.

Witnesses for the State.

John L. Penn. Resided in Colfax Iowa; with Frank McMillan and several others, I got on the train at Winston, we belonged to the stonemason gang, old man McMillan got on too. It was about 9 p.m. Just as we got on, three men entered the door. Westfall, the conductor, was putting checks in our hats; we were standing up receiving the checks. The three men came in with a revolver in each hand. The two rushed up to our crowd and said something, but just what, I don't know. It was "up, up," or "down, down." Then two shots were fired, one going through Westfall. He made a motion like to defend himself, rushed to the rear end of the smoking car, the three men following and firing. Westfall got out on the platform and fell off. The men then returned to the front end of the car, and as they passed us, or just as they went out at the front door, Frank McMillan and I went out the rear door. Just then two shots were fired; looked through the glass of the door and a shot slivered the glass; saw a man on the front end of the car; he seemed to be watching and shooting through the car every few minutes. Frank McMillan and I, on the platform, sat down pretty close. Just then he heard a man halloo in the car. At this time three or four shots were fired. The train was going east, and the man was at the front end, and the shot went through the car. Frank heard the man call out, and said, "it is father," and jumped up, and just then he was shot above the eye and fell off the platform. I tried to catch him, but couldn't. The train was going slow at this time. The train slackened up near the switch, and at this time some man cried out to move on, and the train pulled out slow for three-quarters of a mile, when it stopped. Then three men jumped off the train, like off the baggage car, on the south side, passed me on the platform of the smoking car, went south of the track and disappeared in a hollow. There was shooting in the baggage car; several shots were fired. There were perhaps thirty to forty people in the car during the firing. They got down under the seats as best they could.

Frank Stamper. Was baggageman on the train. The baggage car and express car were together and next to the engine; the express agent was on the car. When the train stopped I stepped in the side door with my light, and was grabbed by the leg and pulled out, and a man pulled a revolver on me and told me to stand still. The train then moved on, and running I got on it, and passing through the passenger coach and sleeper, the passengers asked me what was the matter, and I said "robbers." The train consisted of a sleeper, three coaches, a smoking car and baggage car. The men came up to the side of the car on the north side, four or five, or six of them. They said "come out." No shots were fired until I got out, then there were shots in the smoking car and in the baggage car. Westfall was the conductor; saw Westfall at the station last; the train stopped the last time two miles from the station, and there the robbers left the train.

Had my light in my hand; saw one of the men distinctly when he came up to the door and pulled me out. The man had a long gray beard, wore a gray vest and white shirt; was the same man that stood guard over me. The man was a rather tall and slender man. He was not masked. Not any of them were. There was no masking unless they wore false beards.

Charles M. Murray. Reside at Davenport, Iowa; was on the train at the Winston robbery, and was express agent of the U.S. Express Co. A short distance from Winston the train was stopped and the baggage master rushed to the door to see what was the matter, and was pulled out; heard some firing; there was some sample trunks there and I dropped behind them. The train moved on and then stopped again. Then a man came in and demanded my money. He asked where the safe was, and I showed him; he demanded the key; I gave it to him, and then he directed me to open the safe; did so and he got the money, or I gave it to him, I don't know which. He asked me repeatedly if that was all. He said they had killed the conductor, were going to kill me and the engineer, and ordered me to get down on my knees. I didn't. He told me again, but I didn't, and he struck me over the head and knocked me unconscious; didn't come to until the baggagemaster came to my relief; didn't know how much money or treasure was taken; as to the packages taken could not tell anything as to their value, nor the number; saw three men (robbers) all told, and two came into the express car.

Dick Liddil. Am 31 years old; born and raised in Jackson county; know Frank and Jesse James. First got acquainted with them in 1870, at Robert Hudspeth's, in Jackson county, eight miles from Independence. . . . I have seen two or three of them there together—namely, Jesse James, John Younger and James McDaniel; never saw all five together; they were generally armed and on horseback; they would stay around there maybe a day and a night, or two nights, or maybe not more than two hours; supposed from what I heard and saw that they went together in a band.

There was a gang known as the James boys; belonged to it at one time; joined four years ago this fall. The band was Jesse James, Ed. Miller, Bill Ryan, Tucker Basham and Wood Hite. That was in the fall of 1880, in Jackson county. From there we went to six miles from Independence. I left shortly after that. I went in this summer of 1880 to Nashville with Jesse James. There we found Frank and Jesse James and their families; remained in Nashville nearly a year. The others came there in the winter of 1880–that is, Bill Ryan and Jim Cummings. Bill Ryan was from Jackson county. Bill Ryan, myself and Jesse James went there together. That was my second trip. . . .

Wood Hite was not at Hall's when the plan for the robbery was made. The others left word where they would meet him. Clarence Hite was 20 years old. Wood was 33 or 34 years of age. When in Missouri don't think he wore whiskers. If he did they were thin and light. His name in the gang in Missouri I could not give. We had to change names many times. I was Joe. Frank was Ben in Tennessee and Buck here, and Jesse was Dave in Tennessee. . . .

Frank James had burnsides and mustache. His whiskers were darker than his mustache. . . .

We all had horses. Frank rode the bay mare from Elkhorn. Wood rode a dark bay, taken by Frank and I from old man Frazier in Elkhorn. Frank rode the sorrel I had started on.

We started at night. I assisted in robbing the Winston train on this trip. We started from Mr. Samuels' at dark, coming northeast to Gallatin. We rode till daylight, when we came into a skirt of timber, where we stayed all night till sunrise. I don't reckon we came over fifteen miles that night. Next day we scattered. Frank and Clarence went together, and I, Jesse and Wood Hite together. We three ate dinner at a white house on the road, with an old shed stable back of it. There we met Frank and Clarence late in the evening. That night we stayed in the timber where we next met Wood on the former trip. We left Frank and Clarence together, Jesse and Wood together and I by myself, all going different routes; got my horse shod in Gallatin on the last trip we were here; can pick out the shop; is an old frame shop. There is another shop right below. I also got a pair of fenders to keep my horse from interfering. The saddler who sold them was a heavy man, with a dark mustache and a dark complexion. We were to meet about a mile from Winston. Got dinner on the way, and went on to meet the boys in a skirt of timber near where the road crosses the track. We waited till dark, hitched our horses and went up on foot to the train. Wood and I went together, and met Frank, Jesse and Clarence at the depot.

The arrangement was as follows: I and Clarence should capture the engineer, fireman and engine and start it or stop it as we might be directed by Jesse and Frank. Jesse, Frank and Wood were to get into the passenger cars and at the proper time rob the express car. We carried out the program when the north bound C. R. I. & P. passenger train came along. After getting outside of town

Clarence and I got up back of the tender, and went over on top to the engine. We had two pistols. We kept quiet till the train stopped; then we hollered to go ahead. We shot to scare those fellows, who both ran onto the pilot. The first run was about two hundred yards, then a stop. About this time one of the boys pulled the bell rope and the engineer stopped the train and firing back in the cars commenced. Don't know how many shots. Jesse got into [the] express car through the rear door and Wood and Frank tried to get in through the side door. The baggageman was standing in this side door and Frank seized him by the leg and jerked him out of the car and left him on the ground. Frank, dived into the express car and he or Jesse hollered to us to go ahead. The engineer pretended he could not move the train as the brakes were down. We then struck him with a piece of coal and told him we would kill him if he did not start the train. He then threw open the throttle and started it under a full head of steam. The engineer and fireman then got out of the cab and hid in front of the engine. We, firing a number of shots to frighten them, did not aim to hit them, as we could have easily killed them, being most of the time within a few feet. Started back to the express car, but Clarence called to me and I returned to the engine. Frank came out and shut off steam, and as she slacked we jumped off while it was running. Frank and Clarence got off first. I went back after Jesse who was still in the express car. Jesse jumped first, and I followed. We got $700 or $800 that night in packages. We all got together, except Wood, who had been knocked down as Frank pulled the baggageman out of the car, and we never saw him. Frank talked to me about the robbery afterward. He said he thought they had killed two men. Jesse said he shot one, he knew, and that Frank killed one. He saw him peep in at the window, and thought he killed him. From there we went to our horses, taking our time. The money was divided in a pasture, just before daylight. Jesse divided, giving us about $130 apiece. . . .

Mr. Rush's opening for the defense.

Mr. Rush began by returning thanks for the maintenance of health on the part of all concerned in the case so far, as health was a great factor in an intelligent and wise consideration of so important a case. He then enlarged upon the importance of the case, and declared it the greatest that had ever engaged the attention of a jury in Daviess county. At the outset Mr. Wallace had declared his purpose to establish a conspiracy, and to follow the band of conspirators from its organization in 1879 in Nashville, up to and even into the Winston robbery. He had done this to a certain extent, but by the testimony of Dick Liddil—and his nature and character would be exhibited to the jury in all its immoral enormity. Whatever corroboration other witnesses had given the continuous story of the state—these witnesses and their characters would be exposed for the contemplation of the jury. Coming to the facts alleged to be proved, *Mr. Rush* averred Frank James was not at the Winston robbery. . . . Referring to the witnesses in this section of the country, the speaker promised to show by witnesses present at the blacksmith shop and other places purported to have been visited by "the gang," were mistaken in identifying any one of them as Frank. Moreover, a witness on the train would be introduced to show Frank was not on the Winston train, and that the man seen in the woods a few hours before the robbery, by Ezra Soule, was not Frank James. Coming again to Dick Liddil's evidence, the defense claimed his story in court and his tale to Governor Crittenden did not agree, and that lying thus in any one particular his testimony was unworthy of belief. The speaker then took up the impelling motive of the interested witnesses in this case, and the nature of the prosecution. Dick Liddil's motive was that of revenge, superinduced by cowardice. He killed Wood Hite, feared Jesse and betrayed the band. He agreed to swear them into prison or to the scaffold, and he is merely fulfilling that agreement. . . . The motive of the prosecution was revenge. The officers of Kansas City had been cheated out of the reward offered for his apprehension by the surrender of the defendant. . . . As to the witnesses, one and all, in this region of the country, the speaker in answer to their alleged identification of the defendant would say they had seen a man, but the defense would prove that man was not Frank James. The speaker here enlarged upon the character of the defendant. For fifteen years he had been hunted through a country grid-ironed with railroads and with a web of wires overhead to ascertain his whereabouts. Yet he lived quietly and led a laborious life at Nashville from 1879 to March, 1881. The defense admitted this and confessed he left because of Bill Ryan's arrest. This was not the first time he had been forced to abandon his home, because Jesse, with outlawed companions had driven him out in the world. He, Frank James, was an outlaw, made so against his protest and against his appeals. The speaker then referred to the civilization that denied James citizenship and kept him from his home. He referred to the fact that other men, poor Bill Poole among the number, had been warned away from here, and returning had been shot down from behind. The civilization that permitted a party to sneakingly surround his mother's home, maim her and kill an infant brother in cold blood, warned him not to trust himself near people capable of such deeds of violence. He had been refused amnesty; had had governors refuse him clemency. This was not the place for him, and the defense was prepared to prove he was not in Missouri in 1881, nor at the Winston robbery.

The Witnesses for the Defense.

Samuel T. Brosius. Live at Gallatin; am a lawyer; was on the train that was robbed at Winston. We were about on time. There was a commotion on the front platform of our car, and two men commenced firing as I thought at the time, directly through the car. As the two men came in they called out, "hold up" or "show up," and I looked squarely into the face of the smaller of the two men to see that he noticed me; I held up my hands. As soon as the shooting commenced I saw that the conductor was hit. The two men continued to advance through the car till the larger of the two came up and nearly passed, when the conductor commenced sinking. He caught him, and the other man then came up on the other side. They hustled the conductor out on the platform, then came back, and passed me again, going out at the front end of the car. There was firing on the outside after they passed out. The larger man was full-faced, with beard all over his face, and would weigh one hundred and eighty to two hundred pounds. He was perhaps a full half head taller than the conductor; do not think defendant is the man.

Mrs. Elizabeth Montgomery. Live a mile and a half east of Winston. Remember the Winston robbery. Some strange men ate at our house that night. The clock struck seven before they finished. The younger man was the taller and light complexioned, with burnside whiskers. The older man had dark whiskers and mustache, and dark clothes. One horse was a bay and the other a shade lighter. They had some bundles tied to their saddles.

Mr. Slover. Is the defendant one of those men?

Mrs. Elizabeth Montgomery. I think not, but cannot be positive. Think both horses were bay but one was lighter than the other. The bigger man had whiskers all over his face, chin and all.

General Shelby. Have for thirty-four years resided in Lafayette county. Live nine miles from Lexington and nearer Page City. Remember Jesse James, Dick Liddil, Bill Ryan and Jim Cummings coming to my place in November, 1880. Was spreading hemp at the time, working some twelve or fifteen men, and when I returned home that evening found four men with horses in my yard. Jesse James was there. Young Cummings I knew before, and this man Liddil passed as Mr. Black at that time. In the morning had a conversation with Jesse James in the presence of Dick Liddil, in which I said that a couple of young men had been arrested for supposed complicity with the alleged bank robbery at Concordia, and that I didn't think they had anything to do with it; and asked Jesse James if he knew anything about that affair to tell me, and he said, pointing to Dick Liddil, there is the man that hit the Dutch cashier over the head. Remember in November, 1881, meeting Liddil and Jesse James in my lane, and when I asked Jesse who was ahead of them he replied, Jim Cummings and Hite. Remember meeting Jesse James and Liddil again in the fall of 1881, and of asking Jesse where Frank was, and of his announcement that Frank's health was such that he had been south for years, and that when I asked the same question of Liddil he announced that he had not seen him for two years. Reckon I know Cummings better than any man except Ford's and his own people. He was at my house a dozen times. He was with me in the Confederate army. Have not seen Frank James since 1872. Believe he sits right there now. With the permission of the court, can I be tolerated to shake hands with an old soldier?

The COURT. No, sir, not now.

Gen. Shelby. Did not see him in jail. Have not seen him since 1872. Am correct about it, sir, when I say that the four parties to whom I have alluded by name did not include Frank James, who was not with them. Mrs. Frank James came to Page City in the spring of 1881. She sent for me and said to me, I am in distress. This man Liddil and others are committing depredations in the south, and they are holding my husband amenable for it, as he has been charged with being connected with them. She wanted me to interfere in her husband's behalf with the governor. Told her it was folly to do so, and advised her to go home to her father. She didn't stop at my house. She could have stopped there if she had desired. As to the sewing machine, don't know what time the sewing machine arrived there. She simply gave Mr. Birch, the agent at the depot, directions for shipping it and I don't know where she directed it to be shipped at all. Was only assisting a woman in distress, and if she had been Gennison's wife, the most obnoxious man in the country—. Mrs. James left orders with the agent for the movement of the sewing machine. She was a lone woman, with a little child, and crying, and any man who would have faltered in giving suggestion or aid ought to be ashamed of himself. Have known Frank James since 1862. Have not seen him for twelve years. Got acquainted with him in our army.

Mr. Wallace. This sewing machine you didn't see at all?
Gen. Shelby. Nobody knows better than yourself that I didn't see it.

The Court. Answer the question in a straightforward manner.
Gen. Shelby. I did not.

Mr. Wallace. You didn't have anything to do with it at all?
Gen. Shelby. Nothing in the world.
Mr. Wallace. You are just as sure of that as you are of anything else?

Gen. Shelby. To the Court. I would like to know if the Judge is going to permit a lawyer to insult an unarmed man, who is a witness in this case?

The Court. Every witness comes in here unarmed, sir....

Mr. Wallace. You saw Liddil down at Capt. Ballinger's house, afterward, didn't you? You don't propose to invade the household of Capt. Ballinger, a soldier of the federal army?
Gen. Shelby. It is very wrong for a rebel soldier to make remarks about what occurred in a federal soldier's home.
Mr. Wallace. The war is over.
Gen. Shelby. I don't like to allude to a visit to a gentleman's home. That is indelicate and improper.
Mr. Wallace. Did you see Liddil there?
Gen. Shelby. I did, sir. I saw him like a viper, curled up in a rocking-chair.
Mr. Wallace. You saw him again at the hotel the other night, or was that a drummer that you took for him?

Gen. Shelby. No, sir; by no means.

Mr. Wallace. Were you not about to kill the drummer, thinking he was Dick Liddil?

Gen. Shelby. I have lived thirty-four years in this state and never killed anybody yet.

Mr. Wallace. Answer the question.

Gen. Shelby. I was not.

Mrs. Zerelda Samuels. Have lived for forty years in Clay county. Am the mother of Jesse and Frank James. Frank was forty years old last January. Have lived three miles from Kearney. Have other children—Mrs. Palmer, Mrs. Nicholson, Mrs. Hall, and John T. Samuels. Jesse was killed two years ago next April. Jesse was at my house during 1881. He came there either in May or June. Before that he had not been home for some time. The first time he came Jim Cummings and Dick Liddil were with him—no, only Dick Liddil. Asked Jesse where Buck, or Frank, was, and he said he had left him in Kentucky in bad health. Said, Son, you know he is dead, and I turned to Liddil and he said they had left him in Kentucky. They left my house after the Winston robbery. During that summer the parties that met at my house were Charley Ford, Dick Liddil, Clarence and Wood Hite and Jesse James. My son Frank was not there that summer. Have not seen Frank for seven years till I saw him at Independence. The last time before that I saw him was when Mr. Broome was sheriff of Clay county, and they came to my house and shot at him. Saw Jim Cummings that summer. His relations live three or four miles from my house. One of his sisters married Bill Ford, uncle of the Ford boys. Liddil and the Hites were often at my house that summer previous to the Winston robbery. Did not know that summer where Frank James was. Thought he was dead. Am fifty-five years old. Was fifty years old when I lost my hand.

Frank James (Sworn.)

Judge Philips for the defense.

Judge Philips. Mr. James, you are the defendant in this case?

Frank James. Yes.

Judge Philips. Begin your statement of the history of this case, where the prosecution began, with the time of your departure from Missouri for Tennessee some years ago. Just state when that was?

Frank James. That was in the winter of 1876, if I remember it correctly.

Judge Philips. State where you went and where you stayed.

Frank James. Well sir, it is quite a route to follow it all round. I ranged across southeast Missouri directly into Tennessee, crossing the Mississippi river, think, perhaps about between the first and fifth of January, if I am not mistaken.

Judge Philips. State what time you arrived at Nashville.

Frank James. Didn't arrive at Nashville until July, 1876. Went directly then from Nashville out into what is known as the White creek neighborhood. Rented a farm, which, however, I could not get possession of until January 1, 1878. Remained at Mrs. Ledbetter's during that fall. Put in a crop of wheat and moved there and lived in the place known as the Jesse Walton place one year, that was up to 1878. Next year I rented a place from Felix Smith, on White creek. Remained there a year, and made a crop in the meantime—a general crop, as farmers raise— corn, oats and wheat. The next year lived on what is known as the Jeff Hyde place, on Hyde's ferry, about three and a half miles from Nashville. Remained there a year. During that year didn't farm any. Was working for the Indiana Lumber company. That I think was in 1879. Was working in the woods, logging, as they term it, and I worked off and on all that summer at that business, driving a four mule team, and after that think it was in 1880, moved into Nashville. During that time as it was very hard work logging, I got several strains and my health became impaired, and I found I would have to go at some other business. Thinking I could not stand working ten hours a day for three years as I had, I concluded to move into Nashville and go into some other business.

My first meeting with my brother Jesse was entirely accidental; was farming, as I stated, on the Walton place, and had gone into the store of B. S. Rhea & Son, and while I was sampling oats and talking to one of the clerks, Jesse James walked out of the office, came up to me and says: Why, how do you do? I spoke to him; didn't call any name of course. He was going by; he asked me where I was living, and I told him; he went out home with me, and told me he was living in Humphreys county, one hundred miles west of Nashville. He had been buying grain for this firm of B. S. Rhea & Son. That was in the spring of 1878.

The first time I met Dick Liddil in Tennessee was, in 1879. He and Jesse James came in together. Liddil was there off and on until that fall. He was making trips to and fro, but where I have no idea. Never saw Ryan, Jesse James and Liddil together any great deal in Nashville. When they were out of my sight my impression is they were together, but of course when they were out of my sight I could not state what became of them.

Wood Hite's name was Woodson Hite. He was between thirty-three and thirty-five years of age. His hair was light and his whiskers darker, rather dark sandy. He was a little stoop-shouldered, had a large, prominent nose and high forehead, and would weigh one hundred and fifty pounds. There was a striking family resemblance between us. My attention was first called to it the first time Dick Liddil and Jesse James came to our house. The next morning after breakfast Jesse looked at me and says, Why, Dick, he says, he looks like old Father Grimes. I said: Who is old Father Grimes? He says: he is your counsin, Wood Hite, and Dick laughed and said; Yes; he is. Clarence Hite was slender. You would call him a stripling, very loose in his movements, light complexioned, and, I believe, light-haired, with no whiskers at all. When I saw him in Kentucky he looked just like a green boy. From the Hite's we went to Nelson county, Kentucky. We first arrived at Richard Hoskin's, an old gentleman who lived in the 'knobs,' for it is a very broken country. There I separated from Jesse James and Dick Liddil, and can not tell where they went. Know a man in Nelson county named Robert Hall.

Was not at his place in company with Dick Liddil and Jesse James. There was no agreement entered into between Jesse James, Dick Liddil and myself, or myself with any other parties, to go to Missouri for the purpose of robbing the express at the Kansas City ferry; but, I tried to persuade them not to come to Missouri. Jesse and Dick had been talking of coming to Missouri ever since we left Nashville. Liddil had left his wife here and seemed very anxious to get back. Am not certain who was his reputed wife, but believe it was Miss Mattie Collins. Told Jesse, and Dick not to come to Missouri, because it would endanger the life of our mother. I said: You know already what has been done there. You know there is no protection for my mother and family in the state of Missouri, let alone for you, and I would never go there. My advice to Dick Liddil was to go to work somewhere and then he would have much more money at the end of the year than if he put in his time galloping around the country. But Jesse said they would go anyway. So I separated from them in Nelson county, Kentucky. Was not at Hall's in connection with Liddil and Jesse James. Remained there perhaps till the tenth or fifteenth of May, though I don't just remember the date. Then went to Louisville. Robert Hall took me in a buggy. From there I went to Texas. On the trip from Nashville to Hite's I rode a horse I got from Dick Liddil in 1879. That is the horse he speaks of having sold me. Gave that horse to Mr. Hall for his services in driving me in a buggy to Louisville. From Louisville I went to Texas. Mrs. Palmer is my sister. Got to her house about the first of June, 1881. Remained there five or six weeks. After leaving my sister's I went into the Indian Nation. Got down in that country about the time I heard of the Winston robbery. . . .

Noticed the assassination of Jesse James. Was taking a New York Daily Herald at the time. Had been out walking and when I got back to the house I saw my wife was excited, and she came rushing to me with the paper and says; Jesse James is killed. I says, my God, where and how and who killed him? That was the third of April. After that I paid close attention to my papers. Remember reading in the New York Herald how Governor Crittenden, when asked what hope there was for Frank James, he replied, wherein as none of his friends have never asked anything, I will not state anything about it. That gave me hope. I said to my wife, possibly if you return to Missouri and show a willingness on my part to let the past be buried, and that I am willing to surrender myself up, and be tried and meet every charge they can bring against me, I may have a fair and impartial trial. She went. Left Lynchburg, May 10, 1882, returning to Nelson county, Kentucky. Remained there until I effected my surrender and came to Missouri, October 5, 1882. Was not in Missouri from 1876 to the time I passed through going from Texas to Kentucky.

Went to Kentucky because I wanted to go there to see friends. After getting into Kentucky I kept with them and went to Nelson county for the purpose then of keeping Jesse from going back to Missouri, fully realizing the result would be what it has been, and to prevent another hand grenade raid on my mother's family and the children of the whole family.

Instructions to the Jury

JUDGE GOODMAN. The court instructs the jury on behalf of the state as follows:

If the jury believe from the evidence that defendant Frank James, in the month of July, 1881, at the county of Daviess, in the state of Missouri, willfully, deliberately, premeditatedly, and of his malice aforethought shot and killed one Frank McMillan; or if the jury find that any other person then and there willfully, deliberately, premeditatedly, and of his malice aforethought, shot and killed said Frank McMillan, and that defendant Frank James was present, and then and there willfully, premeditatedly and deliberately and of his malice aforethought aided, abetted, or counseled such other person in so shooting and killing the said Frank McMillan, then the jury ought to find the defendant guilty of murder in the first degree. . . .

The court instructs the jury that under the second count of the indictment the defendant is charged with making an assault in connection with others upon one Charles Murray, and robbing him of certain money, the property of said Murray, and that in perpetration thereof they shot and killed one Frank McMillan. Before the jury can find the defendant guilty under this count they must find and be satisfied beyond a reasonable doubt from the evidence that the defendant made such felonious assault on said Murray and stole from him money as charged in the indictment, and also that in the perpetration of said felony he shot and killed McMillan, or that the defendant acting in connection with one or more of the parties named in the indictment was present aiding, counseling and abetting them in committing said assault and robbery; and that some one or more of said other persons so named in the indictment did shoot and kill said McMillan, and that said killing was so done in the prosecution of said felony. . . .

In order to justify the inference of legal guilt from circumstantial evidence alone, the existence of the inculpating facts must be absolutely incompatible with the innocence of the accused and incapable of explanation upon any other reasonable hypothesis than that of his guilt.

The Speeches to the Jury

Mr. Hamilton began by expressing his unbounded confidence in the character and integrity of the jury and his belief that their verdict would be an acceptable expression of the sense of the community in connection with this crime. He discussed briefly train robbery as a new and ingenious crime which owed its invention to Missourians. He recalled the night when the news flashed over the country that a train had been robbed and two innocent men were killed within a few miles of Gallatin, and reminded the jury how every honest man was filled with indignation at this insult to the law and disgrace to the country. He stoutly denied that the state had used any extraordinary or unfair means to make a case against the defendant. He said that Dick Liddil's testimony, with that of two corroborating witnesses, was of itself abundantly sufficient to convict, but that independent of that man's testimony the state had made out a case. He held that the admitted association of these men in Tennessee and Kentucky, the shipping of the box of guns to the rendezvous of the gang in Missouri, and the absolute and unimpeached proof that the defendant was one of the men in the vicinity of Winston on the day of the robbery were facts of themselves sufficient to convict. The fact that Liddil was a horse-thief was not the fault of the defendant. He chose his own companions and if one of these companions was a horse-thief and afterward proved an informer the defendant was simply unfortunate in his choice. The men who corroborated Liddil, he said, were respectable citizens who could have no motive in sacrificing the life of an innocent man. As far as any part the railroad company had taken in aiding the prosecution, he held that a corporation, as well as a citizen, should aid in hunting down and bringing to punishment any miscreant who perpetrated a crime against it. It was a duty the road owed to the traveling public and to the shippers of treasure. . . .

Judge Philips for the prisoner.

Judge Philips. Long before the prisoner at the bar had surrendered to the governor of the state, he applied to me, through a mutual friend, to know whether, if he should come in and throw himself upon the country, I would undertake his defense and aid in according to him the constitutional privilege of a fair and impartial trial before the courts. He was distinct and candid in the statement that he had not a dollar in the world to offer me. Upon me he had no claims, other than those which spring from the bonds of human sympathy and that charity—the one touch of which makes all the world kin.

In that fierce, internecine strife, which swept the land like a tornado, dividing families, arraying father against son and brother against brother, in deadliest contention, Frank James and I stood in mortal antagonism. It was my fortune to see his flag go down in desperate defeat, while mine went up in permanent triumph. I was victor, he was the vanquished.

Whatever others may say or think, the idea I had and have of the episode of the James brothers was that it came as the bitter fruit of that dire strife. And when, from the summit of peace on which we stand today, we look back over the trampled fields yet marked with the red hot plough-share of war, and recall the history of civil wars, reciting how slowly nations recover from the blight—how long it takes the ghastly wounds in the body politic to heal, I affirm surprise at the rapidity of our recovery. And when I recall all the local bitterness of that day, with its crimination and recrimination, its reprisals and outrages, peculiar to neither side in Missouri, with the bad blood it engendered, and today behold the magnificent picture of a civilized state, reposing in peace, exulting in plenty, and marching on to higher achievements in the arts of peace and social order, my heart swells with pride and gratitude to the God of our deliverance.

And when I saw the so-called James gang—the last remnant in the state of unreconciled and unaccepted parties to the local predatory struggle, suing for reconciliation—offering to throw themselves on the justice of the law and the mercy of the Commonwealth, asking nothing but fair treatment—with but one aspiration and one hope, to devote, if allowed, the remainder of their lives and energies to the duties of a husband, father and good citizenship, my whole heart went out in congratulation to the good people of the state.

To the prisoner, his wife and their little boy, I had but one response to make to their personal appeal to me. No man, no creature made in the image of God, could appeal to me for words of justice, for one throb of sympathy, under such conditions, without my heart beating a little warmly for him and his. . . .

Gentlemen of the jury, common fame has invested this defendant with unmerited notoriety—giving to his life much of romance. How much of truth and how much of fiction there is in it all you and I know not in this trial. Under the broad shield of the constitution of the state he stands before you in this court room as any other citizen. The bond of your oath is that you know him only as the evidence shows him to be. You are to take him where the evidence finds him, and leave him where it places him.

Public rumor is often a false and a foul thing. It has had Frank James identified with every outrage and bold robbery committed between the mountains of West Virginia and the Ozarks of Arkansas and Missouri within the last six years. During these years rumor has placed him simultaneously in the counties of Clay, Jackson, Lafayette, in this state and elsewhere, wherever daring exploit in outlawry startled the country.

But what does the state's own testimony disclose? In 1876 he left this state, with all his earthly possessions—a two-horse wagon and his young wife—and went to the state of Tennessee. Everything about that movement indicated what? To my mind this is impressively significant. The miseries and ghosts of the war hung around his footsteps in Missouri. Weary and heartsick of it all he determined to turn his back upon it, and seek a new home, under an assumed name, in the hope that he might find a new life of peace in humble, honest industry. He had just taken to his bosom and confidence a young, trusting sweet woman. That of itself was highest proof that he was not seeking longer adventure, but that pleasure and happiness which come surest from domestic life and retirement.

I confess myself surprised a the developments of this piece of evidence, touching upon the life and conduct of this man during the years that followed his removal to Tennessee. It strengthens my faith in him. True it is that Jesse James accompanied him from Missouri. But in southeast Missouri they separated, like Abraham and Lot of old, one taking to the right and the other to the left, each pursuing his own course. Frank went to Nashville, not to maraud, not in quest of a new theatre of adventure. He went upon a little farm, and there he toiled, struggled and plead with the generous earth for bread and sustenance. The evidence declares that from early morn of Monday to nightfall on Saturday, week after week, year after year, he delved, drove teams, hauled logs, for one dollar and a half per day; and for nearly five years he was not further from his little home than the nearest trading village or town. Respected and much liked by all his neighbors he ate his bread in peace.

There, too, the first born of happy marriage came to gladden and lend a new charm to that humble home.

There is not on this jury a man who can believe that from the spring of 1876 to the time of the decampment in the spring of 1881 Frank James was engaged in any marauding expedition, or any violation of law, because both the state's testimony and that of the defense establish his constant presence at home in unremit-tent farm labor. . . .

Dick Liddil says they agreed to return to Missouri for pillage and plunder. On the other hand Frank James says that Jesse proposed to return to Missouri, and against that proposition he entered his solemn and earnest protest. Why not be-lieve his story in preference to Dick Liddil? Is it not the more rational? It is cor-roborated by many facts and circumstances in evidence. The defendant says he told his brother they must not go to Missouri, as God knew their dear old mother had already suffered enough on their account. He called up the picture of the sorrow and desolation hitherto wrought in her home, how she had lost her arm by Pinker-ton's detectives throwing hand grenades into her room, and also killing her little child and their brother; that their presence in the state would subject her to espi-onage and additional insult, if not injury and outrage. How natural was this argu-ment and appeal? But Jesse was heady and desperate. On that rock they split.

There is another confirmatory fact, favoring the defendant's story. He sent his wife to her father in Jackson county, Missouri. The family sewing machine was for-warded by express to Page City, Missouri, in care, perhaps, of General Shelby. . . .

Speaker for the prosecution.

What is the evidence in this most important case? As the sun is setting in the west, on the fifteenth day of July, 1881, we see a passenger train rolling slowly un-der the vast shedway at the Union Depot in Kansas City, Missouri, and its engine takes its place by the side of half a dozen or more of others, each panting like so many horses ready for the race. To me, gentlemen, there is something sublime about a locomotive engine; I can look at it and admire it, even if it does belong to a rich corporation, and I have no interest in it. Thank God, in the great realm of vi-sion, we are equally wealthy. Rolling rivers, towering mountains, outstretching plains, bending skies, as well as the splendid specimens of human skill that fret our public streams and highways, are all in the realm of vision the property of rich and poor alike. Yes, what a glorious structure is a railroad engine, what a giant-like tribute to man's inventive genius; how like a thing of life with vast, pulsating heart, it seems to live, and move, and have its being. When like the queen of commerce it comes gliding along, with gorgeous, resplendent coaches for its train, how the law-abiding soul—with never a dream of stopping it in search of plunder—delights to see it speed on, in magnificent splendor and sublimest power. Many a time, a few years since, while loitering about Kansas City, as young lawyers do, have I stood upon the bluffs and watched the trains as they came in and went out; watched them just at night-fall, when they were all departing for the east; watched them as, hurling down the river bottom, with resounding whistle, rolling smoke, and white, stream-ing steam, they plunged into the tunnel of the night, and were seen no more.

So the ill-fated Rock Island train departed in July 15, 1881; so it sped on like a meteor through the darkness until it reached the prairies of your own county. What a splendid spectacle is presented by an approaching train on a western prairie in the night-time! I see that train coming up to Winston now, with its beaming headlight, now partly obscured in a cut, now out, trembling along like a rolling, radiant ball of fire. Yes, yes, gentlemen, I see that train speeding across the prairies of your own free Missouri, where the protecting aegis of the law is spread over every head, and we boast that life, liberty, and the pursuit of happiness is guaranteed to every human being within her borders. I hear the rails clicking by the platform; I see the white steam rise; the whistle sounds out on the pure country air, and in a moment the train is standing at the depot in the town of Winston. Frank James was there to meet that train, gentlemen. Just as surely was he there, as that he is here today. Just as surely was he there as that the village was there— as that Westfall and McMillan were there. Just as surely was he there, as that the All-seeing Eye was there, looking down into the foul intention that dwelt in his heart. Let us look a moment at his surroundings, for here we may get a glimpse at the superb innocence of the "remarkable hero" now on trial. It is said that when a man contemplates doing a wicked deed, if he will look at some splendid painting or upon some scene where nature with her brush has eclipsed all human genius, his vile thoughts may all be taken away. Look at his surroundings on this fatal night. There stands a magnificent train, known to him to be laded with precious immortal beings whose life he is about to hazard. Perchance the mother is there, returning from a visit to her children in the west, or the boy going east to bid farewell to a dying parent. Innocent little children, unborn when civil war brought the defendant his much-talked-of grievance, are there, with tiny hands against the window glass, and eyes peering out, asking his pity and protection. The pure, free atmosphere of his native state is about him. The smoke of the standing engine is towering upward, and as his eyes follow it they meet the tender light from a myriad of twinkling stars, each whispering to him with a silver tongue, pleading with him, as if to woo and win him from his unlawful purpose.

But it is all to no avail. Frank McMillan, old man McMillan, his father and the two Penns—all laborers in a stone-quarry hard by—have gotten into the smoking car. Conductor Westfall, little knowing the sad fate impending, waves his lantern for the last time. The bell rings. The train starts. The robbers get aboard. The fiendish work begins. I am going now by the evidence—no fancy. Dick Liddil and Clarence Hite climb upon the tender to take charge of the engineer and firemen. Jesse James, Frank James, and Wood Hite rush into the smoking-car from the front door; one of them—as seen by the witness Maj. McGee, a most intelligent gentleman, and at present United States Marshal—cuts the bell-rope, and doubtless in doing so gives the signal at the engine which causes the train to stop; but it at once starts up again. The two tall men, as the witness Penn calls them, come right up to conductor Westfall, at this time engaged in putting tabs in the hats of Penn and his companions, saying, "up, up," or "down, down," the witness, affrighted and thunderstruck with the tragedy of double murder, can not say which. Westfall, seeing death was lurking, made some motion thus, as Penn put it; he can not say for what. I believe to defend himself, as duty and God bade him do. Just at that instant the big tall man—all admit now Jesse James—quick as a tiger for his victim, pulls the cruel trigger, and Westfall goes reeling down the aisle to the rear end of the car; as he goes the firing at him is continued. He opens the door, struggles out, and falls dead from the train; dead in the harness! dead on duty!

Again, you are most cunningly urged to acquit because the defendant was a soldier in the "lost cause." Your sympathies and prejudices are continually appealed to in this behalf. In the opening statement for the defense, before they had even introduced their evidence, the counsel boldly told you, that you, yourselves, would remember some man, naming him, an ex-confederate, who at the close of the war returned from the army to your county here—as his client fain would have returned to his county—and was shot down like a dog. He even went away from your county, and named some returning confederate soldier who was similarly shot down on the streets of Lexington, Missouri. Governor Johnson once, or more, referred to the defendant as having been a "gallant soldier"; and any number of times you heard from them the expression, "a soldier with Gen. Shelby." But the climax was reached when Judge Philips, in speaking of the surrender of the defendant said, that when he saw that Frank James had handed his pistols to the Governor of Missouri, he was surprised that the whole matter was closed up so quickly; was astonished that in twenty short years all the "bitter animosities of civil strife were ended"; in plain English, gentlemen, that the surrender of Frank James is to be taken as the end of the "lost cause"—that the "lost cause" wound up in pillage, plunder, train-robbery and murder. Gentlemen, when he said that I thought I heard Robert E. Lee, Stonewall Jackson, Sterling Price, and all the gallant host of southern chiefs who slumber by them, roll over in their graves and murmur "no," "no," "no." Yea, I thought I saw every confederate graveyard throughout the south, yawn in an instant, and each and every sleeping soldier come forth in battle garb from his narrow home, and all shout out in clarion voices "no!" "no!" "no!" And even as they went back, like receding ghosts, I still heard them shouting, "no!" "no!" "no!"

The Verdict

At 12:30 p.m. the *jury* retired, and at 4 p.m. returned the following verdict:

"State of Missouri v. Frank James—murder: We, the jury in the above entitled cause, find the defendant *not guilty* as charged in the indictment.

"Wm. F. Richardson, Foreman."

4
Labor's Martyrs
The Haymarket Trial
1886

The Knights of Labor began in 1869 among Philadelphia garment workers as a secret society mixing idealism and elaborate ritual much like the fraternal lodges so popular among men of that era. After abortive strikes in 1877, workers and small entrepreneurs found attractive the Knights' sociability, idealism, and vague goal of a cooperative commonwealth. The organization spread nationally and early in the 1880s soared in membership. Dropping its male fraternity style, the Knights, began welcoming women and black workers organized in separate Assemblies—the basic unit of the organization. Many workers belonged both to the Knights, which welcomed all workers and opposed strikes, and to a trade union exclusive to their craft, the main weapon of which was the strike. In addition, a number of fringe groups of varying shades of socialism and anarchism noisily struggled with small success to organize the workers as a revolutionary body.

Then in 1884, when a brief period of hard times brought wage cuts, labor militancy flared in a series of strikes. In 1885, railroad workers unexpectedly won union recognition from Jay Gould's Southwestern railroad system. The effect on the Knights of Labor—which had in fact opposed the strikes—was stunning. Between 1885 and mid-1886 membership climbed from about a hundred thousand to seven hundred thousand. Their most attractive demand was for the eight-hour day, the one goal that united virtually all segments of the labor movement. May 1, 1886, was the magic day when all of labor would strike to achieve "Eight hours for work, eight hours for rest, eight hours for what we will."

This scarcely organized national movement provided a tense background for events unfolding independently in Chicago. There Knights, unions, socialists, and anarchists vied for workers' loyalties, and police violence against workers had become, according to a recent study, "routine." Scuffles among police, scabs, and workers that had punctuated a strike going on since February at the McCormick Harvester factory culminated in a bloody clash on May 3, 1886. In response a small group of anarchists, printing a circular—in German and English—headed "REVENGE! WORKINGMEN! TO ARMS!," called a meeting at Haymarket Square for the evening of May 4.

SUGGESTIONS FOR FURTHER READING: Paul Avrich, *The Haymarket Tragedy*, Princeton, New Jersey: Princeton University Press, 1984; Bruce C. Nelson, *Beyond the Martyrs, A Social History of Chicago's Anarchists, 1870–1900*, New Brunswick, New Jersey: Rutgers University Press, 1988.

The meeting was sparsely attended and lackluster. The mayor of Chicago, Carter Harrison, judged the crowd "tame"; impending rain shrunk it further. Yet just as the meeting was about to end, a squad of 180 police arrived and the captain ordered "this meeting immediately and peaceably to disperse." "We are peaceable," the confused speaker replied. Then someone threw a bomb. Chaos ensued and the police opened fire. Possibly some of the crowd fired back. The Haymarket bombing and the trial growing out if it had large consequences. Already weakened after the railroad workers lost a further strike against the Southwestern railroads, the Knights of Labor collapsed. Although labor leaders were unanimous in their condemnation of the bombing, the entire labor movement was tarred with the brush of anarchism. Four anarchists were executed; one committed suicide the day before his scheduled execution; one received a fifteen-year prison sentence; and two had their death sentences commuted to life imprisonment. In 1893, Illinois Governor John Peter Altgeld pardoned the three survivors, a controversial decision that probably cost him reelection.

The Trial of the Eight Chicago Anarchists. *In the Criminal Court of Cook County, Chicago, Illinois, June, 1886.*
HON. JOSEPH E. GARY, *Judge*

On May 28, 1886, the Grand Jury returned into court, indictments for murder, conspiracy and riot, against August Spies, Albert R. Parsons, Adolph Fischer, George Engel, Louis Lingg, Samuel Fielden, Michael Schwab, and Oscar W. Neebe. The prisoners were charged with being accessories before the fact to the murder of one Mathias J. Degan, a policeman, in the city of Chicago, May 4, 1886, by the explosion of a bomb. It was not charged that any of the accused threw the bomb with his own hands. There are sixty-nine counts in the indictment. Some of the counts charge that the eight defendants above named, being present, aided, abetted, and assisted in the throwing of the bomb; others, that, not being present, aiding, abetting, or assisting, they advised, encouraged, aided and abetted such throwing.

All the prisoners with the exception of *Parsons* appeared in court and pleaded *not guilty.*

Julius S. Grinnell, States Attorney; *Francis W. Walker, Edmund Furthmann,* and *George C. Ingham,* for the People.
William P. Black, William A. Foster, Sigmund Zeisler, and *Moses Salomon,* for the prisoners.

Mr. Grinnell. Gentlemen: For the first time in the history of our country are people on trial for their lives for endeavoring to make Anarchy the rule, and in that attempt for ruthlessly and awfully destroying life. I hope that while the youngest of us lives this in memory will be the last and only time in our country when such a trial shall take place. It will or will not take place as this case is determined.
The State now and at no time hereafter will say anything to arouse your prej-

udices or your indignation, having confidence in the case that we present; and I hope I shall not at any time during this trial say anything to you which will in any way or manner excite your passions. I want your reason. I want your careful analysis. I want your careful attention.

On the 4th of My, 1886, a few short weeks ago, there occurred, at what is called Haymarket Square, the most fearful massacre ever witnessed or heard of in this country. The crime culminates there—you are to find the perpetrators. The charge against the defendants is that they are responsible for that act. The testimony that shall be presented to you will be the testimony which will show their innocence or their guilty complicity in that crime.

We have been in this city inclined to believe, as we have all through the country, that, however extravagantly men may talk about our laws and our country, however severely they may criticise our Constitution and our institutions; that as we are all in favor of full liberty, of free speech, the great good sense of our people would never permit acts based upon sentiments which meant the overthrow of law. We have believed it for years; we were taught it at our schools in our infancy, we were taught it in our maturer years in school, and all our walks in life thereafter have taught us that institutions, founded on our Constitution, the Declaration of Independence, and our universal freedom, were above and beyond all Anarchy. The 4th of May demonstrated that we were wrong, that we had too much confidence, that a certain class of individuals, some of them recently come here, as the testimony will show, believe that here in this country our Constitution is a lie. Insults are offered to the Declaration of Independence, the name of Washington is reviled and traduced, and we are taught by these men, as the testimony will show, that freedom in this country means lawlessness and absolute license to do as we please, no matter whether it hurts others or not. In the light of the 4th of May we now know that the preachings of Anarchy, the suggestions of these defendants hourly and daily for years, have been sapping our institutions, and that where they have cried murder, bloodshed, Anarchy and dynamite, they have meant what they said, and proposed to do what they threatened.

We will prove, gentlemen, in this case, that Spies no longer ago than last February said that they were armed in this city for bloodshed and riot. We will prove that he said then that they were ready in the city of Chicago for Anarchy, and when told, by a gentleman to whom he made the declaration, that they "would be hung like snakes," said—and there was the insult to the Father of our Country— then he said George Washington was no better than a rebel, as if there was any possible comparison between those declarations, between that sentiment of Washington's and his noble deeds, and the Anarchy of this man. He has said in public meetings—and the details of them I will not now worry you with—he has said in public meetings for the last year and a half, to go back no further—he and Neebe and Schwab and Parsons and Fielden have said in public meetings here in the city of Chicago that the only way to adjust the wrongs of any man was by bloodshed, by dynamite, by the pistol, by the Winchester rifle. They have advised, as will appear in proof here, that dynamite was cheap, and "you had better forego some luxuries, buy dynamite, kill capitalists, down with the police, murder them, dispose of the militia and then demand your rights." That is Anarchy.

On the 11th day of October, 1885, in a prominent public hall upon the West Side, August Spies, the defendant in this case, and his confreres there, introduced a resolution at a public meeting, in which he said that he did not believe that the eight-hour movement would do the laboring man any good. We will prove in this case that he has always been opposed to the eight-hour law. That is not what he wants. He wants Anarchy. These defendants that I mentioned passed a resolution, which we shall offer in evidence here, and it shall be read to you later—to the effect that the laboring men must arm, must prepare themselves with rifles and dynamite. When? By the 1st of May, 1886, because then would come the contest.

I will prove to you that Parsons—be it said to the shame of our country, because I understand that he was born on our soil—that Parsons, in an infamous paper published by him, called the *Alarm*, has defined the use of dynamite, told how it should be used, how capitalists could be destroyed by it, how policemen could be absolutely wiped from the face of the earth by one bomb; and further has published a plan in his paper of street-warfare by dynamite against militia and the authorities. . . .

I will prove to you further that in January last August Spies told a newspaper reporter of integrity, honesty and fidelity that they were going to precipitate the matter on or about the 1st of May; that he told this man how they could dispose of the police, and in that connection he told that reporter that they would arrange it so that their meeting should be at or near the intersection of two streets. Having this as Randolph street and Desplanes (pointing on map), not calling it any particular name, and that he would have a meeting in which there should be assembled large bodies of laboring men, of which he falsely claims to be the exponent; that they would be located just above the intersection of the streets; that he and his dynamiters would be there; that they would be provided with dynamite bombs at the place of meeting; that they would hold a meeting there; that the police or the militia would walk up towards them; that when they got up there their dynamite-throwers would be situated on different sides of the street near the walks; that when they proceeded up here they would throw the dynamite into their ranks, clean them out and take possession of the town. . . .

He, Spies, did more than what I have said. At that time he handed to the newspaper reporter a dynamite bomb, empty—almost the exact duplicate of the bomb Lingg made which killed the officers; handed it to this witness and said to him: "These are the bombs that our men are making in the city of Chicago, and they are distributed from the *Arbeiter Zeitung* office, because the men who make them have not the facilities for distributing them here."

Those are facts that will be proven here. . . .

Witnesses for the People

Felix D. Buschick. Am a draughtsman. [His testimony had reference simply to maps and plans showing the location of the Haymarket Square, the surrounding streets and alleys, the spot where the bomb was thrown, and the location of the Desplaines Street Station.]

John Bonfield. Am Inspector of Police; was in command of the men at Desplaines Station on the night of May 4; got there about six. . . .

Orders were, that no man should draw a weapon or fire or strike anybody until he received positive orders from his commanding officer. Each officer was dressed in full uniform with his coat buttoned up to the throat and his club and belt on. Capt. Ward and myself had our weapons in our hand; pistols in pockets. As we approached there was a person speaking from the truck. Capt. Ward gave the statutory order to disperse: "I command you, in the name of the people of the State of Illinois, to immediately and peaceably disperse." As he repeated that, he said, "I command you and you to assist." Fielden, who was speaking, stepped off the truck, and said: "We are peaceable." Almost instantly I heard behind me a hissing sound, followed, in a second or two, by a terrific explosion. At once firing from the front and both sides poured in on us. From seventy-five to a hundred pistol shots before a shot was fired by any officer. I turned around quickly, saw almost all the men of the second two lines shrink to the ground, and gave the order to close up. Lieuts. Steele and Quinn with their companies charged down the street; the others formed and took both sides. In a few moments the crowd was scattered in every direction. I gave the order to cease firing and went to pick up our wounded. Matthias J. Degan was almost instantly killed. The wounded, about sixty in number, were carried to the Desplains Street Station. Seven died from the effects of wounds. As we approached there were five or six on the truck. Did not see the direction of the bomb; it came from my rear; was about ten feet from the wagon.

Cross-examined. Was the highest officer on the ground that night. The whole force was under my special direction. As we marched down, the police occupied the full street from curb to curb. Around Desplaines and Randolph streets there were a few persons scattered, apparently paying no attention to the meeting; the crowd attending the speaking was apparently north of that alley; the speakers' wagon being five or six feet north of that alley. Fielden was facing north and west; there were about a thousand people there; don't remember whether it was moonlight; there were no street lamps lit; there was a clear sky. As we marched along the crowd shifted its position; the speaking went right on.

Gottfried Waller. On the evening of 3d May was at Grief's Hall pursuant to an advertisement in the *Arbeiter Zeitung:* "Y—Come Monday night." Before that notice there is the word "Briefkasten," which means letter-box. This notice was a sign for a meeting of the armed section at Grief's Hall; had been there once before, pursuant to a similar notice. There was no other reason for my going there. There were about seventy or eighty men; was chairman. Of the defendants there were present Engel and Fischer. There was talk about the six men who had been killed at McCormick's. There were circulars there headed "Revenge." Mr. Engel stated a resolution of a prior meeting, that if, on account of the eight-hour strike, there should be an encounter with the police, we should aid the men against them. A committee should observe the movement in the city, and if a conflict should occur the committee should report, and we should first storm the police stations by throwing a bomb and should shoot down everything that came out, and whatever came in our way we should strike down. I proposed a meeting of working men for Tuesday morning on Market Square. Fischer said that was a mouse trap; the meeting should be on the Haymarket and in the evening, because there would be more workingmen. Then it was resolved that the meeting should be held at 8 p.m. at the Haymarket; it was stated that the purpose of the meeting was to cheer up the workingmen so they should be prepared, in case a conflict would happen. Fischer was commissioned to call the meeting through handbills; he went away to order them, but came back after half an hour and said the printing establishment was closed. Nothing was said as to what should be done in case the police interfered with the Haymarket meeting. We discussed why the police stations should be attacked. Several persons said, "We have seen how the capitalists and the police oppressed the workingmen, and we should commence to take the rights in our own hands; by attacking the stations we would prevent the police from coming to aid." The plan stated by Engel was adopted with the understanding that every group ought to act independently, according to the general plan. The persons present were from all the groups from the West, South and North sides.

There was no one who expected that the police would get as far as the Haymarket; only, if strikers were attacked, we should strike down the police, however we best could, with bombs or whatever would be at our disposition. If a conflict happened in the daytime they should cause the publication of the word "Ruhe." If at night, they should report to the members personally at their homes. On 4th May we did not understand ourselves why the word "Ruhe" was published. It should be inserted in the paper only if a downright revolution had occurred. Fischer first mentioned the word "Ruhe." Engel moved the plan be adopted. Was present at the Haymarket meeting on Tuesday evening; saw the word "Ruhe" in the *Arbeiter Zeitung* about 6 p.m. On my way to the Haymarket stopped at Engel's; he was not at home; was at Zepf's hall when the bomb exploded. There was some disturbance, and the door was closed. On my way home I stopped at Engel's and told him what had happened at the Haymarket. They had assembled in the back part of their dwelling-place around a jovial glass of beer, and I told them that a bomb was thrown at the Haymarket, and that about a hundred people had been killed there, and they had better go home. Engel said yes, they should go home, and nothing else. . . .

Cross-examined. Nothing was said as to any action to be taken by us at the Haymarket. We did not think that the police would come to the Haymarket. The principal purpose of the Haymarket meeting was to protest against the action of the police at the riot at McCormick's factory. While I was with Fischer at the Haymarket, nothing was said between us about preparations to meet an attack by the police; am indicted for conspiracy; was arrested two weeks after 4th May. . . .

Theodore Fricke. Was business superintendent of the *Arbeiter Zeitung,* once its bookkeeper, identify Spies' handwriting on the manuscript containing the word "Ruhe;" there was a library in the building belonging to the International Working People's Association–a Socialistic association. . . . this book (Johann Most's book) I saw at the library in the *Arbeiter Zeitung* building; have seen that book sold at picnics by Hirschberger, at Socialistic picnics and mass-meetings.

Mr. Black. objected to this line of inquiry, because, as they said, it is not shown that any of the defendants knew or participated in the selling, or that they had anything to do with, or that they saw the selling.

The Court. If men are teaching the public how to commit murder, it is admissible to prove it if it can be proved by items.

Mr. Black. Well, does your Honor know what this teaches?

The Court. I do not know what the contents of the book are. I asked what the book was and I was told that it was Herr Most's "Science of Revolutionary Warfare," and taught the preparing of deadly weapons and missiles, and that was accepted by the other side.

Mr. Black. Does that justify your Honor in the construction that it teaches how to commit murder, or of stating that in the presence of the jury?

The Court. . . . I inquired what sort of book it was, and it was stated by the other side what sort of book it was, and you said nothing about it, so that in ruling upon the question whether it may be shown where it was to be found, where it had been seen, I must take the character of the book into consideration in determining whether it is admissible; whether it is of that character or not we will see when it is translated, I suppose. I suppose the book is not in the English language.

Willilam Seliger. Am a carpenter; have lived in Chicago three years and a half; before that at Charlottenburg, Germany; . . . this "Y–Komme Montag Abend," means that all the armed men should come to the meeting at 54 West Lake street; the armed men were various ones–all the Socialistic organizations; there were several organizations in existence which were drilled in the use of arms; saw a copy of the "Revenge" circular at Zepf 's Hall; Balthasar Rau brought it to the meeting about nine; Lingg had been making bombs at my house; on Tuesday he told me to work diligently at these bombs, and they would be taken away that day; worked at some loaded shells; drilled holes through which the bolt went; Lingg went to the West Side to a meeting; got back probably after one; he said: "You didn't do much; you ought to have worked more diligently;" I said I hadn't any pleasure at the work; Lingg said, "Well, we will have to work very diligently this afternoon;" told me he had not enough of them; Hubner, Muntzenberg, Heuman, were helping; there were forty or fifty bombs made that afternoon; saw dynamite for the first time in Lingg's room, about five or six weeks previous to 4th of May; Lingg said every workingman should get some dynamite and learn to handle these things; Tuesday afternoon Lingg said those bombs were going to be good fodder for the capitalists and the police, when they came to protect the capitalists; there was a re-mark that they were to be used that evening, but nothing positive as to time; the Lehmans were at the house for a little while; we had a little trunk with bombs in; there were round and pipe bombs in it; they were loaded with dynamite and caps fixed; we carried a trunk of them to Neff's Hall; I took two pipe bombs myself; car-ried them in my pocket; Lingg said it might be a beautiful thing if we would walk over and throw one or two bombs into the station; there were two policemen sit-ting in front of the station, and Lingg said if the others came out these two could-n't do much; we would shoot these two down; later a patrol wagon passed; Lingg said that he was going to throw a bomb—that was the best opportunity to throw the bomb . . . we laid the bombs off on our way on Sigel street, between Sedgwick and Hurlbut, under an elevated sidewalk; laid two pipe bombs there; saw Lingg put some bombs there; on Friday before 4th of May, Lingg brought some dynamite to the house in a wooden box; the dynamite with which we filled the bombs on Tues-day was in that box; Lingg once told me he had made eighty to one hundred bombs in all.

G. P. English. Am a reporter for the *Tribune.* I got to the Haymarket meeting on 4th of May about half-past seven. Spies got up on the wagon and said: "Gentle-men, please come to order." Had a notebook and a pencil in my overcoat pocket and made notes in the pocket. Here is what I have of Spies' speech:

"Gentlemen and fellow workmen: Mr. Parsons and Mr. Fielden will be here in a very short time to address you. I will say, however, first, this meeting was called for the purpose of discussing the general situation of the eight-hour strike, and the events which have taken place during the last forty-eight hours. It seems to have been the opinion of the authorities that this meeting has been called for the pur-pose of raising a little row and disturbance. This, however, was not the intention of the committee that called the meeting. The committee that called the meeting wanted to tell you certain facts of which you are probably aware. The capitalistic press has been misleading—misrepresenting the cause of labor for the last few weeks. . . .

Mr. Grinnell introduced in evidence and read to the jury the following ex-tracts—editorials and other articles—from the newspapers *Arbeiter Zeitung,* and *Alarm:*

Arbeiter Zeitung
February 23, 1885. The already approaching revolution promises to be much grander and more terrible than that at the close of the last cen-

tury, which only broke out in one country. The common revolution will be general, for it makes itself felt everywhere and generally; it will demand more sacrifices, for the number of those over whom we have to sit in judgment is now much greater than that of the last century.

March 2, 1885. Our censure is not directed only against the working-men of Philadelphia; it strikes especially and in much higher degree those dirty souls who carry on as a business the quieting of the working class under idle promises of reform in the near future. . . . That thing could not have happened in Chicago without placing for exhibition on the telegraph wires and cornices of houses a dozen cadavers of policemen, in pieces, for each broken skull of a workman. And this is due solely and purely to the revolutionary propaganda on here. . . . [We wonder] whether the working-men of Chicago will take a lesson from this occurrence, and will at last supply themselves with weapons, dynamite, and prussic acid as far as that has not been done yet.

March 11, 1885. The community will soon have to decide whether to be or not to be: either the police must be, and then the community cannot be; or the community must be, and then the police cannot be; one only of the two is possible.

The circular spoken of so often in the evidence as the "Revenge" Circular, and which was written by Spies on the afternoon of May 3, and printed in English, was in the following language:

Revenge

Workingmen! To Arms! The masters sent out their bloodhounds—the police; they killed six of your brothers at McCormick's this afternoon. They killed the poor wretches because they, like you, had the courage to disobey the supreme will of your bosses. They killed them because they dared ask for the shortening of the hours of toil. They killed them to show you, "free American citizens," that you must be satisfied and contented with whatever your bosses condescend to allow you, or you will get killed.

You have for years endured the most abject humiliations; you have for years suffered unmeasurable iniquities; you have worked yourself to death; you have endured the pangs of want and hunger; your children you have sacrificed to the factory lord, —in short, you have been miserable and obedient servants all these years. Why? To satisfy the insatiable greed; to fill the coffers of your lazy, thieving masters. When you ask them now to lessen your burdens, he sends his bloodhounds out to shoot you—kill you. If you are men, if you are the sons of your grandsires, who have shed their blood to free you,—then you will rise in your might, Hercules, and destroy the hideous monster that seeks to destroy you. To arms, we will call you, to arms! Your Brothers.

He at the same time wrote in the German language, of which the following is a translation:

Revenge! Revenge! Workmen! To Arms! Men of labor! This afternoon the bloodhounds of your oppressors murdered six of your brothers at McCormick's. Why did they murder them? Because they dared to be dissatisfied with the lot which your oppressors have assigned to them. They demanded bread, and they gave them lead for an answer, mindful of the fact that thus people are most effectually silenced. You have for many, many years endured every humiliation without protest; have drudged from early in the morning till late at night; have suffered all sorts of privations; have even sacrificed your children. You have done everything to fill the coffers of your masters—everything for them; and now, when you approach them and implore them to make your burden a little lighter, as a reward for your sacrifices, they send their bloodhounds—the police—at you, in order to cure you with bullets, of your dissatisfaction. Slaves, we ask and conjure you, by all that is sacred and dear to you, avenge the atrocious murder which has been committed upon your brothers today, and which will likely be committed upon you tomorrow. Laboring men, Hercules, you have arrived at the crossway. Which way will you decide? — for slavery and hunger, or for freedom and bread. If you decide for the latter, then do not delay a moment; then, people, to arms! Annihilation to the beasts in human form who call themselves rulers! Uncompromising annihilation to them! This must be your motto. Think of the heroes whose blood has fertilized the road to progress, liberty, and humanity, and strive to become worthy of them. Your Brothers.

Twenty-five hundred copies were printed and distributed in various parts of the city.

The Opening Speech for the Prisoners

July 31.

Mr. Salomon said the defendants had steadily refused to believe that any man on the jury would be willing to convict any of the defendants because of being an Anarchist or a Socialist. Mr.Grinnell failed to state to you that he had a person by whom he could prove who threw the bomb, and he never expected to make this proof until he found that without this proof he was unable to maintain this prosecution against these defendants; and it was as this case neared the prosecution end of it that the State suddenly changed front and produced a professional tramp and a professional liar, as we will show you, to prove that one of these defendants was connected with the throwing of it. They then recognized, as we claimed and now claim, that that is the only way they can maintain their case here.

They are not charged with Anarchy; they are not charged with Socialism; they are not charged with the fact that Anarchy and Socialism is dangerous or beneficial to the community; but, according to the law under which we are now acting, a charge specific in its nature must be made against them, and that alone must be sustained, and it is the duty of the jury to weigh the evidence as it bears upon that charge; and upon no other point can they pay attention to it. Now, gentlemen, the charge is shown by this indictment. This is the accusation. This is what the case involves, and upon this the defendants and the prosecution must either stand or fall. This indictment is for the murder of Mathias J. Degan. It is charged that each one of these defendants committed the crime, each defendant individually; and it is charged in a number of different ways. Now, I desire to call your attention to the law governing this indictment and to read it to you; and I am presenting the law to you now, gentlemen, so that you can understand how we view this case and how the evidence is affected by what the law is.

The law says, no matter whether these defendants advised generally the use of dynamite in the purpose which they claimed to carry out, and sought to carry out, yet if none of these defendants advised the throwing of that bomb at the Haymarket, they cannot be held responsible for the action of others at other times and other places. What does the evidence introduced here tend to show? It may occur to some of you, gentlemen, to ask: What, then, can these defendants preach the use of dynamite? May they be allowed to go on and urge people to overturn the present government and the present condition of society without being held responsible for it and without punishment? Is there no law to which these people can be subjected and punished if they do this thing? There is, gentlemen, but it is not and never has been murder, and if they are amenable, as the evidence introduced by the prosecution tends to show, It Is under another and a different law, and no attempt on the part of the prosecution to jump the wide chasm which separates these two offenses can be successful unless it is done out of pure hatred, malice, ill-will, or because of prejudice. . . .

We expect to show you that these defendants never conspired, nor any one of them, to take the life of any single individual at any time or place; that they never conspired or plotted to take, at this time or at any other time, the life of Mathias Degan or any number of policemen, except in self-defense while carrying out their original purpose. We expect, further, to show you that on the night of the 4th of May these defendants had assembled peaceably, that the purpose of the meeting was peaceable, that its objects were peaceable, that they delivered the same harangue as before, that the crowd listened, and that not a single act transpired there, previous to the coming of the policemen, by which any man in the audience could be held amenable to law. They assembled there, gentlemen, under the provision of our Constitution, to exercise the right of free speech, to discuss the situation of the workingmen, to discuss the eight-hour question. They assembled there to incidentally discuss what they deemed outrages at McCormick's. No man expected that a bomb would be thrown; no man expected that any one would be injured at that meeting; but while some of these defendants were there and while this meeting was peaceably in progress, the police, with a devilish design, as we expect to prove, came down upon that body with their revolvers in their hands and pockets, ready for immediate use, intending to destroy the life of every man that stood upon that market square. That seems terrible, gentlemen, but that is the information which we have and which we expect to show you. We expect to show you further, gentlemen, that the crowd did not fire, that not a single person fired a single shot at the police officers. We expect to show you that Mr. Fielden did not have on that night, and never had in his life, a revolver; that he did not fire, and that that portion of the testimony here is wrong. We expect to show you further, gentlemen, that the witness Gilmer, who testified to having seen Spies light the match which caused the destruction coming from the bomb is a professional and constitutional liar; that no man in the city of Chicago who knows him will believe him under oath, and, indeed, I might almost say that it would scarcely need even a witness to show the falsity of his testimony, because it seems to me that it must fall of its own weight. We expect to show you, gentlemen, that Thompson was greatly mistaken; that on that night Schwab never saw or talked with Mr. Spies; that he was at the Haymarket early in the evening, but that he left before the meeting began and before he saw Mr. Spies on that evening at all. We expect to show that Mr. Parsons so far from thinking anything wrong, and Fischer, were quietly seated at Zepf 's Hall, drinking, perhaps, a glass of beer at the time the bomb exploded, and that it was as great a surprise to them as it was to any of you. We expect to show you that Engel was at home at the time the bomb exploded, and that he knew nothing about it. With the whereabouts of Lingg you are already familiar. It may seem strange why he was manufacturing bombs. The answer to that is, he had a right to have his house full of dynamite. He had a right to have weapons of all descriptions upon his premises, and until he used them, or advised their use, and they were used in pursuance of his advice, he is not liable any more than the man who commits numerous burglaries, the man who commits numerous thefts, who walks the streets, is liable to arrest and punishment only when he commits an act which makes him amenable to law. . . .

Witnesses for the Defense

Carter H. Harrison. Am Mayor of Chicago. On the 4th of May, was present during part of the Haymarket meeting so-called. On the day before there was a riot at McCormick's factory, which was represented to have grown out of a speech by Spies; next morning I received information of the issuance of a circular of a peculiar character and calling for a meeting at the Haymarket that night; directed the Chief of Police if anything should be said at that meeting that might call out a recurrence of such proceedings as at McCormick's factory, the meeting should be dispersed; believed it was better for myself to be there; went to the meeting to disperse it in case I should feel it necessary for the safety of the city; arrived about five minutes before eight; there was a large concourse of people about the Haymarket, but it was so long before any speaking commenced that two-thirds of the people left; about half-past eight the speaking commenced and the meeting congregated around Crane's building, or the alley near.

Mr. Spies may have been speaking one or two minutes before I got near enough to hear what he said; left the meeting between 10 and 10:05 o'clock that night; heard Spies' speech, and all of Parsons' up to the time I left; when I went over to the station, spoke to Capt. Bonfield, and determined to go home, but I went back to hear a little more; stayed there about five minutes longer and then left. Within about twenty minutes I heard the sound of the explosion of the bomb at my house. While at the meeting thought Spies had observed me when I lighted a cigar, as the tone of his speech suddenly changed. Prior to that change in the tone of Spies' speech I feared his remarks would force me to disperse the meeting; was there for that purpose; it was my own determination to do it against the will of the police. After that the general tenor of Spies' speech was such that I remarked to Capt. Bonfield that it was tame.

Took no action about dispersing it. There were occasional replies from the audience, as "Shoot him," "Hang him" or the like, but I do not think there were more than two or three hundred actual sympathizers with the speakers. Several times cries of "Hang him" would come from a boy in the outskirts, and the crowd would laugh; felt that a majority of the crowd were idle spectators, and the replies nearly as much what might be called "guying" as absolute applause. Some of the replies were evidently bitter. The audience numbered from eight hundred to one thousand. The people in attendance were laborers or mechanics, and the majority of them not English-speaking people—mostly Germans. There was no suggestion made by either of the speakers calling for immediate use of force or violence toward any person that night; if there had been I should have dispersed them at once. . . .

Cross-examined. Bonfield told me he had just received information that the Haymarket meeting, or a part of it, would go over to the Milwaukee and St. Paul freight house then filled with "scabs," and blow it up. There was also an intimation this meeting might be held merely to attract the attention of the police to the Haymarket, while the real attack, if any, should be made that night on McCormick's. In listening to the speeches, I concluded it was not an organization to destroy property that night, and went home. My order to Bonfield was that the reserves held at the other stations might be sent home, because I learned that all was quiet in the district where McCormick's factory is situated. Bonfield replied he had already ordered the reserves in the other stations to go in their regular order.

Barton Simonson. Am a traveling salesman; concluded, after taking supper, to take in the Haymarket meeting.

The speakers were northeast from me, in front of Crane's building, north of the alley. Spies said: "Please come to order. This meeting is not called to incite any riot." He then said McCormick had charged him with the murder of the people at the meeting the night before; that McCormick was a liar. McCormick was himself responsible. Somebody had opposed his speaking at the meeting near McCormick's because he was a Socialist. The people he spoke to were good Christian church-going people. While he was speaking, McCormick's people had come out. Some of the men and boys had started for them, and had had some harmless sport throwing stones at the windows, etc. Then he said that some workingmen were shot at and killed by the police. . . .

A dark cloud with cold wind came from the north. Many people had left before, but when the cloud came a great many people left. Somebody said: "Let's adjourn," —to some place, I can't remember. Fielden said he was about through, there was no need of adjourning. He said two or three times, "Now, in conclusion," or something like that, and I became impatient. Then I heard a commotion and a good deal of noise in the audience, and somebody said, "Police;" looked south and saw a line of police when it was at about the Randolph street car tracks. The police moved along until the front of the column got about up to the speakers' wagon. Heard somebody near the wagon say something about dispersing; saw some persons upon the wagon; could not tell who they were. I distinctly heard two words coming from the vicinity of the wagon or from the wagon; don't know who uttered them. The words were "peaceable meeting" a few seconds before the explosion of the bomb. As the police marched through the crowd the latter went to the sidewalks on either side, some went north, some few went on Randolph street, east, and some west; did not hear any exclamation as "Here come the bloodhounds of the police; you do your duty and I'll do mine," from the locality of the wagon or from Mr. Fielden. At the time the bomb exploded I was still in my position upon the stairs. No pistol shots anywhere before the explosion of the bomb. Just after the command to disperse had been given saw a lighted fuse or something come up from a point twenty feet south of Crane's alley, from about the center of the sidewalk on the east side of the street, from behind some boxes; am positive it was not thrown from the alley. I first noticed it about six or seven feet in the air, a little above a man's head. It went in a northwest course and up about fifteen feet from the ground, and fell about the middle of the street. The explosion followed almost immediately within two or three seconds. After the bomb exploded there was pistol shooting. I could distinctly see the flashes of the pistols; fifty to one hundred and fifty pistol shots from about the center of where the police were; did not observe the flshes of pistol shots or hear the report of any shots from the crowd upon the police prior to the firing by the police; stayed in my position from five to twenty seconds. There was shooting going on in every direction, as well up as down; could see from the flashes of the pistols that the police were shooting up. The police were not only shooting at the crowd, but I noticed several of them shoot just as they happened to throw their arms. . . .

In conversation I had with Capt. Bonfield at the station before the meeting that night, I asked him about the trouble in the southwestern part of the city. He says, "The trouble there is that these" —whether he used the word Socialists or strikers, I don't know—"get their women and children mixed up with them and around them and in front of them, and we can't get at them. I would like to get three thousand of them in a crowd, without their women and children" —and to the best of my recollection, he added, "and I will make short work of them;" noticed a few women and children at the bottom of the steps where I was; don't think there were any in the body of the crowd around the wagon.

Cross-examined. The bomb struck the ground and exploded just a little behind the front line of police.

The firing began from the police, right in the center of the street; did not see a single shot fired from the crowd on either side of the street; didn't know what became of the men in the wagon; don't think there were any shots fired in the neighborhood of the wagon. My firm discharged me.

John Ferguson. Am a resident of Chicago; in the cloak business; passed the Haymarket, and, noticing a crowd there, stopped to listen to the speeches; was accompanied by an acquaintance. During Parsons' speech, when he mentioned Jay Gould's name, somebody said: "Throw him in the lake;" and a man standing almost in front of me took his pipe from his mouth and halloaed out: "Hang him." Parsons replied that would do no good; a dozen more Jay Goulds would spring up in his place.

August Spies' Statement

Spies. May 4 last I was one of the editors of the *Arbeiter Zeitung*. Occupied that position since 1880. Prior to that I was engaged in the furniture business. Am a member of the Socialistic Publishing Society, which is organized under the laws of the State of Illinois, and by which the *Arbeiter Zeitung* was published. Was an employe of that society in my position as editor, and was subject to their control as to the general policy of the paper.

At a meeting of the Central Labor Union of Sunday, May 2, at 54 West Lake street, which I attended in the capacity of a reporter, I was invited to address a meeting of the Lumber-shovers' Union on the afternoon of May 3. As there were no other speakers, I went out. When I came there was a crowd of 6,000 to 7,000 people assembled on the prairie. When I was invited nothing was said to me about any relationship of Mr. McCormick's employes to that meeting. I did not know that the locality of the meeting was in the immediate neighborhood of McCormick's. When I arrived there several men were speaking from a car in the Bohemian or Polish language. Balthasar Rau introduced me to the chairman of the meeting. I spoke from fifteen to twenty minutes. Told the people, who in my judgment were not of a very high intellectual grade, to stand together and to enforce their demands at all hazards; otherwise the single bosses would one by one defeat them. Abut two hundred persons, standing a little ways apart from the main body, detached themselves and went away. Five minutes later I heard firing, and about that time I stopped speaking and inquired where the pistol shots came from, and was told that some men had gone up there to stone McCormick's "scabs," and that the police had fired upon them. Two patrol wagons came up in great haste on the Black Road, driving towards McCormick's, followed immediately by about seventy-five policemen on foot, and then other patrol wagons came. I jumped from the car

and went up to McCormick's. They were shooting all the while. In front of Mc-
Cormick's factory there are some railroad tracks, on which a number of freight
cars were standing. The people were running away and hiding behind these freight
cars as much as they could to keep out of the way of the pistol firing. The fight
was going on behind the cars. When I came up there on this prairie, right in front
of McCormick's, I saw a policeman run after and fire at people who were fleeing,
running away. My blood was boiling, and, seeing unarmed men, women and children, who were running away, fired upon, I think in that moment I could have
done almost anything. At that moment a young Irishman, who probably knew me
or had seen me at the meeting, came running form behind the cars and said:
"What kind of a -business is this? What h–l of a union is that? What people are
these who will let those men be shot down here like dogs? I just come from there;
we have carried away two men dead, and there are a number of others lying on the
ground who will most likely die. At least twenty or twenty-five must have been shot
who ran away or were carried away by friends;" I took a car and went down town;
the same evening I wrote the report of the meeting which appeared in the *Arbeiter
Zeitung* of the next day; immediately after I came to the office I wrote the so-called
Revenge circular, except the heading, 'Revenge.' At the time I wrote it I believed
the statement that six workingmen had been killed that afternoon at McCormick's;
I believe 2,500 copies of that circular were printed, but not more than half of them
distributed, for I saw quite a lot of them in the office of the *Arbeiter Zeitung* on
the morning I was arrested; at the time I wrote it I was still laboring under the excitement of the scene and the hour; I was very indignant.

On May 4th was invited to address a meeting on the Haymarket that evening;
that was the first I heard of it; had no part in calling the meeting; I put the announcement of the meeting into the *Arbeiter Zeitung* at the request of a man who
invited me to speak. The *Arbeiter Zeitung* is an afternoon daily and appears at 2 p.m.;
about eleven o'clock a circular calling the Haymarket meeting was handed to me
to be inserted in the *Arbeiter Zeitung*, containing the line, 'Workingmen, arm yourselves and appear in full force;' I said to the men who brought the circular that, if
that was the meeting which I had been invited to address, I should certainly not
speak there, on account of that line; he stated that the circulars had not been distributed, and I told him if that was the case, and if he would take out that line, it
would be all right; Mr.. Fischer was called down at that time, and he sent the man
back to the printing-office to have the line taken out; I struck out the line myself
before I handed it to the compositor to put it in the *Arbeiter Zeitung*; the man
who brought the circular to me and took it back with the line stricken out was on
the stand here—Grueneberg I believe is his name.

I left home that evening about half-past seven o'clock and walked down with
my brother Henry, arriving at the Haymarket. . . .

Spoke about fifteen or twenty minutes; began by stating that I heard a large
number of patrol wagons had gone to Desplaines Street Station; that great preparations had been made for a possible outbreak; that the militia had been called under arms, and that I would state at the beginning that this meeting had not been

called for the purpose of inciting a riot, but simply to discuss the situation of the eight-hour movement and the atrocities of the police on the preceding day; then I referred to one of the morning papers of the city, in which Mr. McCormick said that I was responsible for the affair near his factory; that I had incited the people to commit violence, etc., and I stated that such misrepresentations were made in order to discredit the men who took an active part in the movement; I stated that such outbreaks as had occurred at McCormick's, in East St. Louis, in Philadelphia, Cleveland and other places, were not the work of a band of conspirators, of a few Anarchists or Socialists, but the unconscious struggle of a class for emancipation; that such outbreaks might be expected at any minute and were not the arbitrary work of individuals; I then pointed to the fact that the people who committed violence had never been Socialists or Anarchists, but in most instances had been up to that time the most lawful citizens, good Christians, the exemplary so-called honest workmen, who were contrasted by the capitalists with the Anarchists; I stated that the meeting at McCormick's was composed mostly of humble, church-going good Christians, and not by any means atheists, or materialists, or Anarchists. . . .

I wrote the word 'Ruhe' for insertion in the *Arbeiter Zeitung* on May 4th; received a batch of announcements from a number of labor organizations and societies a little after eleven o'clock, in my editorial room, and went over them. Among them was one which read: "Mr. Editor, please insert in the letter-box the word 'Ruhe,' in prominent letters." This was in German; there is an announcement column of meetings in the *Arbeiter Zeitung*, but a single word or something like that would be lost sight of under the announcements. In such cases people generally ask to have that inserted under the head of 'Letter-box.' Upon reading that request, I just took a piece of paper and marked on it 'Briefkasten' (Letter-box), and the word 'Ruhe.' The manuscript which is in evidence is in my handwriting; at the time I wrote that word and sent it up to be put in the paper, I did not know of any import whatever attached to it; my attention was next called to it a little after three o'clock in the afternoon; Balthasar Rau, an advertising agent of the *Arbeiter Zeitung*, came and asked me if the word 'Ruhe' was in the *Arbeiter Zeitung*. I had myself forgotten about it, and took a copy of the paper and found it there. He asked me if I knew what it meant, and I said I did not. He said there was a rumor that the armed section had held a meeting the night before, and had resolved to put in that word as a signal for the armed sections to keep themselves in readiness in case the police should precipitate a riot, to come to the assistance of the attacked. I sent for Fischer, who had invited me to speak at the meeting that evening, and asked him if that word had any reference to that meeting. He said, 'None whatever;' that it was merely a signal for the boys—for those who were armed to keep their powder dry, in case they might be called upon to fight within the next days. I told Rau it was a very silly thing, or at least that there was not much rational sense in that, and asked him if he knew how it could be managed that this nonsense would be stopped; how it could be undone. Rau said he knew some persons who had something to say in the armed organizations, and I told him to go and tell them that the word was put in by mistake. . . .

The Verdict

The *Jury* entered and took their places.

JUDGE GARY. All spectators, every one, except the officers of the Court, must be seated and every one must preserve absolute silence. Gentlemen, have you agreed upon your verdict?

Foreman Osborne. We have.

JUDGE GARY. Have you written it out?

Foreman Osborne. We have [handing a paper to the clerk].

Clerk Doyle [reading]: We, the jury, find the defendants, August Spies, Michael Schwab, Samuel Fielden, Albert R. Parsons, Adolph Fischer, George Engel and Louis Lingg guilty or murder in the manner and form as charged in the indictment, and fix the penalty at death.

5
Shame of the Cities
The Edward Butler Trial
1902

"Tweed Days in St. Louis" by Claude Wetmore and Lincoln Steffens, which appeared in McClure's Magazine for October 1902, created from the battles in Missouri between Edward Butler and Joseph W. Folk the plot line of the journalism called "muckraking." For the next half-dozen years, sensational exposés of corruption commanded a national audience. Folk, who prosecuted the case against Edward Butler, was the model progressive: young, ruthlessly upright, the uncompromising enemy of the traffic in bribery between corrupt politicians and equally corrupt businessmen. "Bribery is treason," Folk told a jury, "and the givers and takers of bribes are traitors of peace." And Edward Butler precisely fitted the stereotype of the political boss: Irish-born, scarcely educated, the unelected chief of St. Louis politics for a generation, self-described as "active in politics—tact for organization—never desired to hold office himself." Or, as he boasted, "I've been stealing elections in St. Louis for 30 years."

Folk, only thirty-one years old when he became St. Louis's chief prosecuting attorney, immediately attacked the system of open bribery that went with municipal government decisions to make public expenditure such as garbage disposal or to award franchises such as street car routes. Indicting both boodling politicians and bribing businessmen, he quickly became a controversial figure, gaining enthusiastic supporters as well as powerful opponents. By 1902 he was ready to tackle the elderly Butler. Folk found his opportunity when Butler attempted to bribe a member of the Board of Health to award to firms in which Butler had a financial stake the contract for "the sanitary removal of all slops, offal, vegetable and animal matter of the city." A grand jury indicted Butler, and Folk's successful prosecution of the case made him a national figure. He became governor of Missouri, in which office he pushed through a host of progressive reforms to limit lobbying, regulate public utilities, and reform political processes. His adversary Butler, although sentenced to three years in prison, had the decision reversed on appeal to the Missouri Supreme Court, which bizarrely decided that the removal of garbage was unrelated to public health and therefore should not have been a matter for the Board of Health.

SUGGESTIONS FOR FURTHER READING: Steven L. Piott, *Holy Joe: Joseph W. Folk and the Missouri Idea*, Columbia, Missouri: University of Missouri Press, 1997

The Trial of Edward Butler for Bribery, *Columbia, Missouri, November 1902*
HON. JOHN A. HOCKADAY, *Judge.*

MR. GENTRY, *for the defense.*
MR. FOLK, *for the prosecution.*

On this day the grand jury of the city of St. Louis returned an indictment against Edward Butler, charging him with attempting to bribe one Dr. Henry M. Chapman, a member of the Board of Health of St. Louis, by offering him the sum of $2,500, if he would vote as a member of that board to accept the bid of the St. Louis Sanitary Company for the reduction of the garbage of the city.

Edward Butler, by his counsel applied to the St. Louis court for a change of venue to some other place, "because the minds of the inhabitants of the city of St. Louis are so prejudiced against the defendant that a fair trial cannot be given him." The prisoner filed an affidavit that "the public mind has been improperly inflamed against him by editorials, cartoons, sermons and miscellaneous articles, published in the daily newspapers of said city of St. Louis for the purpose of preventing him from securing a fair trial in said city; that said editorials, cartoons, sermons and miscellaneous articles were published in the *Globe-Democrat, Republic, Post-Dispatch, Star* and *Chronicle,* and said articles by declaring directly and by innuendo that defendant was the Boss Boodler have caused the minds of the inhabitants of St. Louis to become so prejudiced against him that a fair trial cannot be had in said city."

Howard A. Blossom, Joseph V. Martin and Stephen Peck, all citizens of St. Louis, made affidavits to the same effect.

JUDGE O'NEILL RYAN; of the Circuit Court of the City of St. Louis, ordered that the cause be removed to the Circuit Court of Boone County, it not being alleged that prejudice against the Prisoner exists in said county of Boone.

The trial of Edward Butler on an indictment for bribery found by the grand jury of St. Louis and removed here for trial began today.

Mr. Gentry said that the defense wished to file a demurrer to the indictment, which he read as follows:

First. The indictment alleges, that by virtue of Ordinance 20476, of the city of St. Louis, Henry M. Chapman would be required as a member of the St. Louis Board of Health to vote, or pass upon any matter which might be brought before said Board by virtue of said ordinance, but the indictment shows that such matter of inquiry could not by law, be brought before the said Board in that the ordinance was and is void, because it is not alleged to have been recommended, or proposed by the Board of Public Improvements and accompanied by an estimate of cost; it having been an ordinance relating to public work, which under the charter, is required to have had such origin, or recommendation and accompaniment.

Secondly. The indictment depends upon the validity of an ordinance, which undertook to vest the Board of Health with power to contract with reference to public work, and the said ordinance being void for want of authority in the Municipal Assembly to pass any ordinance for such purpose, the matter of passing upon bids for removing garbage was not one which could by law be brought before the Board of Health for any action, vote, or decision of its members.

Mr. Folk read to the jury the formal indictments and then stated to them what the State expected to prove against the prisoner. He said that the city of St. Louis, in order to insure better sanitation had provided that all garbage and refuse matter which naturally accumulates in a city be removed and destroyed by a process called the "Merz" process, and that bids were received for the removal of this garbage by the Board of Health. Those bids were to be received on or before October 1, 1901, Dr. Chapman was a member of the Board of Health who had power to vote upon the bids submitted to the Board of Health for the removal of said garbage. The prisoner was one of the owners of a company which did hauling, called the Sanitary Company, and this company had sent a bid covering the removal of the garbage for a certain period of time; that he [Edward Butler] had before the time set for the action of the Board of Health upon the bids, called upon Dr. Chapman at his home, had gone to the door, rung the bell and inquired for Dr. Chapman. On being told that he was not at home, he had gone away, but had returned on the same day and saw Dr. Chapman in his private study, and had offered to give him $2,500 if he would vote for the acceptance of the bid by the Sanitary Company. Dr. Chapman positively refused, saying that this would be bribery and that Mr. Butler's company would get the contract if their bid should be the lowest. Mr. Butler said that he did not mean a bribe, but that he only wanted to make Mr. Chapman a present of the $2,500. Dr. Chapman again refused the money and Mr. Butler departed, returning again some days later with the money and tendered it to Dr. Chapman, which he positively refused, after which Mr. Butler left him; also that the defendant had gone to Dr. Albert Merrell, a member of the Board of Health and had offered him the same amount of money at two different times and been refused in the same way, and that Mr. Butler had tried to force the money upon him, but was emphatically refused.

The Evidence for the State

Geo. F. Mockler. Am secretary of the St. Louis City Council. I read minutes of various Council meetings and the action taken pertaining to the passage of the bill providing for the removal of the slops and garbage.

The original bid was offered, documents and official records were read in order to determine all the particulars as to dates and the votes upon the passage of the bill in question. Bill No. 71 was offered in evidence, was objected to by defense, but objection was overruled. An ordinance was also introduced which was objected to by defense because it had not been passed by a majority of members. The objection was overruled by the JUDGE. This ordinance which was entitled one for the protection and preservation and protection of the public health provided for the sanitary disposal of all slops, garbage, vegetable matter and animal matter by a process known as the "Merz" process. It was passed by both houses and signed by President Hornsby on September 11, 1901, was sent to the Mayor, Rolla Wells, and approved by him on September 17th. . . .

Max Kauffman. Am clerk of the Board of Health; sealed proposals for the disposition of garbage under the Merz process were duly advertised for as my records show. A bid was opened at the meeting of the Board on October 1st, 1901, from the St. Louis Sanitary Co.; Dr. Chapman moved that the consideration be laid over until October 3rd, which was carried and on the afternoon in executive session the contract was awarded to that company by a unanimous vote.

Walter J. Blakely. Am Secretary of the St. Louis Sanitary Co., Charles F. Herman is President; Mr. Butler has no connection with it except that he is a stockholder; he owned 185 shares in October, 1899. We put up a deposit of $50,000 with the bid. In October, 1901, Edward Butler was receiving $2,500 a year from the Sanitary Company; it was for good will and services; we wanted good feeling between the Sanitary Company and the Excelsior Hauling Co. There was an agreement between them as to the bid. I have it here.

JUDGE HOCKADAY. I will allow it for the purpose of showing Butler's interest in the contract let to the Sanitary Company.

Mr. Folk read the contract, which was dated September 30, 1901, and it provided that if the Sanitary Company secured the contract from the city for the reduction of garbage after the expiration of the contracts it then held it would pay to the Excelsior Hauling Co. $45,000 in cash and $17,000 a year for each of the three years covered by its contract.

Edward Dierkes. Am deputy auditor of St. Louis; have been since June, 1891; I have the custody of the warrants, for money paid out by the city. Have warrants in my possession in favor of the Excelsior Hauling Co.

Mr. Krum. We object to this as irrelevant to the charge.

Mr. Folk. We propose to show that the prisoner signed these warrants.
The COURT. I think it is admissible.

Dierkes. Here is one dated October 30, 1901, for $10,000 signed Excelsior Hauling & Transfer, signed Edward Butler, Vice President, and there are several others for smaller sums. Under the new contract the Sanitary Company receives $130,000 a year; under its old contract it received about $65,000.

Dr. Henry N. Chapman. Am a physician; my office is in my house, No. 1538 Mississippi avenue, St. Louis. Attended the medical college here in Columbia. Have been for nearly four years a member of the City Board of Health; know the prisoner; saw him on the 16th or 17th of last November at my office in my house about twilight—seven or eight o'clock in the evening.

Mr. Butler was in the front room of my place, the front office when I was sent in. Did not open the door; he came in, some one let him in and I followed into the room after him. We shook hands, and be began to speak about the Garbage Reduction Works in South St. Louis, telling me what a very fine place it was, all of which I appreciated, for I had seen it, and he told me of the great expenses that the Sanitary Company had been put to in fitting up these works, and how it was the most complete works in the United States, and how perfectly they were ready to take and handle any amount of garbage, and he then went on to speak of the ordinance that had been passed for a new garbage contract. He said "our company intends to put in a bid, and we would like to get it," he said. "In fact we think it is due us. We have worked there for ten years and made no money, and the city rather owes it to us to throw it our way if possible." I said to him that if there was more than one bid the Board of Health would be compelled to give it to the lowest bidder and that if he was the lowest bidder—if his bid was the lowest, of course he would get it. He then went on to speak of the terms of the ordinance and he said: "You know, Doctor, that in the ordinance it calls for a $50,000 cash bond to be put up by the bidder, who is successful in receiving the bid. You know," he said, "this $50,000 is intended to cover the faithful completion of the works," he said. "You know we have the complete works down there and therefore this cash bond will not have to stay up very long, and at the time this comes down and the Board of Health signs the release and takes it down I would like to come to you, Doctor, and make you a present of twenty-five hundred dollars if you will vote for our Company to get this contract."

I said "Mr. Butler, I can't do that. It would not be money that I could take and spend with any satisfaction to myself, and I can't do it." He then said, "Well, Doctor, I will see you again," and shook hands with me and left the house. Think this occurred on 16th September. Next saw him about the first of November the same year about six in the evening; was told a gentleman wanted to see me and went into my office, the same room in which the previous interview occurred. When I went into the room Mr. Butler was standing in a dim light. There was no light in the house, but in front of my house is a gas lamp which reflects distinctly into the office and shows up fairly a good deal of light, enough to recognize people in the room. When I stepped in he was standing close to the folding door that separated the two rooms. I walked up and said, "Good evening, Mr. Butler." He responded and then peered about the room, and said to me, "Doctor, I am a man of my word, and I am here." "Mr. Butler, I thought I made it plain to you that I would not take that money." He said, "Well, Doctor, you are not a millionaire," and I said, "No, I am not a millionaire, and further than that, I could use and place every penny of the money you are offering to me, but I won't take it, and I can't use it." He then appeared to get somewhat excited, and said, "Well, Doctor, you are one man in a million," and he turned and said, "I hope you won't hold it against me." I said, "No, Mr. Butler, I suppose, according to your light it is right, but according to my lights it is wrong." He said, "If I can ever do anything for you, call on me," and he said "Good evening," and stepped out. Butler did not sit down all the time he was with me; he did not go into the next room to my office; peered in as if looking for somebody; when I told him I would not take the money he made a motion towards me as though he was trying to put the roll in my coat; his first visit was before I knew any bids had been put in. . . .

Was present at the meeting of the Board when the bid was opened; did not tell any of my fellow members about the attempt to bribe me; nor on the 3rd of October when we accepted the bid.

Had talked to Dr. Merrell about it; we had discussed if it was possible for anything to be done and we had concluded there was nothing we could do and we let it alone. Talked to a few other people but I made up my mind that it was simply my word against Mr. Butler's word; told a friend, Mr. Hodder, of it as an interesting incident; took no action until I was summoned before the grand jury in the winter of 1901–2.

Mr. Krum. You were satisfied in your own mind that it was a deliberate attempt to bribe you and you took no action with reference to the incident at all? I did take action, sir. I spoke to Dr. Merrell and discussed it; spoke to half a dozen men and asked if there was any possible way by which we could reach this thing before the meeting of 1st October, the conclusion we all came to was that there was nothing that could be done, since there was no one present at the interview but him and I. Therefore I gave it up, sir. . . .

Mr. Krum. And therefore you did nothing about it, except to discuss it among your friends? I am talking about impossibilities. I talked among my friends, in the way of discussing impossibilities.

Mr. Krum. You went on and voted for the contract, and moved the adoption of it yourself, and the letting of the contract, and did not inform Dr. Starkloff, the Health Commissioner, the Mayor, the Acting Mayor or the member of the Board of Police Commissioners, or any other member of the Board with the exception of Dr. Merrell? You did not say a word to any of them, with the exception of Dr. Merrell? No, sir, not a word. And all the explanation that you have to give for your silence is what you have given here? Yes, sir.

Dr. Chapman. Went with the Board one day to visit the Sanitary Company's works; don't remember if it was before or after my interview with prisoner; know Mr. Claude H. Wetmore; he was at my house early in October; did say to him then that I could not recall the exact date of Butler's visit; had not called to mind the date of Mrs. Bell's return at that time. Wetmore came to interview me for a newspaper. Did not say to him that Butler said to me, "Doctor, we have $50,000 tied up with our bid. As soon as that is released I would like to make you a present of $2,500 or so"; when Butler came to my house I knew that the reduction ordinance was pending in the Municipal Assembly; did not know whether it had passed; did not tell Wetmore that I was sure there was about $2,500 in the roll Butler offered or that I saw a $500 bill; in November the second visit Butler came in a buggy; saw no one with him; told Mr. Wetmore that I could not understand why Butler made such an offer to me because under the ordinance we could only award the contract to a concern that employed the Merz system and the companies in which Butler was interested were the only ones that used that system.

Mr. Folk. When Mr. Wetmore came out to see you what did he say? Whom was he representing? He said he was representing the *McClure Magazine.* What did he say he wanted to do? He says, "Doctor, I am going up to Columbia Friday or Saturday, and I want to get an article in the October number of *McClure's Magazine,* and to prepare another for the November number. We are getting photographs and material together, and I want that when I get to Columbia I will only have to telegraph details of the trial; I would like to interview you for that purpose." He said, "Doctor, it will not be published before November 1st, in *McClure's Magazine.*" What was it you said to him regarding the $50,000, if it was mentioned. What I said to Mr. Wetmore was in substance what I have already said, that Butler said to me in my house. He spoke about the reduction works which he had in the southern part of the city, their capability of taking care not only of the city's garbage but a great deal more and his company would put in a bid. Butler said to me, "our company will put in a bid, and if we receive the bid we will have to put up a $50,000 cash bond for the faithful building of the works. After you have examined those works this $50,000 will be taken down and released, which, as you know, we have our work nearly completed, it won't stay up very long, and then if you will vote for this contract for our company I would like to make you a present of twenty-five hundred dollars."

Dr. Chapman. Besides the two persons I have named I told the story of the attempt to bribe me to my wife and to John R. Harkins, E. A. Bell, Earl Lehman, Mrs. Morison, of Chester, Ill., and her daughter, Ada, Dr. E. W. Saunder, Dr. Wessler, Phil. Bardemeyer, Mr. Rotty and Captain William R. Hodges; when any of the wives of these gentlemen were present they heard the story, too; it was a matter very freely discussed by me among my neighbors and friends.

To Mr. Krum. In my talks with these people I gave them to understand it was an attempt to bribe me as a member of the Board of Health. . . .

Dr. Albert Merrell. Am a practicing physician living at 3814 Washington avenue, St. Louis. Have been a member of the Board of Health since spring of 1895; the prisoner called at my house in September, 1901, my office is in my house, about half past ten a.m. and remained till after 11. He spoke of the pending bids, these bids that were to be submitted by the Sanitary Company for the purpose of renewing or obtaining a new contract for the disposal of the garbage. He remarked that they were very anxious to secure it because of the fact that he claimed they had made no money on their former contract and had been at very large expense for repairs and reconstruction, and that they were desirous of securing the contract—especially desirous of securing it for that reason, even for the brief period which was proposed, three years, although he had hoped to secure it for seven years. He spoke about their ability to take care of the garbage, the extent and perfection of their equipment for that purpose, which I was already aware of, and assented to, and I remarked that with such an equipment they certainly ought to be able to make the best bid for another contract. He then stated, "I will tell you right now the bid will be higher than it was before"; he didn't say how much higher or what the bid would be, but that it would be higher. I said I was sorry it was to be higher, as I thought they were in a position to do as least as well, if not better than before, on the old contract. I mean in price. He said nothing about my vote or about the votes of other members of the Board; but he did say "You will not be reappointed on the Board of Health, and if I got this contract—" not that wording, the words were "When the contract is approved and becomes a law, I will make you a present of twenty-five hundred dollars." I said "I don't want any of your money; if I were to accept one penny in the situation I am placed in, I would feel as though I was accepting a bribe, and I know every one else would believe I was too." He then said he had no such intention. That practically ended the conversation. He left very soon afterwards. . . .

The Witnesses for the Defense

Joseph Hornsby. Am President of the St. Louis City Council and a member of the Board of Health. Remember the letting of the garbage contract to the Sanitary Co. There was only one bid received; know of no person or corporation that could have performed that work except the Sanitary Co.; don't think it was possible for other works to have been erected in time; was spoken to by others about bids; but they offered nothing definite.

Dr. Max C. Starkloff. Am Health Commissioner of St. Louis and a member of the Board of Health; the only plant in the city capable of doing the work required by the garbage ordinance was the St. Louis Sanitary Co.; am familiar with such plans; don't think it possible any plant could have been erected in time to do the work after the old contract expired; about 250 tons of garbage were reduced daily in 1901 as against 100 in 1895 when I became Health Commissioner.

To Mr. Folk. The salary of the medical members of the Board of Health was $500 a year.

Andrew Blong. Am a police commissioner of St. Louis and a member of the Board of Health. Do not know what company had the Merz process. Understood that there was no other company in St. Louis but the Sanitary Co. that could reduce the garbage, so I voted for its bid—the only one made.

E. C. Bryant. Have been superintendent of the St. Louis Sanitary Co. since 1891; in 1891 the time of our first contract with the city we had only one plant;

the next year we built another one. There was no other works in the city in 1901 capable of doing the work called for; a new one would find it hard to get a location; people object to it; call it a stink factory, I don't think it's so bad but other people do; new works to take charge of all the garbage of the city would cost from $300,000 to $350,000.

Edward Butler, Jr. Am son of Edward Butler, am 38 years old, a horseshoer in St. Louis. On September 16th last father was laid up with the gout. Saw him confined to his room on that day.

To Mr. Folk. On 17th of September father telephoned to me from his room about the garbage contract. Saw him that day; he was in his room but able to get up.

Claude H. Wetmore. Reside at Webster Groves, 10 miles from St. Louis; am a writer of books and magazine articles. In October, 1902, was associate editor of the St. Louis *Chronicle;* published an article entitled in the *Chronicle* on the 11th of October from material I obtained from Dr. Chapman at his office in his house on the 8th or 9th, I think; I made notes of what he said on a pad; am not a short hand writer. I requested Dr. Chapman to give me an interview and he consented; I asked him to give me the details of Ed. Butler's first interview with him.

Mr. Krum (reading from the *Chronicle*). Did he give you this answer: "It was in the evening that Col. Butler called, about dusk, he drove up in a storm buggy, and was shown into the parlor. As I said, I do not remember the exact date. You see the Municipal Assembly had passed an ordinance specifying that the contract for disposing of the garbage should be awarded to a Company which would use the Merz process of reduction. After this ordinance had been passed the Board of Health advertised for bids." Cannot state that he made it exactly in those words; but the substance as I can remember it now, is the way he stated it to me. I wrote it out within an hour afterwards from the notes I had. In writing it out I intended to tell the truth, to give substantially what had been stated to me.

Mr. Krum. Did Dr. Chapman make this statement to you on that occasion: "Well, we talked along those lines for some little time, and then he said to me. 'Doctor, we have $50,000 tied up with our bid; as soon as that is released, I would like to make you a present of $2,500?' " That is in substance; there was a great deal Dr. Chapman said that was not there, in reference to what he and Butler had been talking about the garbage works, and I did not bring that into my interview, so the sentence commencing "Well, after we had talked along those lines for a certain time" is the sum and substance of what he stated. Did Dr. Chapman tell you on this occasion that Butler said to him, "Doctor, we have $50,000 tied up with our bid, and as soon as that is released, I would like to make you a present of $2,500"? Yes. Did you ask Dr. Chapman this question: "Did Col. Butler make you the offer of $2,500 for your vote on the garbage contract?" Yes. Did he give you this answer: "No, not in those words. He simply said that he wished to make me a present"? Yes. Did you ask Dr. Chapman: "Why did he wish to make you this present?" I probably did. Did he then make you this answer: "That I could never understand. There was no necessity for his offering anything to any member of the Board of Health. Under the ordinance passed by the Municipal Assembly, they could award the contract only to a company which employed the Merz system of reduction, and the works in which Col. Butler is interested are the only ones that employ this system, besides Col. Butler's company was the only one to introduce a bid"? Yes, he said that and more on the same line. That is a condensed statement of his rather lengthy conversation about expressing surprise that such a thing should have been done. Did Dr. Chapman furnish you with a picture or a photograph from which a picture was taken for the paper? Yes.

Mr. Folk. In getting up newspaper interviews, you don't attempt to use the exact language. This is written in your own language, is it not? Yes, sir. It is written in—well in the general run of interviews, they are written in the language of the writer, but in special cases he tries to adhere as closely as possible to the phraseology of the person interviewed. He gives his own impression of the substance of the interview with the person he is interviewing. Is that correct? Yes. Of course reporters sometimes make mistakes, don't they? You have heard of that? I have heard of it. You know that newspapers are not always accurate, don't you? They are not; they try to be; try harder than most people believe that they do. And having to come out every day, in the rush and hurry of getting the news, they sometimes get pretty much mixed up? They do at times get mixed up, certainly. We all err. . . .

The Verdict and Sentence.

The sheriff was ordered to bring in the Jury. The jurors entered and the foreman [Mr. Hickman] handed a paper to the sheriff who passed it to the Judge who read it aloud: "We, the Jury, find the defendant, Edward Butler, guilty as charged and assess his punishment at imprisonment in the penitentiary for a term of three years."

6

Progressive Jurisprudence
Muller v. Oregon
1908

On Labor Day 1905, Emma Gotcher, an employee of the Grand Laundry of Port-land, Oregon, was ordered to work overtime in violation of a recently passed state law that forbade employing women for more than a ten-hour day. The state filed criminal charges against Curt Muller, the owner of the laundry. Arguing against the constitutionality of the law, Muller's attorney appealed to a recent United States Supreme court decision in Lochner v. New York *which earlier in the year 1905 had rejected a New York State law limiting the hours bakers could work. In that case, the court had found that in preventing the bakers from con-tracting to work additional hours, the law violated the liberty of contract guar-anteed by the Fourteenth Amendment. When the Oregon courts rejected this argument, Muller, financed by a consortium of Portland laundry owners, ap-pealed to the Supreme Court.*

Reformers, particularly women progressives in the largely female National Consumers' League, feared that a decision based on Lochner would void existing legislation in twenty states setting limits on the hours women could work. Were such a precedent to be established, the Supreme Court might easily decide that virtually any interference with the theoretical right of workers to contract freely with employers violated the Fourteenth Amendment, destroying the legal basis for legislation to improve the harsh working conditions typical of the era.

The National Consumers' League under the energetic leadership of the vet-eran labor reformer Florence Kelley sought legal counsel to defend the Oregon law. Eminent lawyers one after another turned down the League. "Big strong laundry women," trumpeted Joseph Choate, a leading constitutional lawyer. "Why shouldn't they work longer?" Finally the NCL hired Louis D. Brandeis, a successful lawyer and a progressive reformer.

Brandeis represented a new current in early twentieth-century legal thinking first called "sociological jurisprudence," then later "legal realism." This school of thought, inspired largely by Oliver Wendell Holmes, Jr., who became a Supreme Court justice in 1902, believed that the law had to change with social conditions. The facts behind a case were more important than abstract legal reasoning.

SUGGESTIONS FOR FURTHER READING: Nancy Woloch, *Muller v. Oregon, A Brief History with Docu-ment*, Boston & New York: Bedford Books, 1996; Susan Lehrer, *Origins of Protective Labor Legisla-tion for Women, 1905–1925*, Albany, NY: State University of New York Press, 1987.

Judges had to be aware of economics and sociology. That would enable the law to catch up with what Brandeis termed "the facts of life."

Taking the case without a fee, Brandeis applied this theory in the brief he presented for the state of Oregon. Setting ten researchers to work, he had them collect all the data they could find in major libraries about the ill effect of long hours on the health and welfare of working women and the benefits of shorter work days. He then wrote a mere two-page account of legal precedents arguing that the Lochner precedent forbade limiting freedom of contract only when the Court was offered no reasonable ground to show that "there is material danger to the public health . . . or to the health . . . of the employees." The rest of the brief piled on a hundred pages of "facts" from numerous states and foreign countries to demonstrate that the Oregon legislature had "reasonable ground" for believing that limiting the hours of work for women would improve the health and welfare of the state's population.

The Brandeis Brief, as it came to be called, was an enormous success and worked a revolution in American jurisprudence. The Supreme Court not only decided for Oregon but complimented Brandeis by name in its decision. Commentators at the time, almost unanimous in their praise, recognized that Brandeis had initiated an era in constitutional interpretation that might bring about much of the agenda of progressive reform.

Recent students of the case have been more sparing in their praise. Did the brief offer relevant tested facts, they ask, or was it a hodgepodge of material that proved little? Many of the facts cited were old or unauthenticated; little of the material distinguished effects on women from effects on men; none of it specifically addressed women laundry workers. And what did it say about women: that they were more frail than men? That they could not work so long and needed special protection? That they were defined by their household and nurturing duties? The question arises whether this special concern for women in fact placed a roadblock in the way of gender equality. The Courts in the past generation, steadily eliminating protective legislation in favor of equal rights, certainly appear to be of that opinion.

Brief for Curt Muller

The Act of the Oregon Legislative Assembly called in question is as follows:

"An Act to regulate and limit the hours of employment of females in any mechanical or mercantile establishment, laundry, hotel, or restaurant; to provide for its enforcement and a penalty for its violation.

Curt Muller is accused of the crime of requiring a female to work in a laundry more than ten hours in one day. Muller contends that the statute pursuant to which the information was filed is unconstitutional, and that a violation thereof does not constitute a crime, for the following reasons, to wit:

(1) Because the statute attempts to prevent persons, *sui juris*, from making their own contracts, and thus violates the provisions of the Fourteenth Amendment, as follows:

"No state shall make or enforce any law which shall abridge the privileges or immunities of citizens of the United States; nor shall any state deprive any person of life, liberty or property without due process of law, nor deny to any person within its jurisdiction the equal protection of the laws."

(2) Because the statute does not apply equally to all persons similarly situated, and is class legislation.

(3) The statute is not a valid exercise of the police power. The kinds of work proscribed are not unlawful, nor are they declared to be immoral or dangerous to the public health; nor can such a law be sustained on the ground that it is designed to protect women on account of their sex. There is no necessary or reasonable connection between the limitation prescribed by the Act and the public health, safety or welfare. . . . The argument based on sex ought not to prevail, because women's rights are as sacred under the Fourteenth Amendment as are men's.

Is there any difference between the case of a healthy, adult woman, contracting for service for more than ten hours in a laundry, and that of a man employed as a baker for more than ten hours a day? Certainly conditions are as favorable in a laundry as in a bakery. The character of labor is not such in the case of a laundry to justify the assumption that it is more dangerous than that of the work of a baker.

The facts before the court in *Lochner* v. *New York* (1905) and the conclusion to which the Court there arrived, justify the contention that a statute which attempts to restrict the hours of service of all women, without relation to the dangers of the employment or the character of the service, is invalid. In that case a statute of the State of New York provided that no employees should be required or permitted to work in bakeries more than sixty hours in a week, or ten hours a day, and this statute was held to be invalid and not within the police power of the state, although it was there claimed and apparently conceded that the labor of the baker was not only laborious, but performed under conditions peculiarly injurious to his health. It is true that in that case it appeared that the employees were all men, but it is not perceived that a difference in sex would or could have made any difference in the decision. . . .

"The Brandeis Brief"

The world's experience upon which the legislation limiting the hours of labor for women is based on

I. The dangers of long hours

A. Causes

(1) Physical Differences between Men and Women

The dangers of long hours for women arise from their special physical organization taken in connection with the strain incident to factory and similar work.

Long hours of labor are dangerous for women primarily because of their special physical organization. In structure and function women are differentiated from men. Besides these anatomical and physiological differences, physicians are agreed that women are fundamentally weaker than men in all that makes for endurance: in muscular strength, in nervous energy, in the powers of persistent attention and application. Overwork, therefore, which strains endurance to the utmost, is more disastrous to the health of women than of men, and entails upon them more lasting injury.

Report of Select Committee on Shops Early Closing Bill, British House of Commons, 1895.

Dr. Percy Kidd, physician in Brompton and London Hospitals:

The most common effect I have noticed of the long hours is general deterioration of health; very general symptoms which we medically attribute to over-action, and debility of the nervous system; that includes a great deal more than what is called nervous disease, such as indigestion, constipation, a general slackness, and a great many other indefinite symptoms.

Are those symptoms more marked in women than in men?

I think they are much more marked in women. I should say one sees a great many more women of this class than men; but I have seen precisely the same symptoms in men, I should not say in the same proportion, because one has not been able to make anything like a statistical inquiry. There are other symptoms, but I mention those as being the most common. Another symptom especially among women in anæmia, bloodlessness or pallor, that I have no doubt is connected with long hours indoors. (Page 215.)

Report of Committee on Early Closing of Shops Bill, British House of Lords, 1901.

Sir W. MacComac, President of the Royal College of Surgeons:

Would you draw a distinction between the evil resulting to women and the evil resulting to men?

You see men have undoubtedly a greater degree of physical capacity than women have. Men are capable of greater effort in various ways than women. If a like amount of physical toil and effort be imposed upon women, they suffer to a larger degree. (Page 219.)

Report of the Maine Bureau of Industrial and Labor Statistics, 1888.

Let me quote from Dr. Ely Van der Warker (1875):

Woman is badly constructed for the purposes of standing eight or ten hours upon her feet. I do not intend to bring into evidence the peculiar position and nature of the organs contained in the pelvis, but to call attention to the peculiar construction of the knee and the shallowness of the pelvis, and the delicate nature of the foot as part of a sustaining column. The knee joint of woman is a sexual characteristic. Viewed in front and extended, the joint in but a slight degree interrupts the gradual taper of the thigh into the leg. Viewed in a semi-flexed position, the joint forms a smooth ovate spheroid. The reason of this lies in the smallness of the patella in front, and the narrowness of the articular surfaces of the tibia and femur, and which in man form the lateral prominences, and thus is much more perfect as a sustaining column than that of a woman. The muscles which keep the body fixed upon the thighs in the erect position labor under the disadvantage of shortness of purchase, owing to the short distance, compared to that of man, between the crest of the ilium and the great trochanter of the femur, thus giving to man a much larger purchase in the leverage existing between the trunk and the extremities. Comparatively the foot is less able to sustain weight than that of man, owing to its shortness and the more delicate formation of the tarsus and metatarsus. (Page 142.) . . .

(2) THE NEW STRAIN IN MANUFACTURE

Such being their physical endowment, women are affected to a far greater degree than men by the growing strain of modern industry. Machinery is increasingly speeded up, the number of machines tended by individual workers grows larger, processes become more and more complex as more operations are performed simultaneously. All these changes involve correspondingly greater physical strain upon the worker.

Reports of Medical Commissioners on the Health of Factory Operatives. Parliamentary Papers, 1833, Vol. XXI.

The first and most influential of all disadvantages of factory work is the indispensable, undeviating necessity of forcing both their mental and bodily exertions to keep exact pace with the motions of machinery propelled by unceasing, unvarying power. (Page 72.)

Factory and Workshop Act Commission, 1875. *British Sessional Papers*, 1876.

We have already referred more than once to the unremitting and monotonous character of all labor at a machine driven by steam. If the day's work of a housemaid or even of a charwoman be closely looked at and compared with that of an ordinary mill hand in a card room or spinning room, it will be seen that the former, though occasionally making greater muscular efforts than are ever exacted from the latter, is yet continually changing both her occupation and her posture, and has very frequent intervals of rest. Work at a machine has inevitably a treadmill character about it; each step may be easy, but it must be performed at the exact moment under pain of consequences. In hand work and house work there is a certain freedom of doing or of leaving undone. Mill (*i.e.* machine) work must be done as if by clockwork. . . . The people are tied as it were to machinery moving at a great speed in certain operations; again it has been alleged that the state of the atmosphere is very unhealthy, and the temperature at a great height, and from the employment of machinery the speed has been so much increased, that the wear and tear, not merely of the body but of the mind also, of the operatives were too great for them to bear.

The Working Hours of Female Factory Hands. From the Reports of Factory Inspectors, collated in the Imperial Home Office. Berlin, 1905.

From Frankfurt am Oder it is reported that the insurance records for two textile mills show steady deterioration in the health of the women employed eleven hours a day. One reason for this is believed to be the speeding up of the machinery. Vigorous weavers stated repeatedly that the old, slow looms exhausted them less in twelve and thirteen hours than the swift new looms in eleven hours. The more intensive work requires better nourishment; but there is no adequate increase in wages to afford this improved food, and the eleven-hour day of more rapid work is presumably responsible for the deteriorated health. (Page 119.)

B. Bad Effect of Long Hours on Health

The fatigue which follows long hours of labor becomes chronic and results in general deterioration of health. Often ignored, since it does not result in immediate disease, this weakness and anæmia undermines the whole system; it destroys the nervous energy most necessary for steady work, and effectually predisposes to other illness. The long hours of standing, which are required in many industries, are universally denounced by physicians as the cause of pelvic disorders.

(1) General Injuries from Long Hours

Reports of Medical Commissioners on the Health of Factory Operatives. DAVID BARRY. *British Sessional Papers,* 1833, Vol. XXI.

Evidence of Francis Sharp, at Leeds, member of College of Surgeons in London, student of medical profession for fourteen years, house surgeon of Leeds Infirmary for four years:

The nervous energy of the body I consider to be weakened by the very long hours, and a foundation laid for many diseases. . . . Were it not for the individuals who join the mills from the country, the factory people would soon be deteriorated. (Pages 12, 13.)

Females whose work obliges them to stand constantly, are more subject to varicose veins of the lower extremities and to a larger and more dangerous extent than ever I have witnessed even in foot-soldiers. (Page 73.) . . .

Reports of Commissioners on the Hours of Labor. Massachusetts Legislative Documents. House, 1867, No.44.

Women are held under the present customs and ideas to at least five hours each half day of continuous work, often in the most tedious, minute, and monotonous employ. It is assumed . . . that they have no lower limbs to ache with swollen or ruptured veins, no delicacy of nerve, or versatility of mind, to revolt from such severity of application. (Page 66.)

Massachusetts Bureau of Statistics of Labor. Domestic Labor and Woman's Work, 1872.

In the cotton mills at Fitchburg the women and children are pale, crooked, and sickly-looking. The women appear dispirited, and the children without the bloom of childhood in their cheeks, or the elasticity that belongs to that age. Hours, 60 to 67¾ a week. (Page 94.)

Report of the British Chief Inspector of Factories and Workshops, 1873, Vol. XIX.

The house surgeon of a large hospital has stated that every year he had a large number of cases of pulmonary disease in girls, the origin of which he could distinctly trace to long and late hours in overcrowded and unhealthy workrooms. (Page 43.)

Factory and Workshops Act Commission, 1875. Miss A. E. Todd. *Great Britain Sessional Papers,* 1876, Vol. XXIX, Appendix D.

I would say that factory work is often, but not always, injurious to those engaged in it; country girls especially suffer from the close air and confinement; many of them fall into consumption or bad health of some kind. I have known many deaths from this cause in this class. I have also found much derangement of the liver, stomach, and digestive organs, owing, I think, partially to the rapidity with which they are obliged to eat their meals. (Page 164.)

Report of the Maine Bureau of Industrial and Labor Statistics, 1888.

Many saleswomen are so worn out, when their week's work is ended, that a good part of their Sundays is spent in bed, recuperating for the next week's demands. And one by one girls drop out and die, often from sheer overwork. This I know from observation and personal acquaintance. (Page 142.) . . .

(2) Specific Evil Effects on Childbirth and Female Functions

The evil effect of overwork before as well as after marriage upon childbirth is marked and disastrous.

Report of Select Committee on Shops Early Closing Bill. British House of Commons, 1895.

Testimony of Dr. W. Chapman Grigg (formerly out-patient physician for the diseases of women at Westminster Hospital, and senior physician to the Queen Charlotte Lying-in Hospital and the Victoria Hospital for Children).

Would you please tell us in a general way your experience as to the effects of these prolonged hours on health?

It has a very grave effect upon the generative organs of women, entailing a great deal of suffering and also injuring a very large body of them permanently, setting up inflammation in the pelvis in connection with those organs. . . .

I have had a great many sad cases come before me of women who were permanent invalids in consequence.

If the matter could be gone into carefully, I think the committee would be perfectly surprised to find what a large number of these women are rendered sterile in consequence of these prolonged hours.

I believe this is one of the greatest evils attached to these prolonged hours. I have seen many cases in families where certain members who have pursued the calling of shop-girl assistants have been sterile, while other members of the family have borne children. I know of one case where four members of a family who were shop-girls were sterile, and two other girls in the family, not shop-girls, have borne children; and I have known other cases in which this has occurred. . . . I have patients come to me from all parts of London. It appears to be a most common condition.

When these women have children, do you find that the children themselves suffer from the woman having been affected by these very long hours?

I have seen many cases where I have attributed the mischief arising in childbed to this inflammatory mischief in the mother, which, after delivery, has set up fresh mischief, and I have seen serious consequences resulting. (Page 219.) . . .

D. Bad Effects of Long Hours on Morals

The effect of overwork on morals is closely related to the injury to health. Laxity of moral fibre follows physical debility. When the working day is so long that no time whatever is left for a minimum of leisure or home-life, relief from the strain of work is sought in alcoholic stimulants and other excesses.

Massachusetts Legislative Document. House, 1866, No. 98.

Overwork is the fruitful source of innumerable evils. Ten and eleven hours daily of hard labor are more than the human system can bear, save in a few exceptional cases. . . . It cripples the body, ruins health, shortens life. It stunts the mind, gives no time for culture, no opportunity for reading, study, or mental improvement. It leaves the system jaded and worn, with no ability to study. . . . It tends to dissipation in various forms. The exhausted system craves stimulants. This opens the door to other indulgences, from which flow not only the degeneracy of individuals, but the degeneracy of the race. (Page 24.)

Relations between Labor and Capital. U. S. Senate Committee, 1883. Vol. I. *Testimony of* Robert Howard, *Mule-Spinner in Fall River Cotton Mills.*

I have noticed that the hard, slavish overwork is driving those girls into the saloons, after they leave the mills evenings . . . good, respectable girls, but they come out so tired and so thirsty and so exhausted . . . from working along steadily from hour to hour and breathing the noxious effluvia from the grease and other ingredients used in the mill.

Wherever you go . . . near the abodes of people who are overworked, you will always find the sign of the rum-shop.

Drinking is most prevalent among working people where the hours of labor are long. (Page 647.) . . .

Report of the British Association for the Advancement of Science: the Economic Effect of Legislation Regulating Women's Labor, 1902.

On the morals of the workers there has been a marked effect [by the Factory

Acts]. "Saint Monday" is now a thing of the past, and just as irregularity conduces to drunkenness and irregular living, and the rush of overtime at the end of the week, with nothing to do in the early parts, induced an irregular and careless mode of life, so the comparative steadiness of the present methods have tended to raise the standard of morality and sobriety. (Page 287.)

E. Bad Effect of Long Hours on General Welfare

The experience of manufacturing countries has illustrated the evil effect of overwork upon the general welfare. Deterioration of any large portion of the population inevitably lowers the entire community physically, mentally, and morally. When the health of women has been injured by long hours, not only is the working efficiency of the community impaired, but the deterioration is handed down to succeeding generations. Infant mortality rises, while the children of married working-women, who survive, are injured by inevitable neglect. The overwork of future mothers thus directly attacks the welfare of the nation.

(1) THE STATE'S NEED OF PROTECTING WOMAN

Report of the Massachusetts State Board of Health, 1873. Edward Jarvis, M.D.

All additions to the physical, moral, or intellectual power of individuals—in any individual are, to that extent, additions to the energy and the productive force—the effectiveness of the State; and on the contrary, all deductions from these forces, whether of mind or body—every sickness, and injury or disability, every impairment of energy—take so much from the mental force, the safe administration of the body politic. . . .

The State thus has an interest not only in the prosperity, but also in the health and strength and effective power of each one of its members. . . .

The first and largest interest of the State lies in the great agency of human power—the health of the people. (Page 336.)

Report of the New York Bureau of Labor Statistics, 1900.

The family furnishes the really fundamental education of the growing generation—the education of character; and the family life thus really determines the quality of the rising generation as efficient or non-efficient wealth producers. If a reduction in the hours of labor does promote the growth of a purer and better family life, it will unquestionably result in the production of greater material wealth on the part of the generation trained under its influence; nothing else in fact will so effectively diminish the vast number of criminals, paupers, and idlers, who, in the present generation, consume the people's substance. When one or both parents are away from home for twelve or thirteen hours (the necessary period for those who work ten hours) a day, the children receive comparatively little attention. What was said in the opening paragraph of this section in discussing the importance of a good family life in the training of character needs repeated emphasis, for it is the fundamental argument for a shorter working day. (Page 69.)

III. The general benefits of short hours

History, which has illustrated the deterioration due to long hours, bears witness no less clearly to the regeneration due to the shorter working day. To the individual and to society alike, shorter hours have been a benefit wherever introduced. The married and unmarried working woman is enabled to obtain the decencies of life outside of working hours. With the improvement in home life, the tone of the entire community is raised. Wherever sufficient time has elapsed since the establishment of the shorter working day, the succeeding generation has shown extraordinary improvement in physique and morals.

A. Good Effect on the Individual Health, Home Life, etc.

Report of the Massachusetts Bureau of Labor Statistics, 1871.

Their hours of labor should not exceed ten hours per day, for, as we have seen, 85+per cent of the working girls of Boston do their own housework and sewing either wholly or in ·part, and this homework must be done in addition to that performed for their employers. (Page 558.) . . .

Report of the New York Bureau of Labor Statistics, 1900.

The wife's life is darkened even more by the long-hour day, especially if she also be a working woman. Even if the day be one of only ten hours, she must arise as early as five o'clock to prepare breakfast for her husband and herself, so that they may be at their work places at seven. Beginning at that early hour her day will be a very long one. (Page 69.)

B. Good Effect on the General Welfare

Report of the Massachusetts Bureau of Statistics of Labor, 1873. On Results of Ten-Hour Labor Law in England.

Lord Ashley said: Upon the good moral and social influence of the change, the testimony is most favorable from the clergymen and school teachers throughout Yorkshire and Lancaster. How have the women used their time? Hundreds of them are attending evening school—learning to read and write and to knit and sew, things that they could not have learned under the twelve-hour system.

A burial society testifies to the diminution of burial although the cholera was upon the town, and that the diminution was among children under five years of age, and he assumes as a reason that mothers can get home earlier and give that attention to children which no hired nurse can ensure.

The Catholic priests at Stockport and Bolton testify that the number of factory workers attending schools has more than doubled and that there was not the slightest doubt that the moral, social, and physical condition of the people had improved. (Page 491.)

Report of the New Jersey Bureau of Statistics of Labor and Industry, 1886.

The Factory Acts were believed to be the death-blow to English manufactures, and they have made labor more efficient, more intelligent, more decent, and more continuous without trenching on profits.

In 1851 and 1852 those who advocated that ten hours should be a legal day's work were denounced as demagogues, and the ten-hour plan as a humbug which could only tend to reduce the wages proportionately, while all kinds of evil results were sure to follow its application, especially to agricultural labor. But we have seen ten hours become the rule; wages have not fallen, and many of those who prophesied disaster are now as loud in their praises of its beneficence as the friends of the change. (Page 231.)

Report of the Massachusetts Chief of the District Police, 1889.

The good results of shortening the hours of labor were soon apparent, in the substantial disappearance of discontent among those affected thereby; in the maintenance of the standard of factory productions, both as to quantity and quality; and in placing Massachusetts in the lead, where by her history and her aspirations, she rightfully belonged.

. . . If experience has shown anything in this matter, it has been the wisdom and statesmanship of the body of laws in our Public Statutes and additions thereto, which are known as industrial legislation. It is sixteen years since the ten-hour law was enacted; and it is entirely safe to say that, if it were stricken from the statutes to-day, not an influential voice would be raised within our borders in favor of the restoration of the order of things which that law changed. The increase of public interest in matters of this kind is a very significant fact. (Page 7.)

IV. Economic aspect of short hours

A. Effect on Output

The universal testimony of manufacturing countries tends to prove that the regulation of the working day acts favorably upon output. With long hours, output declines; with short hours, it rises. The heightened efficiency of the workers, due to the shorter day, more than balances any loss of time. Production is not only increased, but improved in quality.

(1) SHORTER HOURS INCREASE EFFICIENCY, AND THUS PREVENT REDUCTION OF OUTPUT.

Report of the United States Industrial Commission, 1900.

Those States which are just now advancing to the position of manufacturing communities might well learn from these examples the lesson that permanent industrial progress cannot be built upon the physical exhaustion of women and children. . . . A reduction in hours has never lessened the working-people's ability to compete in the markets of the world. States with shorter work-days actually manufacture their products at a lower cost than States with longer work-days. (Page 788.) . . .

Massachusetts Bureau of Statistics of Labor. 1872.

The testimony of those who have adopted the shorter time is almost unanimous in its favor. Many reported an improved condition of the employees. No instance is given of decreased wages, though many report an increase, not only in wages, but in production. All of the arguments against reduction made by those working eleven hours and over are answered by those who have adopted the shorter time, and worked under that system for years. The advocates of eleven hours have utterly failed to sustain themselves in their continued adhesion to a system that England outgrew twenty-two years ago; a system unworthy of our State and nation, and one that would not last a month if the victims of it were men instead of women and children, as most of them are. (Page 240.)

B. Effect on Regularity of Employment

Wherever the employment of women has been prohibited for more than ten hours in one day, a more equal distribution of work throughout the year has followed. The supposed need of dangerously long and irregular hours in the season-trades are shown to be unnecessary. In place of alternating periods of intense overwork with periods of idleness, employers have found it possible to avoid such irregularities by foresight and management.

Report of Conference of Members of Women's Trade Unions on the Factory and Workshops Act, 1875. Vol. XXIX.

The permission granted to season trades for the extension of the hours to fourteen per day, during certain periods of the year, should be withdrawn, with the view of equalizing the work throughout the year. . . .

Bookbinders complained that the trade was most unnecessarily considered by the law a season-trade. . . . The existence of the modification made employers careless of due economy in time. (Page 193.)

Report of the British Chief Inspector of Factories and Workshops, 1892.

I am convinced that there is no necessity for this overtime; the season-trade work or the press orders would be executed just the same if overtime were illegal, as it is in the textile and many of the non-textile trades; the work would only be spread over a longer period or mean the employment of more hands. Much of the good done by the Factory Act is undone by allowing delicate women and girls to work from 8 A.M. to 10 P.M. for two months of the year. (Page 89.)

C. Adaptation of Customers to Shorter Hours

Experience shows how the demands of customers yield to the requirements of a fixed working day. When customers are obliged to place orders sufficiently in advance to enable them to be filled without necessitating overtime work, compliance with this habit becomes automatic.

Factory and Workshops Acts Commission, 1875. *British Sessional Papers*, 1876. Vol. XXIX.

A very large number of the orders of customers (to printers, milliners, dressmakers, etc.), which it has been usual to keep back to the last minute and then throw upon the already fully-burdened workers, not merely can be quite as easily given so as to have plenty of time for their completion, but also will be so given, and are in fact so given, when and so often as the customer is made to recognize that he otherwise runs the risk of not having his orders completed in time to suit his own convenience. . . .

We trust in time that the use of overtime in trades of this class may be restricted down to the vanishing point. (Page 41.)

Report of the British Association for the Advancement of Science, 1903.

The tendency to put off giving orders to the last moment is easily checked when the customer can be met with a universal legal prohibition. (Page 7.)

D. Incentive to Improvements in Manufacture

The regulation of the working day has acted as a stimulus to improvement in processes of manufacture. Invention of new machinery and perfection of old methods have followed the introduction of shorter hours.

Reports of the Wisconsin Bureau of Labor Statistics, 1903–1904.

Wherever a uniform standard of wages, hours of labor, and wholesome sanitary conditions have been uniformly enforced, the result has been that laborers have been stimulated to render greater services to their employers, and, in turn, employers strive to excel in improved machinery and devices for the protection of employees, sanitation, and methods of production in general. (Page 138.)

That the enforcing of a certain standard in regard to hours of labor, wages, and sanitary conditions compels employers to continually seek more improved machinery and methods of production is as true in practice as in theory. (Page 140.)

E. Effect on Scope of Women's Employment

The establishment of a legal limit to the hours of woman's labor does not result in contracting the sphere of her work.

Foreign Work and English Wages. By Thomas Brassey, *1st Baron Brassey.* London, 1879.

The argument that the tendency of the Factory Acts is to place an artificial restriction on the employment of women, and thus to depreciate the market value of this labor, is refuted on every hand by practical experience in the textile manufactories. Here the restrictions upon women's work are the most stringent, and yet the tendency for a long series of years has been the opposite—the proportion of women employed has steadily increased. The same observation applies to many of the trades and occupations carried on in London. As for the rate of wages paid, there is not an employer in the metropolis who will hesitate to acknowledge that there has been during the last ten or fifteen years a very substantial and important advance in the remuneration given to women for their work. (Pages 338, 339.)

The Case for the Factory Acts. Edited by Mrs. Sidney Webb. *London,* 1901.

But, it may be objected, that although Factory Legislation would improve the women, it annoys the employer, and makes him inclined to get rid of women altogether and employ men. As a matter of fact, this course, though often threatened beforehand, is not in practice followed. Where women can be employed, their labor is so much cheaper than that of men that there is no chance of their being displaced. The work of men and women tending automatically to differentiate itself into separate branches, it follows that there is very little direct competition between individual men and women. (Page 209.)

VI. The reasonableness of the ten-hour day

Factory inspectors, physicians, and working women are unanimous in advocating the ten-hour day, wherever it has not yet been established. Some indeed consider ten hours too long a period of labor; but as opposed to the unregulated or longer day, there is agreement that ten hours is the maximum number of working hours compatible with health and efficiency.

A. Opinions of Physicians and Officials

British Sessional Papers. Dr. Loudon. 1833. Vol. XXI.

From fourteen (years of age) upwards, I would recommend that no individual should, under any circumstances, work more than twelve hours a day; although if practicable, as a physician, I would prefer the limitation of ten hours for all persons who earn their bread by industry. Ten working hours a day are in fact thirteen hours, allowing an hour for dinner, half an hour for breakfast, half an hour for tea-time, half an hour for going, and the same for returning from work. (Page 24.)

Report of Special Committee to inquire as to the Propriety of reducing the Hours of Labor. Massachusetts Legislative Document. House, 1865.

This (system of ten hours) is now very generally in use—the exceptions being in manufacturing towns and corporations—where they now require . . . women and children to work eleven hours daily—one hour more than in England—a disgrace in our opinion to Massachusetts and an outrage on humanity. (Page 2.)

Report of the Special Commission on the Hours of Labor. Massachusetts Legislative Documents. House, 1866, No. 98.

Dr. Tewksbury has been a practising physician eighteen years in Lawrence, and a close observer of the health and morals of operatives. Thinks long confinement in mills and insufficient time for meals injurious, and that ten hours a day is better than eleven or twelve hours.

Dr. Sargent, many years practising physician in Lawrence: Ten hours a day enough for strong men; too long for delicate women. (Page 63.)

Conclusion

We submit that in view of the facts above set forth and of legislative action extending over a period of more than sixty years in the leading countries of Europe, and in twenty of our States, it cannot be said that the Legislature of Oregon had no reasonable ground for believing that the public health, safety, or welfare did not require a legal limitation on women's work in manufacturing and mechanical establishments and laundries to ten hours in one day.

LOUIS D. BRANDEIS,
Counsel for State of Oregon.

7
Dissent During World War I
The Kate O'Hare Trial
1919

The Espionage Act, proposed by the administration of Woodrow Wilson and passed by Congress in June 1917, went substantially beyond providing sanctions against acts of espionage. It raised questions of rights under the first amendment to the Constitution by providing jail terms of up to twenty years for making or publishing statements that interfered with the armed forces or obstructed the military draft. Many of the defendants were socialists like Kate Richards O'Hare (1877–1948). While during World War I it was typical of major European socialist and social-democratic parties to support their home countries, the American Socialist Party divided on the issue, many of its leaders arguing against American involvement in what they viewed as a capitalists' war in which workers had nothing to gain. A special American condition explaining some of the difference between European and American socialists on the war issue is the support the American party drew from people of German descent, many of whom were unsympathetic to the Allied cause.

O'Hare, a leading speaker for the party whose fiery evangelical rhetoric was particularly effective in converting to socialism poor dirt farmers in the Plains states, spoke against the war in Bowman, North Dakota, on July 17, 1917, repeating what she had said in dozens of speeches across the country. The local political situation, however, on this occasion greatly amplified the effect of her words. Until 1915 the socialists had enjoyed steady support in North Dakota. Then the Nonpartisan League, a broader farmers' movement that included many socialists, swept to power in the state. The Nonpartisan League uneasily balanced support for the war effort with intense criticism of war profiteering. Its major party enemies, the Democrats, seeking to identify the League with O'Hare's militant opposition to the war, made an issue of her speech, and that led to her arrest for obstructing recruitment and enlistments in the armed forces.

At her trial, O'Hare faced a judge who had made public statements opposing both socialism and women who were active in public life. Her jury—in a county with many depressed farmers who had joined the Nonpartisan League—was com-

SUGGESTIONS FOR FURTHER READING: Sally M. Miller, *From Prairie to Prison, The Life of Social Activist Kate Richards O'Hare*, Columbia, Missouri: University of Missouri Press, 1993; David M. Kennedy, *Over Here: The First World War and American Society*, New York: Oxford University Press, 1980.

posed of twelve businessmen, none of them members of the League. She received a five year sentence that was upheld on appeal. In a little over a year, the Justice Department in response to a nationwide amnesty campaign on behalf of those jailed under the Espionage Act commuted her sentence. Eventually she received a full pardon from President Calvin Coolidge. Her incarceration having made her an ardent advocate of prison reform, she remained active in that cause until her death in 1948. She also founded a school for workers' education and campaigned for Upton Sinclair in his 1934 race for governor of California.

The Trial of Kate Richards O'Hare for Disloyalty, *Bismarck, North Dakota, 1917*
HON. MARTIN J. WADE, *Judge.*

The prisoner, *Kate Richards O'Hare*, had been indicted by the grand jury on Jully 27 for violating section 3 of the Espionage act, which declares that "whoever, when the United States is at war . . . shall willfully obstruct the recruiting or enlistment service of the United States, to the injury of the service or of the United States," shall be punished as therein provided. The indictment alleges that the prisoner stated, in substance, in a public speech in the town of Bowman, N. Dak., in the presence of 125 people—

"that any person who enlisted in the army of the United States for service in France would be used for fertilizer, and that is all he was good for; and that the women of the United States were nothing more or less than brood sows to raise children to get into the army and be made into fertilizer";

and that statement so made was made with the intention of willfully obstructing the recruiting service of the United States, to the injury of the service of the United States.

Kate Richards O'Hare, being arraigned today, pleaded *not guilty.*

The witnesses for the Government

J. E. James. Am a farmer near Bowman; on 27th April last went to Mrs. O'Hare's lecture there at the Cozy Theatre; Bowman has about 800 population; she spoke about two hours; she said she had spent the last five years traveling here and in Europe delivering addresses on Socialistic reform; that she was the original editor of the Ripsaw, which had been stopped going through the mails, and author of several books on Socialism; that we were drawn into this terrible catastrophe and that she was going to do all she could against it. She said if mothers became pregnant for the purpose of bringing sons into this world for cannon fodder they were no better than farmers' sows. She said if any young man is foolish enough to enlist and go over there and fight, why, we can not help that; he is either—he was good for either German or French fertilizer. At this time we were arranging to carry out the draft law in our country and the town was placarded with appeals to enter the army and navy.

Cross-examined. Before this I had read a little from one or two of her books; there were about 150 in the audience, mostly adults . . . have not been much interested in politics lately; there was a good deal of feeling between rival factions in Bowman at this time; my son enlisted in May; thought her talk reflected on our family and was seditious too; it rather angered me . . .

She said . . . she was out working for the betterment of mankind, uplift of society and trying to stop this horrible war. She wasn't going to sit by with her hands folded and let her son be made into fertilizer.

Dr. A. A. Whittimore. Am a physician, practicing in Bowman; was at Mrs. O'Hare's lecture; think there were 200 or 250 people there; some were young men. There were two or three things that made a special impression on my mind at the time, and the first thing I can recall now is that she stated she had no objection to men volunteering for the army if they were fools enough to do so, but that they would make good fertilizer anyway. She objected very strongly to these men going because they had to go in the draft and stating that if the mothers would—she was contrasting the difference between the Government's power to call men and the mother's right to determine the destiny of her sons, as I understand it, and she said that if the Government had a right to conscript or draft men into the service it was placing the women on a level with the ordinary brood sow. And another thing that impressed me was her statement regarding the cause of the war. She said it was not in order to make democracy safe or to protect the lives of American citizens, but to protect J. P. Morgan's millions that he had loaned to the Allies for the war and to enrich the munition factory owners; another statement that—I think she was taking about the clergymen or the church regarding their sympathies and actions in the war—and she said they were making the churches recruiting stations and that the priests and preachers were recruiting officers. That is all that I can recall at this moment.

Cross-examined. There has been strong political feeling in Bowman at times; Socialists have a good many adherents there; a good many foreigners in the city and county; mostly Scandinavians, but some Germans.

Joe Hawks. Am a stockman at Bowman; heard the lecture from the door of the theatre. . . . I remember she spoke about the causes of the war. She said she didn't think it was for democracy; it was for the Morgan millions. . . . Part of the audience seemed to approve what she said; have heard of the political fight in Bowman; take a side myself, but don't bother much about politics; think most of the audience were foreigners.

Mrs. George Olson. My husband is a grain buyer; we live at Bowman. Heard Mrs. O'Hare from an auto just outside the door. . . . Hate to have him undergo the same fate that the soldiers abroad were undergoing at that time; but if he saw fit to enlist and didn't know any better, any boy that would do that was only fit for fertilizing. She also went on to say that the Republicans and Democrats seemed to accuse the Socialists of wanting war, but it was done without any aid on their part. She goes on to say that we elected President Wilson in 1916 because we thought he would keep us out of the war, but that we had forgotten that Morgan's millions had to be gotten back from the old country. Therefore he called upon some of the best young men in the country to help him recover them. She goes on to tell that the public at large didn't want war. She said there was only three classes of men to her knowledge who did not care whether we had war or not. One of the classes were the Catholic priests and so-called ministers, who, under the cloak of the church, were excused from the draft. Those men didn't care whether we had war or not. The second class of men was the profit-makers, the munition makers and the big men who profited by the war. Those men didn't care how long the war lasted. The third class of men was the has-beens, the men who were bald-headed and had a paunch on them that they couldn't drag to war if they wanted to. Those were the men who didn't care whether we had war or not. She goes on to mention about conditions in the Belgian country and the suffering women were undergoing. She tried to demonstrate that such things might befall the American women if the war was continued. That women had no right to speak for their boys. If they were called by the country they must go. That all they were called upon to do was to suffer to bring the boys into the world. After that they had no say in the matter. In other words, they had no more to say in the birth of their children than a common sow.

Witnesses for the Defense

Mrs. Kate R. O'Hare. I am the defendant here; I delivered a lecture at Bowman in July last; I believe in the tenets and doctrines of the Socialistic party. I have held every elective position within the gift of the Socialist party of the United States. The Socialist party has an international organization embracing the Socialist parties of every civilized country on the globe. Internationally the executive body of the international organization is known as the International Bureau, and to this bureau every labor organization and Socialist party in the world elects their representatives or their delegates as they are called. I have been a representative of this country in the International Bureau, sitting with the prominent Socialists of European countries, such as Kerensky. The position of the Socialist party is absolutely against settling the problems of the world by physical force; that they should be settled by ballot.

Since the United States declared war I have not opposed but have hoped that it would be the last war; since its adoption I have not opposed conscription, though asked a thousand times to do so; I have not opposed it by word or writing or in any other way. I have never tried to interfere with the Government plans for carrying on the war nor with the Liberty loan or the Red Cross work. The lecture I gave at Bowman was a carefully prepared one; have delivered it as least 135 times. I very carefully prepare my outline, decide the phases I want to cover, then work up the explanatory matter and in that way work out a lecture.

This lecture at Bowman was subheaded into six general divisions. The first, a statement about the Socialist party being charged with trying to do certain things, one of them being to plunge the world into war; another to destroy civilization; another to destroy Christianity; another to degrade women; another that the Socialists believe that the child is the property of the state and not of the parent and to confiscate the property of the people. That was the statement. And I went on to prove that all of these things—that the war had come and the Socialists were not responsible for the war and all these other things had come as a result of war. Then my conclusion was that I, like other Socialists, hated war, wanted to see the end of war and the hope I had that this war might be the end of all war and that the only hope was in overthrowing the economic system that creates war. I went on to show that the economic system that creates war was being actually overthrown by this war and that I was very hopeful of the future because of the fact.

I always adjust the vocabulary of a lecture to the intellectual requirements of my audience. If I am speaking to a group of college students I use the academic language common in college. If I am speaking to a Southern audience I use the words common to the south. If I am speaking to a farmer audience I use the words and terms most commonly used by farmers in order to bring the thing directly to their mind. In this lecture I had no purpose to obstruct enlisting or recruiting; I never said what the indictment charges as to "fertilizers" and "brood sows." I said, "Please understand me and do not misquote me and say I am opposed to enlistment; I am not. If any young man feels that it is his duty to enlist in the army of the United States then he should enlist and God bless him." I said, "His blood may enrich—or possibly fertilize—speaking to farmers—"His blood may enrich the soil of France." Then I stopped and questioned. Perhaps that may be the best use for it. As to the other, what I said was, when the governments and churches of the European countries demanded of the women of Europe that they should give themselves to the soldiers going away to war in marriage or not, in order that those soldiers might breed before they died—that when the church and government demanded that of women they reduced them to the status of breeding animals or brood sows on a stock farm.

I had absolutely no intention of bringing American women into it in this connection. To have done so would have involved myself, my mother, my grandmothers and all my ancestors back into revolutionary times.

My father served in the Federal army all through the Civil war and I have had relatives in the service of the United States in every war since the Revolution. I am American born of Irish-Welsh extraction, and my family has been in this country for many generations. I was afterwards prevented from delivering this lecture at Devils Lake in this State by my arrest.

Mr. Hildreth. Before you started your lecture you looked around the room and sized up the class of people that were to listen to you, did you not?

I always do and did at this time.

And having sized up the people that were there you reached the conclusion that it would be necessary for you to use a vocabulary that would fit the minds of the people that were there to listen to you, is that true?

I decided that it would be wisdom on my part to use the words commonly used by the majority of my audience. . . .

I decided that the majority of the people were farmers largely of foreign extraction, judging from their faces, and that it would be wisdom on my part to use the vocabulary of their every-day life. The object of my lecture was to attempt to convince people that my attitude to all war was well founded.

Were you on the platform as a free lecturer or did you receive compensation?

I am employed by a lecture bureau and receive compensation.

I have been in touch with the Socialist leaders in Europe up to last week; but not those of Germany since the war. They were all opposed to the war; I told the people in Bowman that I was against the war, but told the young men that if they felt it their duty to enlist to do so and God bless them.

The grand objective of my lecture was to prove to the people that we all hated war and that my belief was that the way to kill war was by eliminating the profits from war.

Edward P. Totten. Am judge of the County Court of Bowman; attended Mrs. O'Hare's lecture with my wife and a stenographer; heard it all; did not hear her say what she is charged with in the indictment as to "fertilizers" and "brood sows," nor did she say anything in opposition to enlistment and recruiting; I remember hearing Mrs. O'Hare say at that time in substance if any young man desires to enlist or volunteer, let him go and God bless him.

Cross-examined. The audience were nearly all farmers; she was applauded but not by my wife or myself; she subpoened me here and is to pay my expenses.

As I understood the lecture, it was solely a defense of—an explanation of the attitude of the Socialist party and of Socialists against the charges of enemies of socialism and an explanation of the position of the party with relation to war generally.

Mrs. E. P. Totten. Am wife of last witness; attended the lecture; did not hear her say the things charged in the indictment; heard her say if any man desired to enlist, let him go and God bless him; the crowd was largely adult. She told of her trip to Europe just prior to the war and described the beautiful country that was now being devastated by war and spoke of it as being blood-soaked. She said that the young men that went from here to France their blood might fertilize the French fields. She was developing her point that she was making about the Socialists—that they had not brought about the destruction of the home, but that war had; and that the war had so lowered the position of women in Europe it placed them in the position of brood sows on a Montana stock farm.

Mrs. M. A. Johnson. My husband is a farmer in Bowman County; I heard the lecture. She said, "Don't quote me as saying that I object to enlistment, because I do not. If any young man feels it his duty to go, let him go and God bless him." She said his blood might enrich the soil of France and perhaps it might do that. She didn't say it would. She just put it as a question. She said at the beginning of the European war the European women were asked by the church or by the State to give themselves to the solders regardless of marriage so the soldiers could breed before they died to increase the birth rate as well as the death rate and the women were put on the same basis as a brood sow on a Montana stock farm.

Mrs. E. K. Couet. Live in Bowman; my husband is a barber; was at the lecture; did not hear her use the language charged; so far as I can remember she was referring to the war in Europe and went on to tell about how women were being degraded by having to give themselves to the soldiers, so they could breed before they died. That is the way I understood it. She said that the women were being carried down, put down with the brood sows; did not hear her use the word scum.

Cross-examined. We used to take the Ripsaw; I practically agreed with all she said; I applauded it; the only young man I saw there was my brother; I did not know that my husband had been reported to the Federal authorities as a man who was having congregated in his shop from time to time individuals that were opposing the measures of the Government with reference to recruiting. I never knew my husband to say anything.

Speeches to the Jury

Mr. Lovell argued to the jury that the evidence did not sustain the charge; that the witnesses for the Government were prejudiced; that the prosecution was the outcome of a political quarrel; and that the great preponderance of the evidence showed that the defendant did not use the language attributed to her.

Mr. Hildreth. Gentlemen of the jury: The Congress of the United States declared war on Germany on the 6th day of April, 1917. The purposes of that war are known to all men. It is to settle the great question as to whether democracy shall rule the world or autocracy. Our soldiers are now crossing the seas. Back of the men who go into the line of entrenchments to do or die must rest the great reserve forces of the Nation.

Our Government has called to the colors under the draft act young men between the ages of 21 and 31 years. The man power of the Nation not only is involved, the resources of the Nation are not only involved, but greater than all of these elements of national strength is the spirit of our people. Whatever tends to destroy the spirit of the people, the patriotism of the people, to lessen it here at home while our troops are fighting the battles of the Nation in Europe, lessens our strength as a Nation, minimizes the patriotism of our people, and contributes in no small degree to strengthening the armies of the Central Powers.

One of the methods that have been used in the past in the wars of the Republic to injure the patriotism of the people has been the abuse of free speech. In every war we have been engaged in we have been confronted with the propagandist, the agitator, and the corruptionist. These forces have made it difficult for us to win battles, have prolonged wars, injured the unity of the Nation and been destructive of complete success on the battlefield. It was true of the Revolutionary War, the War of 1812, the Mexican War, and of the great Rebellion; and it is true today that in this country, where we have a written Constitution, trial by jury, freedom of the press, and liberty of speech, we are met with a hostility on our own shores far more dangerous than the guns of our European foes.

This great evil was known to all men. Therefore Congress, on the 15th day of June, 1917, passed this Espionage act, and the defendant is charged in this indictment with having violated that act.

She went to Bowman and before an audience of from 100 to 150 people made a speech which, in some respects, has no parallel in the English language. She said: "Any person who enlists in the army of the United States of America will be used for fertilizer, and that is all that he is good for; and the women of the United States are nothing more or less than brood sows to raise children to get into the army and be made into fertilizer." Search the annals of history and you will find no parallel in any country in the world. It was a direct blow at the spirit of the people, at the patriotism of the people. It was made intentionally and for the purpose charged. It was made to willfully obstruct the enlistment service of the United States, to the injury of the service of the United States, and to obstruct the recruiting service of the United States. . . .

This lecture, this speech, stirred this Commonwealth as no other speech. Why? Because this woman had gone upon the rostrum and, before the people of a great country, had instilled in their hearts and minds that this was [the financier J. P.] Morgan's war and not the war of the United States; that this was a war to protect the investments of financiers and not the democracy of the world; that this was a war that was brought about by moneyed interests; that this was a war not intended to break down the autocracy of Europe, but to build up the moneyed interests of the country; that this war was unjust and was being waged for that purpose and that alone, when she knew that the United States had suffered injury after injury at the hands of the German Government, when she knew that its ships that had a right to sail upon the seas had been sunk and the bodies of thousands of men, women, and children consigned to a watery grave under circumstances of the greatest atrocity and in violation of every principle of the laws of nations and of humanity. And yet she was telling the people that this was a war not in the defense of the American people on the sea and on the land, but that it was a war for the benefit of the moneyed interests of the country. False and pernicious doctrine! A doctrine that, if instilled in the minds of the people of this country, would prevent us from raising armies and navies and would be more potential in behalf of the Central Powers than the soldiers that are across the seas to fight the battles of the Republic. That was her attitude; that was her position; and that is her position here today. She rather justifies her position. She declares that it was a war in behalf of special interests, and not one for the cause of the people of the earth.

Gentlemen of the jury, we are not concerned with the politics of this defendant. We are indifferent as to whether she is a Socialist, a Democrat, or a Republican. But we are not indifferent to her violation of this statute which forbade her efforts upon the rostrum to carry out the evil intentions which this statute was aimed to prevent. . . .

Gentlemen of the jury, this cause is one of the most important that has ever been tried in the United States. The defendant made her speech on the 17th of July, 1917. She has repeated that speech in many places throughout this Commonwealth. Here in this State, where its men and women have been taught to love the land of their adoption, where men and women have been taught that under our system of free schools, universities, and where a million church spires point to heaven, she would instill in the minds of the young, not the patriotism of the fathers of the Republic but the zeal of those who would destroy this Government, destroy its institutions, and drag this flag in the dust of Socialism.

Take the case. Render such a verdict that when the hand that shall write it is traceless in the grave it shall live the embodiment of the hope of a free people and a monument to the stability of our institutions.

The Charge of the Court

JUDGE WADE. Gentlemen of the jury. It does not make any difference how many men have violated this law and have not been prosecuted. Get that out of your mind. It does not make any difference what has been said in Congress by certain parties. Get that out of your mind. Let us all hope that persons who have violated this law or any other law will receive proper punishment ultimately.

I do not want you, from anything that I may say, to even infer that I have any opinion as to how this case ought to be decided, because that is not my duty, nor is it my power. You have the sole power in that field and you will give it no consideration if I should express my opinion. . . This Republic is a government of majorities, as every republic must be. The majority of the people determine the policy of the government. The majority may not always be right, but the only way you can have a republic is that the minority shall yield for the time being to what the majority says the law shall be. We take the position in this country that we would rather be bound and governed by a majority that maybe sometimes wrong than to be bound by the will of a monarch who is usually wrong.

The bringing of an indictment or a person before the court for trial is no evidence whatsoever of guilt. It is a medium by which persons are brought before the court charged with an offense. By this indictment the people of North Dakota, speaking through the grand jury, simply, for the purpose of bringing her to trial, charged this woman with committing an offense against the laws of the United States, and the offense charged in this indictment is that at a place up here called Bowman, in the county of Bowman, this defendant, Kate Richards O'Hare, did willfully, unlawfully, and feloniously, at a public meeting held in a hall in the city of Bowman, in the said county of Bowman and State of North Dakota, in a public speech made by her in the presence of 125 people state, in substance, that any person who enlisted in the army of the United States of America for service in France would be used for fertilizer and that is all that he was good for, and that the women of the United States were nothing more or less than brood sows to raise children to get into the army and be made into fertilizer. That such statement so made was made with the intention of willfully obstructing the enlistment service of the United States, to the injury of the service of the United States. And in another count the same language is charged, it being stated that her intention was to interfere with the recruiting service of the United States. So, you see, the charge is that she made a speech in which she said certain things with a certain intent and purpose. Now, all you gentlemen have to determine is whether that is true or not.

And in this connection something has been properly said with reference to free speech in this country. I hope there may be no misunderstanding upon that point by anyone. The Constitution of the United States and the Constitution of North Dakota both guarantee rights of free speech. But under these constitutions it has always been the law that every person will be held liable for the abuse of that right. This case does not involve any restraint upon the physical act of speaking and saying things. It simply charges that in the exercise of the constitutional right of free speech she abused that right by violating a law passed by the Congress of the United States. . . .

Bear in mind that it does not make any difference in a criminal case whether a man on trial knew about the law or not. The whole process of government in any country must proceed upon the theory that every man understands the law; because if a man should steal your horse or break into your home or kill your family and could defend himself upon the theory that he did not know it was a violation of the law, it would result in a strange perversion of justice. This woman is not charged with an intent to violate the law. She is charged with doing things with an intent to have a certain effect which the law says shall be punished. The intent relates to a purpose that she has in saying things and is utterly oblivious as to whether she had in her mind a law she was trying to violate or not.

Now, in order to understand this law and appreciate its obligation you have a right to take into consideration the things of general knowledge that the world knows, that you know—that this Nation has been drawn into this awful world conflict and that we are at war since April 6, 1917. You have a right to take into consideration the general purpose and feeling on the part of the great majority of the American people that this war must be won; that no other result would be tolerated. You have a right to take into consideration the general knowledge which you must have, as everyone else, that there is only one way to win the war and that is to have soldiers, and the only way to get men for soldiers is either by voluntary enlistment or by conscription. The evidence shows, and your own knowledge brings you to the fact, that at and prior to the time this speech was made the Government was exercising its power and its duty to get men to serve as soldiers, and was then recruiting, as the expression is—asking men to enlist voluntarily as well as at that time preparing methods of conscription. It appears from the evidence that this effort at getting enlistment was being made at Bowman, in this county. Now, of course, the Government, having this obligation and this duty and responsibility, had the right to protect itself against those who would interfere with the performance of that function, not against the many but against the few who might assume to obstruct, so far as they might, this duty on the part of the Government. The Government in this country speaks only through Congress, and Congress, representing all the people of the United States, on June 15, 1917, passed a law which has been referred to as the Espionage law, having a great many restrictions upon acts and conduct which are never exercised in times of peace but which Congress deemed advisable in a time of war. And one of these restrictions is that "whoever, when the United States is at war, shall willfully cause, or attempt to cause, insubordination, disloyalty, mutiny, or refusal of duty in the military or naval forces of the United States or shall willfully obstruct the recruiting or enlistment service of the United States, to the injury of the service of the United States, shall be punished." Now, it is the latter of those two clauses which the indictment charges here that the defendant violated. "Whoever shall willfully obstruct the recruiting or enlistment service of the United States . . . shall be punished." That is the law of this country. You will observe that it does not say how the act shall be done, but any way that a person obstructs, willfully, the recruiting or enlistment service. That is the thing the grand jury charged against her and specified the things which they said she did. . . .

The Verdict and Sentence

The *Jury* retired, and after a short time, returned to the court room. The foreman handed the following written verdict to the clerk: "We, the jury, find the defendant *guilty* as charged in the indictment. –A. L. Peart, Foreman."

JUDGE WADE. Is there anything to be said now why sentence should not be imposed upon this defendant?

Mrs. O'Hare. Yes, your Honor: I was taught in high school that law was pure logic. Abstract law may be pure logic but the application of the law of testimony in this case seems to have gone far afield from logic. As your Honor knows, I am a professional woman, following the profession of delivering lectures whereby I hope to induce my hearers to study the philosophy of socialism. In the regular course of my profession and work I delivered during this year lectures all over the United States—in North Carolina when the draft riots were at their height; in Arizona two or three days following the deportations from Bisbee, and on the day when the strike vote was taken, when excitement ran high and passions were having their sway; in San Francisco during the Mooney case, and in Portland, Idaho, and the Northwestern lumber regions during the great I. W. W. [Industrial Workers of the World] excitement; and at all of these lectures conditions were as tense as conditions could be. The men who were in the employ of the United States in the Department of Justice were present at my meetings. These men were trained, highly efficient, and highly paid, detectors of crime and criminals. In all these months, when my lecture was under the scrutiny of this kind of men, there was no suggestion at any time that there was anything in it that was objectionable, treasonable or seditious. It was the custom of my meetings to send complimentary tickets to the district attorney and the marshal and deputy marshals of the district in order that they might hear the lecture.

And then in the course of the trip I landed at Bowman—a little, sordid, wind-blown, sun-blistered, frost-scarred town on the plains of Western Dakota. There was nothing unusual in my visit to Bowman, except the fact that it was unusual to make a town of this size. The reason I did was because there was one man whose loyalty and faithfulness and unselfish service to the cause to which I had given my life wanted me to come, and I felt he had a right to demand my services. I delivered my lecture there just as I had delivered it many, many times before. There was nothing in the audience that was unusual except the fact that it was a small audience—a solid, substantial, stolid type of farmer crowd. There was not the great enthusiasm that had prevailed at many of my meetings. There was nothing to stir me or arouse me or cause me to make a more impassioned appeal than usual. There was nothing at all in that little sordid, wind-blown town, that commonplace audience, that should have for a moment overbalanced my reason and judgment and common sense and have caused me to have been suddenly smitten with hydrophobia of sedition. But I found there were peculiar conditions existing at Bowman, and they are common to the whole state of North Dakota. In this State in the last year and a half the greatest and most revolutionary social phenomena that has occurred since the foundation of this Government, has taken place. The story is one that is so well known that I need spend little time on it. Here to these wind-blown, frost-scarred plains came men hard of face and feature and muscle who subdued this desert and made it bloom and produce the bread to feed the world; and these men, toiling in their desperate struggle with adverse conditions and with nature, gradually had it forced on their minds that in some way they were not receiving a just return for the labor expended; that after their wheat was raised and garnered in the processes of marketing, men who toiled not and suffered none of the hardships of production were robbing them of the product of their labor. . . .

And your Honor, it seems to me one of those strange grotesque things that can only be the outgrowth of this hysteria that is sweeping over the world today that a judge on the bench and a jury in the box and a prosecuting attorney should attempt to usurp the prerogatives of God Almighty and look down into the heart of a human being and decide what motives slumber there. There is no charge that if my intent or my motive was criminal that that intent or motive ever was put into action—only the charge that in my heart there was an intent, and on that strange charge of an intent so securely buried in a human heart that no result and no effect came from it, I went to trial. . . .

Your Honor, there are 100,000 people in the United States who know me personally. They have listened to my voice, looked in my face and have worked side by side with me in every great reform movement of the last twenty years. My life has been an open book to them. They know down to this time I have given all that I am, all that I have, from my earliest girlhood, my girlhood, my young womanhood, even my motherhood. And, your Honor, no judge on earth and no ten thousand judges or ten thousand juries can ever convince these hundred thousand people who know me and have worked with me, and these millions who have read my writings, that I am a criminal, or that I have ever given anything to my country except my most unselfish devotion and service. You cannot convince the people who know me that I am dangerous to the United States Government. They are willing to admit I am dangerous to some things in the United States, and I thank God that I am. I am dangerous to the invisible government of the United States; to the special privileges of the United States; to the white-slaver and the saloonkeeper, and I thank God that at this hour I am dangerous to the war profiteers of this country who rob the people on the one hand and rob and debase the Government on the other, and then with their pockets and wallets stuffed with the blood-stained profits of war, wrap the sacred folds of the Stars and Stripes about them and shout their blatant hypocrisy to the world. You can convince the people that I am dangerous to these men; but no jury and no judge can convince them that I am a dangerous woman to the best interests of the United States. . . .

JUDGE WADE. It is never a pleasant duty for me to sentence any one to prison, and it certainly is not a pleasant duty to send a woman to prison; in the course of a trial, in all the years I have been on the bench in the State and Federal courts, I have made it a rule to try to find out who I am sending to prison, because we all make mistakes in this world at times. On the spur of the moment and under excitement, sometimes people are misled and commit offenses, and I have a hard time to reconcile my view of things with heavy sentences in those cases. Therefore, when this case was closed, I made up my mind that I would find out before imposing sentence in this case what were the activities of this defendant.

She testified here to her loyalty, and her support of the President, and I was hoping in my heart that somewhere I would find out that after all, she was such a woman as she has here pictured herself today, and that thus a small penalty for this offense might be adequate, because I realize this is a serious business. The Nation is at war. Every sane man and woman knows that there is only one way that this war can be won, and that is by having men and money and spirit. Those three things are necessary—spirit in the men, in the service, and spirit in the men and women behind the men. And it was because of these absolute essentials that Congress enacted the Espionage law, to reach out and take hold of those who are trying to kill the spirit of the American people, in whole or in part; trying to put in their hearts hate toward this Government and towards the officials of this Government conducting the war. And realizing that this was such a grave matter, I investigated it as far as possible to find out really what character of woman this defendant is, and has been, in her work. I heard the evidence in this case. I had nothing to do with the question of whether she was guilty or innocent. The jury settled that question, and in my judgment, settled it right.

I received information from another town in North Dakota, and this information was given in the presence of counsel for the defendant that at Garrison, in her lecture there, she made the statement that mothers who reared sons to go into the army, were no better than animals on a North Dakota farm; that this war was in behalf of the capitalists, and that if we had loaned our money to Germany instead of to the allies, we would be now fighting with Germany instead of with the allies. That she had boys, but that they are not old enough to to go to war, but that if they were, they would not go. That the way to stop the war was to strike, and if the laboring men of this nation would strike, the war would soon be ended Of course that was an *ex parte* matter. I have heard enough of testimony in my life, and I have seen enough of human nature to know that sometimes these things are stretched because of the feeling on one side or another of the question. So I thought I would go back and see what she had been doing. I wired the Postoffice Department at Washington, and I received a telegram which states:

"Party is on editorial staff of publication, *Social Revolution*, Saint Louis, Missouri, which has been barred from the mails for gross violations of Espionage Act, and is successor to *Ripsaw*. The party appears to be of the extreme type who have attempted to handicap the Government in every way in the conduct of the present war."

That was only a statement of an opinion. I tried to get copies of the *Social Revolution*, and have not succeeded in getting either the number for June or July. At some period during that time the Postmaster General barred this from the mails. I have the April and May numbers. In April they publish from Eugene Debs this statement:

"As we have said, the bankers are for bullets—for the fool patriots that enlist at paupers' wages to stop the bullets, while the bankers clip coupons, boost food prices, increase dividends, and pile up millions and billions for themselves. Say, Mr. Workingman, suppose you have sense enough to be as patriotic as the banker, but not a bit more so. When you see the bankers on the firing line with guns in their hands ready to stop bullets as well as start them, then it is time enough for you to be seized with the patriotic itch and have yourself shot into a crazy-quilt for their profit and glory. Don't you take a fit and rush to the front until you see them there. They own the country and if they don't set the example of fighting for it, why should you?

This was in April, before the war was declared. Up to that time I realize that every person in this country had the right to discuss the war, express their opinions against the war, give any reasons they might have against the war. But you will find here in this statement the note which rings out from the statement of the defendant here in court this afternoon and which forms the foundation of the entire gospel of hate which she and her associates are preaching to the American people: That the Nation is helpless, prostrate, down-trodden by a few capitalists, and that the average man has not a chance on earth; that this war is a war of capitalism; that it was brought about by capital and in the interest of capital; that 100, 200. Or 300 millionaires and billionaires if you please, in these United States dominate the souls and consciences of the other 99,000,000 American people. . . .

The Department of Justice furnishes me the following resolutions adopted at a meeting of the extreme wing of the Socialist Party, to which the defendant belongs, at their St. Louis convention after war was declared. The Secret Service, in sending in their report, says in a letter:

> "We have been unable to secure anything specific on her that would be a violation of the Federal law in this district, but we have placed her in a class whose hearts and souls we are morally certain are for Germany against our country."

This defendant was chairman of the committee that brought in these resolutions. A newspaper of the city of St. Louis, in describing this convention, states:

> "The Socialist Party, in a national convention at the Planters' Hotel last night, adopted resolutions proclaiming its "unalterable opposition to the war just declared by the Government of the United States. The majority report of the committee on war and militarism containing the resolutions received 140 votes. An even more radical report by Louis Boudin, of New York, received 31 votes. The conservative minority report of John Spargo, of New York, declaring that Socialists should support the war, received only 5 votes. The vote was taken after hours of speech-making. Thomas William, of California, was hissed when he said he was an American, charged the delegates with being pro-German, and declared they did not represent the true sentiment of American Socialists. Mrs. Kate Richards O'Hare, of St. Louis, defied the Government and civil authorities. She declared that Socialists would not be molested in St. Louis for what they said because the city was against war, and the authorities were afraid to molest them."

Fine stuff for the boys and girls of the United States to be reading at this hour!

Mrs. O'Hare. May I make a statement to your Honor?

The COURT. No, no; I have heard you. . . .

This defendant does not take pride in her country. She abhors it. From the Atlantic to the Pacific there is nothing she can approve; she can only condemn. She is the apostle of despair, and carries only a message of hate and defiance. She is sowing the seed of discontent. She preaches defiance of authority. She poses as a

Socialist, but she is breeding anarchy. Even in those sad times of bitter stress she cannot refrain from inspiring class hatreds. She asserts here today that if at liberty she could aid the Government. "Aid the Government!" Why every day she is at liberty she is a menace to the Government. She proclaims that if she is punished her followers will assert themselves and that the cause she represents will gain in strength and power. Let them "assert themselves"; they will find that while this Nation is kind and generous, she is also powerful, and that when the loyal people of the country are fully aroused, traitors will receive the reward of their treachery.

Every person sentenced by a court must not only serve to expiate his own wrong, but he must serve as a warning to others. For these reasons the judgment of the court is that you, Kate Richards O'Hare, shall serve a period of five years in the Federal prison at Jefferson City, Missouri, and pay the costs of this suit.

8
Evolution and the Bible
The Scopes Trial
1925

In March 1925, the state of Tennessee made it a crime to teach in a state-supported school "any theory that denies the story of the Divine Creation of man as taught in the Bible, and to teach instead that man has descended from a lower order of animals." This law, the Butler Act, expressed the beliefs of many fundamentalist Protestants who accepted the word of the Bible literally. Such views were particularly popular in the South, a region labeled by the iconoclastic social critic and journalist H. L. Mencken as the "Bible belt." Many other American Protestants, often termed liberals, had accommodated their interpretation of the Bible to the findings of modern science. This included Charles Darwin's theory of evolution, which held that all species, including man, had evolved in response to environmental pressures and competition with other species. Behind these theological differences lurked sharp cultural contrasts. The stronghold of fundamentalism was in the countryside and small towns, where populations, especially in the South, had remained homogeneously of old American stock. Liberalism grew in the cities with their peoples of diverse origins and values. The conflict among the churches between fundamentalists and liberals had its counterpart in a split between country and city Democrats that had paralyzed the party through 103 ballots during its 1924 national convention.

Aware that all biology textbooks relied on evolutionary theory and hoping to give the town some publicity, several citizens of Dayton, Tennessee, persuaded a young instructor at the local high school, John T. Scopes, to test the Butler Law. Both fundamentalists and defenders of modernity and the scientific outlook quickly seized upon the event. William Jennings Bryan, three times the Democratic candidate for president and the nation's most famous defender of the literal truth of the Bible, joined the state's legal team. Clarence Darrow, a criminal defense lawyer almost as well known as Bryan on the opposite side, led Scopes's defense. The little town for a moment became a media capital. Journalists and radio broadcasters crowded in for the first nationally broadcast trial.

The state intended to limit the case to demonstrating what Scopes had already conceded: that he had violated the Butler Act by teaching evolution in a

---

SUGGESTIONS FOR FURTHER READING: Ray Ginger, *Six Days or Forever? Tennessee v. John Thomas Scopes*, New York: Beacon Press, 1958; Lawrence W. Levine, *Defender of the Faith: William Jennings Bryan; the Last Decade, 1915–1925*, New York: Oxford University Press, 1965.

public high school. Darrow planned to bring a flock of scientists to testify to the truth of evolution. The judge, John T. Raulston, in the tiny Dayton courtroom—he later moved the proceedings out of doors to accommodate the crowds—ruled against Darrow's strategy for defending Scopes. Since obedience to the law and not the truth of the theory of evolution was the issue before the court, no expert witnesses would be allowed to testify. The resourceful Darrow, however, asked Bryan to take the witness stand as an authority on the Bible. Having engaged in many such debates and finding another one irresistible, Bryan allowed Darrow to question him. The judge, obviously uncertain how to respond, permitted Bryan's testimony but not in the jury's presence. Had Bryan questioned Darrow in return, as had also been proposed, perhaps his faith in science as a guide for human behavior would have seemed as naive as Bryan's belief in the Bible as a description of the physical world. We shall never know, for the next day Judge Raulston expunged from the record Bryan's testimony and hurried the case to the jury. Scopes was found guilty and sentenced to a small fine that he was never made to pay.

The State of Tennessee v. John T. Scopes 1925

The Court—Mr. Bryan, you are not objecting to going on the stand?

Mr. Bryan—Not at all.

The Court—Do you want Mr. Bryan sworn?

Mr. Darrow—No.

Mr. Bryan—I can make affirmation; I can say, "So help me God, I will tell the truth."

Mr. Darrow No, I take it you will tell the truth, Mr. Bryan.

Q—You have given considerable study to the Bible, haven't you, Mr. Bryan?

A—Yes, sir, I have tried to.

Q—But you have written and published articles almost weekly, and sometimes have made interpretations of various things.

A—I would not say interpretations, Mr. Darrow, but comments on the lesson.

Q—If you comment to any extent these comments have been interpretations?

A—I presume that any discussion might be to some extent interpretations, but they have not been primarily intended as interpretations.

Q—Then you have made a general study of it?

A—Yes, I have; I have studied the Bible for about fifty years, or some time more than that, but, of course. I have studied it more as I have become older than when I was but a boy.

Q—Do you claim that everything in the Bible should be literally interpreted?

A—I believe everything in the Bible should be accepted as it is given there; some of the Bible is given illustratively. For instance: "Ye are the salt of the earth." I would not insist that man was actually salt, or that he had flesh of salt, but it is used in the sense of salt as saving God's people.

Q—But when you read that Jonah swallowed the whale—or that the whale swallowed Jonah—excuse me please—how do you literally interpret that?

A—When I read that a big fish swallowed Jonah—it does not say whale.

Q—Doesn't it? Are you sure?

A—That is my recollection of it. A big fish, and I believe it; and I believe in a God who can make a whale and can make a man and make both do what He pleases.

Q—Mr. Bryan, doesn't the New Testament say whale?

A—I am not sure. My impression is that it says fish; but it does not make so much difference; I merely called your attention to where it says fish—it does not say whale.

Q—But in the New Testament it says whale, doesn't it?

A—That may be true; I cannot remember in my own mind what I read about it.

Q—Now, you say, the big fish swallowed Jonah, and he there remained how long? Three days? And then he spewed him upon the land. You believe that the big fish was made to swallow Jonah?

A—I am not prepared to say that; the Bible merely says it was done.

Q—You don't know whether it was the ordinary run of fish, or made for that purpose?

A—You may guess; you evolutionists guess.

Q—But when we do guess, we have a sense to guess right.

A—But do not do it often.

Q—You are not prepared to say whether that fish was made especially to swallow a man or not?

A—The Bible doesn't say, so I am not prepared to say.

Q—You don't know whether that was fixed up specially for the purpose?

A—No, the Bible doesn't say.

Q—But you do believe He made them—that He made such a fish and that it was big enough to swallow Jonah?

A—Yes, sir. Let me add: one miracle is just as easy to believe as another.

Q—It is for me.

A—It is for me.

Q—Just as hard?

A—It is hard to believe for you, but easy for me. A miracle is a thing performed beyond what man can perform. When you get beyond what man can do, you get within the realm of miracles; and it is just as easy to believe the miracle of Jonah as any other miracle in the Bible.

Q—Perfectly easy to believe that Jonah swallowed the whale?

A—If the Bible said so; the Bible doesn't make as extreme statements as evolutionists do.

Mr. Darrow—That may be a question, Mr. Bryan, about some of those you have known.

A—The only thing is, you have a definition of fact that includes imagination.

Q—And you have a definition that excludes everything but imagination.

Gen. Stewart [a colleague of Bryan]—I object to that as argumentative.

The Witness—You—

Mr. Darrow—The witness must not argue with me, either.

Q—Do you consider the story of Jonah and the whale a miracle?

A—I think it is.

Q—Do you believe Joshua made the sun stand still?

A—I believe what the Bible says. I suppose you mean that the earth stood still?

Q—I don't know. I am talking about the Bible now.

A—I accept the Bible absolutely.

Q—The Bible says Joshua commanded the sun to stand still for the purpose of lengthening the day, doesn't it? And you believe it?

A—I do.

Q—Do you believe at that time the entire sun went around the earth?

A—No, I believe that the earth goes around the sun.

Q—Do you believe that men who wrote it thought that the day could be lengthened or that the sun could be stopped?

A—I don't know what they thought.

Q—You don't know?

A—I think they wrote the fact without expressing their own thoughts.

Q—Have you an opinion as to whether or not the men who wrote that thought—

Gen. Stewart—I want to object, your Honor; it has gone beyond the pale of any issue that could possibly be injected into this lawsuit, except by imagination. I do not think the defendant has a right to conduct the examination any further and I ask your Honor to exclude it.

The Court—I will hear Mr. Bryan.

The Witness—It seems to me it would be too exacting to confine the Defense to the facts; if they are not allowed to get away from the facts, what have they to deal with?

The Court—Mr. Bryan is willing to be examined. Go ahead.

Mr. Darrow—Have you an opinion as to whether—whoever wrote the book, I believe it is, Joshua, the Book of Joshua, thought the sun went around the earth or not?

A—I believe that he was inspired.

Mr. Darrow—Can you answer my question?

A—When you let me finish the statement.

Q—It is a simple question, but finish it.

The Witness—You cannot measure the length of my answer by the length of your question.

Mr. Darrow—No, except that the answer be longer.

A—I believe that the Bible is inspired, an inspired author, whether one who wrote as he was directed to write understood the things he was writing about, I don't know.

Q—Whoever inspired it? Do you think whoever inspired it believed that the sun went around the earth?

A—I believe it was inspired by the Almighty, and He may have used language that could be understood at that time.

Q—Was—

The Witness—Instead of using language that could not be understood until Mr. Darrow was born.

Q—So, it might not; it might have been subject to construction, might it not?

A—It might have been used in language that could be understood then.

Q—That means it is subject to construction?

A—That is your construction. I am answering your question.

Q—Is that correct?

A—That is my answer to it.

Q—Can you answer?

A—I might say, Isaiah spoke of God sitting upon the circle of the earth.

Q—I am not talking about Isaiah.

The Court—Let him illustrate, if he wants to.

Mr. Darrow—Is it your opinion that passage was subject to construction?

A—Well, I think anybody can put his own construction upon it, but I do not mean that necessarily that is a correct construction. I have answered the question.

Q—Don't you believe that in order to lengthen the day it would have been construed that the earth stood still?

A—I would not attempt to say what would have been necessary, but I know this, that I can take a glass of water that would fall to the ground without the strength of my hand and to the extent of the glass of water I can overcome the law of gravitation and lift it up, whereas without my hand it would fall to the ground. If my puny hand can overcome the law of gravitation, the most universally understood, to that extent, I would not set power to the hand of Almighty god that made the universe.

Mr. Darrow—I read that years ago. Can you answer my question directly? If the day was lengthened by stopping either the earth or the sun, it must have been the earth?

A—Well, I should say so.

Q—Yes? But it was language that was understood at that time, and we now know that the sun stood still as it was with the earth. We know also the sun does not stand still.

A—Well, it is relatively so, as Mr. Einstein would say.

Q—I ask you if it does stand still?

A—You know as well as I know.

Q—Better. You have no doubt about it?

A—No. And the earth moves around.

Q—Yes?

A—But I think there is nothing improper if you will protect the Lord against your criticism.

Q—I suppose He needs it?

A—He was using language at that time the people understood.

Q—And that you call "interpretation?"

A—No, sir; I would not call it interpretation.

Q—I say, you would call it interpretation at this time, to say it meant something then?

A—You may use your own language to describe what I have to say, and I will use mine in answering.

Q—Now, Mr. Bryan, have you ever pondered what would have happened to the earth if it had stood still?

A—No.

Q—You have not?

A—No; the God I believe in could have taken care of that, Mr. Darrow. . . .

[*Applause in the Courtroom*]

Mr. Darrow—Great applause from the bleachers.

The Witness—From those whom you call "yokels.

Mr. Darrow—I have never called them yokels.

The Witness—That is the ignorance of Tennessee, the bigotry.

Mr. Darrow—You mean who are applauding you?

The Witness—Those are the people whom you insult.

Mr. Darrow—You insult every man of science and learning in the world because he does not believe in your fool religion.

The Court—I will not stand for that.

Mr. Darrow—For what he is doing?

The Court—I am talking to both of you.

Gen. Stewart—This has gone beyond the pale of a lawsuit, your Honor. I have a public duty to perform under my oath, and I ask the Court to stop it. Mr. Darrow is making an effort to insult the gentleman on the witness stand and I ask that it be stopped, for it has gone beyond the pale of a lawsuit.

The Court—To stop it now would not be just to Mr. Bryan. He wants to ask the other gentleman questions along the same line.

Gen. Stewart—It will all be incompetent.

The Witness—The jury is not here.

The Court—I do not want to be strictly technical.

Mr. Darrow—Then your Honor rules, and I accept.

Gen. Stewart—The jury is not here.

Q—B.C. You believe that all the living things that were not contained in Noah's ark were destroyed.

A—I think the fish may have lived.

Q—Outside of the fish?

A—I cannot say.

Q—You cannot say?

A—No, I accept that just as it is; I have no proof to the contrary.

Q—I am asking you whether you believe?

A—I do.

Q—That all living things outside of the fish were destroyed?

A—What I say about the fish is merely a matter of humor.

Q—I understand.

The Witness—Due to the fact a man wrote up here the other day to ask whether all the fish were destroyed, and the gentleman who received the letter told him the fish may have lived.

Q—I am referring to the fish, too.

A—I accept that as the Bible gives it and I have never found any reason for denying, disputing, or rejecting it.

Q—Let us make it definite, 2,348 years?

A—I didn't say that. That is the time given there [indicating the King James edition of the Bible] but I don't pretend to say that is exact.

Q—You never figured it out, these generations, yourself?

A—No, sir; not myself.

Q—But the Bible you have offered in evidence says, 2,340 something, so that 4,200 years ago there was not a living thing on the earth, excepting the people on the ark and the animals on the ark and the fishes?

A—There have been living things before that.

Q—I mean at that time.

A—After that.

Q—Don't you know there are any number of civilizations that are traced back to more than 5,000 years?

A—I know we have people who trace things back according to the number of ciphers they have. But I am not satisfied they are accurate.

Q—You are not satisfied there is any civilization that can be traced back 5,000 years?

A—I would not want to say there is because I have no evidence of it.

Q—Would you say there is not?

A—Well, so far as I know, but when the scientists differ from 24,000,000 to 306,000,000 in their opinion as to how long ago life came here. I want them to be nearer, to come nearer together, before they demand of me to give up my belief in the Bible.

Q—Do you say that you do not believe that there were any civilizations on this earth that reach back beyond 5,000 years?

A—I am not satisfied by any evidence that I have seen.

Q—I didn't ask you what you are satisfied with. I asked you if you believe it?

The Witness—Will you let me answer it?

The Court—Go right on.

The Witness—I am satisfied by no evidence that I have found that would justify me in accepting the opinions of these men against what I believe to be the inspired Word of God.

Q—And you believe every nation, every organization of men, every animal, in the world outside of the fishes—

The Witness—The fish, I want you to understand, is merely a matter of humor. . . .

Q—You believe that every civilization on the earth and every living thing, except possibly the fishes, that came out of the ark were wiped out by the flood?

A—At that time.

Q—At that time. And then whatever human beings, including all the tribes, that inhabited the world, and have inhabited the world, and who run their pedigree straight back, and all the animals, have come onto the earth since the flood?

A—Yes.

Q—Within 4,200 years. Do you know a scientific man on the face of the earth that believes any such thing?

A—I cannot say, but I know some scientific men who dispute entirely the antiquity of man as testified to by other scientific men.

Q—Oh, that does not answer the question. Do you know of a single scientific man on the face of the earth that believes any such thing as you stated, about the antiquity of man?

A—I don't think I have ever asked one the direct question.

Q—Quite important, isn't it?

A—If I had nothing else to do except speculate on what our remote ancestors were and what our remote descendants have been, but I have been more interested in Christians going on right now to make it much more important than speculation on either the past or the future.

Q—You have never had any interest in the age of the various races and people and civilization and animals that exist upon the earth today, is that right?

A—I have never felt a great deal of interest in the effort that has been made to dispute the Bible by the speculations of men, or the investigations of men.

Q—Are you the only human being on earth who knows what the Bible means?

Gen. Stewart—I object.

The Court—Sustained.

Mr. Darrow—You do know that there are thousands of people who profess to be Christians who believe the earth is much more ancient and that the human race is much more ancient?

A—I think there may be.

Q—And you never have investigated to find out how long man has been on the earth?

A—I have never found it necessary—

Q—For any reason, whatever it is?

A—To examine every speculation; but if I had done it I never would have done anything else.

Q—I ask for a direct answer.

A—I do not expect to find out all those things, and I do not expect to find out about races.

Q—I didn't ask you that. Now, I ask you if you know if it was interesting enough or important enough for you to try to find out about how old these ancient civilizations were?

A—No; I have not made a study of it.

Q–Don't you know that the ancient civilizations of China are 6,000 or 7,000 years old, at the very least?

A–No; but they would not run back beyond the creation, according to the Bible, 6,000 years.

Q–You don't know how old they are, is that right?

A–I don't know how old they are, but probably you do. I think you would give preference to anybody who opposed the Bible, and I give the preference to the Bible.

Q–I see. Well, you are welcome to your opinion. Have you any idea how old the Egyptian civilization is?

A–No.

Q–Do you know of any record in the world, outside of the story of the Bible, which conforms to any statement that it is 4,200 years ago or thereabouts that all life was wiped off the face of the earth?

A–I think they have found records.

Q–Do you know of any?

A–Records reciting the flood but I am not an authority on the subject of any records, that describe that a flood existed 4,200 years ago, or about that time, which wiped all life off the earth.

A–The recollection of what I have read on that subject is not distinct enough to say whether the records attempted to fix a time, but I have seen in the discoveries of archaeologists where they have found records that described the flood.

Q–Mr. Bryan, don't you know that there are many old religions that describe the flood?

A–No, I don't know.

Q–You know there are others besides the Jewish?

A–I don't know whether these are the record of any other religion or refer to this flood.

Q–Don't you ever examine religion so far to know that?

A–Outside of the Bible?

Q–Yes.

A–No; I have not examined to know that, generally.

Q–You have never examined any other religions?

A–Yes, sir.

Q–have you ever read anything about the origins of religions?

A–Not a great deal.

Q–You have never examined any other religion?

A–Yes, sir.

Q–And you don't know whether any other religion ever gave a similar account of the destruction of the earth by the flood?

A–The Christian religion has satisfied me, and I have never felt it necessary to look up some competing religions. . . .

Q–Would you say that the earth was only 4,000 years old?

A–Oh, no; I think it is much older than that.

Q–How much?

A—I couldn't say.

Q—Do you say whether the Bible itself says it is older than that?

A—I don't think the Bible says itself whether it is older or not.

Q—Do you think the earth was made in six days?

A—Not six days of twenty-four hours?

Q—Doesn't it say so?

A—No, sir. . . .

Mr. Bryan—[Darrow's] purpose is to cast ridicule on everybody who believes in the Bible, and I am perfectly willing that the world shall know that these gentlemen have no other purpose than ridiculing every Christian who believes in the Bible.

Mr. Darrow—We have the purpose of preventing bigots and ignoramuses from controlling the education of the United States and you know it, and that is all.

Mr. Bryan—I am glad to bring out the statement. I want the world to know that this evidence is not for the view Mr. Darrow and his associates have filed affidavits here stating, the purpose of which, as I understand it, is to show that the Bible story is not true.

Mr. Malone—Mr. Bryan seems anxious to get some evidence in the record that would tend to show that those affidavits are not true.

Mr.. Bryan—I am not trying to get anything into the record. I am simply trying to protect the Word of God against the greatest atheist or agnostic in the United States. I want the papers to know I am not afraid to get on the stand in front of him and let him do his worst. . . .

Mr. Darrow—I wish I could get a picture of these clackers. . . .

Mr. Darrow—Mr. Bryan, do you believe that the first woman was Eve?

A—Yes.

Q—Do you believe she was literally made out of Adam's rib?

A—I do.

Q—Did you ever discover where Cain got his wife?

A—No, sir; I leave the agnostics to hunt for her?

Q—You have never found out?

A—I have never tried to find out.

Q—You have never tried to find out?

A—No.

Q—The Bible says he got one, doesn't it? Were there other people on the earth at that time?

A—I cannot say.

Q—You cannot say. Did that ever enter your consideration?

A—Never bothered me.

Q—There were no others recorded, but Cain got a wife.

A—That is what the Bible says.

Q—Where she came from you do not know? All right. Does the statement, "The morning and the evening were the first day," and "The morning and the evening were the second day," mean anything to you?

A—I do not think it necessarily means a twenty-four-hour day.

Q—You do not?

A—No.

Q—What do you consider it to be?

A—I have not attempted to explain it. If you will take the second chapter—let me have the book. The fourth verse of the second chapter says: "These are the generations of the heavens and of the earth, when they were created in the day that the Lord God made the earth and the heavens." The word "day" there in the very next chapter is used to describe a period. I do not see that there is any necessity for construing the words, "the evening and the morning," as meaning necessarily a twenty-four-hour day, "in the day when the Lord made the heaven and the earth."

Q—What do you think about it?

A—That is my opinion. I do not know that my opinion is better on that subject than those who think it does.

Q—You do not think that?

A—No. But I think it would be just as easy for the kind of God we believe in to make the earth in six days as in six years or in 6,000,000 days or in 6,000,000,000 years. I do not think it important whether we believe one or the other.

Q—Do you think those were literal days?

A—My impression is they were periods, but I would not attempt to argue as against anybody who wanted to believe in literal days.

Q—Have you any idea of the length of the periods?

A—No; I don't.

Q—Do you think the sun was made on the fourth day?

A—Yes.

Q—And they had evening and morning without the sun?

A—I am simply saying it is a period.

A—I believe in creation as there told, and if I am not able to explain it I will accept it. Then you can explain it to suit yourself.

Q—Mr. Bryan, what I want to know is, do you believe the sun was made on the fourth day?

A—I believe just as it says there.

Q—Do you believe the sun was made on the fourth day?

A—Read it.

[*Darrow reads aloud from Genesis 1:14-19.*]

Q—Do you believe, whether it was a literal day or a period, the sun and the moon were not made until the fourth day?

A—I believe they were made in the order in which they were given there. . . .

Q—Can you not answer my question?

A—I have answered it. I believe that it was made on the fourth day, in the fourth day.

Q—And they had the evening and the morning before that time for three days or three periods. All right, that settles it. Now, if you call those periods, they may have been a very long time.

A—They might have been.

Q—The creation might have been going on for a very long time?

A—It might have continued for millions of years.

Q—Yes. All right. Do you believe the story of the temptation of Eve by the serpent?

A—I do.

Q—. . . thenceforth and forever should suffer the pains of childbirth in the reproduction of the earth?

A—I believe what it says, and I believe the fact as fully—

Q—That is what it says, doesn't it?

A—Yes.

Q—And for that reason, every woman born of woman, who has to carry on the race, the reason they have childbirth pains is because Eve tempted Adam in the Garden of Eden?

A—I will believe just what the Bible says. I ask to put that in the language of the Bible, for I prefer that to your language. Read the Bible and I will answer.

Q—All right, I will do that.

[*Darrow reads from Genesis 3:15–16.*]

A—I accept it as it is.

Q—And you believe that came about because Eve tempted Adam to eat the fruit?

A—Just as it says.

Q—And you believe that is the reason that God made the serpent to go on his belly after he tempted Eve?

A—I believe the Bible as it is, and I do not permit you to put your language in the place of the language of the Almighty. You read that Bible and ask me questions, and I will answer them. I will not answer your questions in your language.

Q—I will read it to you from the Bible: "And the Lord God said unto the serpent, Because thou hast done this, thou art cursed above all cattle, and above every beast of the field; upon thy belly shalt thou go and dust shalt thou eat all the days of thy life." Do you think that is why the serpent is compelled to crawl upon its belly?

A—I believe that.

Q—Have you any idea how the snake went before that time?

A—No, sir.

Q—Do you know whether he walked on his tail or not?

A—No, sir. I have no way to know.

Q—Now, you refer to the cloud that was put in the heaven after the flood, the rainbow. Do you believe in that?

A—Read it.

Q—All right, I will read it for you.

Mr. Bryan—Your Honor, I think I can shorten this testimony. The only purpose Mr. Darrow has is to slur at the Bible, but I will answer his question. I will answer it all at once, and I have no objection in the world, I want the world to know that this man, who does not believe in a God, is trying to use a court in Tennessee—

Mr. Darrow—I object to that.

Mr. Bryan—[continuing] to slur at it and while it will require time I am

Mr. Darrow—I object to your statement. I am examining you on your fool ideas that no intelligent Christian on earth believes.

The Court—Court is adjourned.

9
Racial Justice
The Scottsboro Boys
1931-37

On March 31, 1931, following reports of a scuffle between white and black young men among the hoboes on a freight train bound from Chattanooga to Memphis, a hastily gathered posse of deputized citizens boarded the train near Scottsboro, Alabama. Searching the cars, they found one white and nine black youths and the far more disturbing sight of two young white women dressed in men's caps and overalls. The two women, after first attempting to flee the posse, accused the black youths of gang rape. So began what would soon be known throughout much of the world as the case of the Scottsboro Boys.

What happened that day the reader will decide from the contested stories told here by witnesses and accusers as well as by a judge who presided during one of the many trials and retrials of the nine defendants. But doing that reveals only a piece of the Scottsboro saga. The implications of the case were powerful and contradictory.

From those trials in remote Alabama courtrooms flowed a spreading stream of personal grief and public shame. Leaders of the Alabama bar and political system—all white—were committed to seeing the nine young men die for the rape of white women whether or not the evidence was sound. The trials confirmed every stereotype Northern newspaper readers had of the South. The Communist Party, attempting to recruit blacks, competed with the National Association for the Advancement of Colored People and other liberal groups in providing legal counsel to the defendants. To spread their political message, the Communists shamelessly exploited the young men, which doubtlessly hardened Southern juries against them. The lawyer who contributed most to their defense, Samuel S. Leibowitz, endured the vilest antisemitism for his painful and unpaid efforts. And the young men, ages thirteen through twenty years old, had their lives shattered: Charlie Weems, Ozie Powell, Clarence Norris, Willie Roberson, Olen Montgomery, Eugene Williams, Andrew Wright, Leroy Wright, and Haywood Patterson. Trials and retrials, in which the individual defendant would hear the death sentence pronounced over him, continued for six years. While none was executed, they

---

SUGGESTION FOR FURTHER READING: Dan T. Carter, *Scottsboro, A Tragedy of the American South*, Revised Edition, Baton Rouge: Louisiana State University Press, 1979.

were all imprisoned during the period of their trials and five eventually were sentenced to terms in the penitentiary. When finally freed—one in fact escaped from prison and became permanently free when a Northern governor refused to extradite him to Alabama—most found themselves with too few skills, too little literacy, and too much fame to establish any reasonable track for their lives. The two accusers, Victoria Price who steadily maintained she had been raped and Ruby Bates who recanted her testimony, lived hard poor bitter lives seeking some public vindication even as late as 1977 with an unsuccessful lawsuit they brought over their portrayal in a television docudrama on the case. Judge James Edwin Horton, who broke the Southern code of the era in the analysis you will read of one of the trials, ended his promising political career with this brave gesture.

Emerging from this painful story were constitutional developments of great significance for legal procedure and the protection of civil rights. In the first round of trials in 1931, the judge had made a point of naming a lawyer to represent the defendants assuming that this would prevent legal challenges. But the U.S. Supreme Court in Powell v. Alabama *(1932), noting that little opportunity had been allowed for the lawyer to prepare a case for his clients, reversed the convictions, strengthening the right to counsel in capital cases. Then in the second set of trials, the defense prepared another appeal to the Supreme Court, demonstrating that the panels from which jury members were selected systematically excluded eligible blacks. The high court in* Norris v. Alabama *(1935) agreed, sending the young men back into court. Faced with such pressure, Alabama juries compromised the principle that a white woman's accusation of rape against a black man automatically called for the death penalty. The full story of the "Scottsboro Boys" was a painful tale of progress.*

The Original Trial

[Direct Examination]:

My name is Victoria Price; I live at Huntsville, Alabama. On or about the 25th of March, 1931, I was on a freight train traveling through this county from Stevenson, Alabama, to Paint Rock, Alabama. Ruby Bates, another woman, was with me. I saw this defendant, Haywood Patterson; I saw him come over the top of the train. At that time I was in a gondola car. When I first saw the defendant come over the top of it, the train had just left out of Stevenson about ten minutes; that was after it had left out of Stevenson about ten minutes. The train was traveling towards Scottsboro, in this County. There were eleven more colored men with the defendant when he came over the top of the train. I stated that I was riding in a gondola car. There were Ruby Bates and seven white boys in the car with me. When these colored men came over the top of the car, this defendant told these white boys to get down, to unload. There were twelve of those negroes, as I stated. After that time, they commenced knocking the white boys off and shot a time or two. The defendant was among them.

In that fight, I saw this defendant knock a boy in the head with a gun, a .38 pistol. I saw him do something else in that fight with the white boys. He put his hands on me and had sexual intercourse with me there in that car; that occurred while the train was running this side of Stevenson, in this County. Others there had hold of me while he had intercourse with me, but I do not know their names; that little one sitting over yonder (indicting) had hold of me while the defendant was having sexual intercourse with me, and that one over yonder (indicating); both of them held me while he ravished me. This defendant's private parts penetrated my private parts. The defendant was in that bunch there and he helped to take my clothes off. He had a knife and a gun, and I don't know what all, and he was cursing them and calling them all sorts of names and everything. I got off of the train in Paint Rock, Alabama. This defendant was on the train when I got off there. Those twelve negroes were not on there at the time I got off, but nine of them were on there.

When the train stopped at Paint Rock, I crawled up by the side of the gondola and finished getting my clothes fixed up and started to get off of the train and got next to the bottom step and fell off, and when I came to myself I was sitting down at a store. I made complaint to several who were down there at the store about the way this defendant had treated me. Somebody took my clothes off; this defendant had something to do with that; he sat on my overalls after they were taken off; that was after he had had intercourse with me, that he sat down on my overalls. The overalls were then off of me and were about a foot or a foot and a half from me at that time. After I had gotten off of the gondola car, when I came to myself, I was sitting at a store and the doctor was there and I left there and came to the jail. The store at which I was when I came to myself is at Paint Rock, Alabama, in this County. I came to the jail at Scottsboro.

After I came to Scottsboro, the doctor made an examination of me while another doctor was present, but only one made the examination. It was about an hour and a half, somewhere along there, after I got off the train at Paint Rock before this doctor made the examination of me here in Scottsboro. . . .

[Cross Examination]:

I was afraid when I saw the negroes coming over the top of that car. I screamed and cried out when I saw them coming over the car. They had pistols and knives out; two of them had pistols. I counted them as they came into that car and counted two pistols and all of them had knives but two. They had their knives out and open. They came up there and shot over the gondola where we were and said, "unload." All of them did not have pistols; I said that two of them had pistols; it looked like all of them had knives; I never saw the like in my life. The knives were open.

They came down there and told the boys to "unload," and Ruby Bates and I started to get off the train and they grabbed us. I was grabbed by that one over yonder (indicating), that black one, the big one. I know how they came over the top of the car; the big one came first and the others followed him, one right after the other. This defendant here was the second one to come into the car. There is the third one (indicating) to come into the car, that one over there at the left. The fourth one was that one sitting right over yonder (indicating). I know there were four of them came in there and they just stood there knocking the white boys off and the rest of them just came and jumped in there. They began to jump two at a time and you couldn't tell who they were. I know four of them, because I was standing up there in the corner. Ruby Bates and I were standing up there in the corner looking at them.

I did not ask the boys whether any of them were cut with the knives these negroes had. All the colored boys had knives, and these knives were opened. I did not examine the knives to see whether they were long-bladed knives or not, but I saw the knives. I did not say that everyone of the negroes had knives; I said I saw knives on them and it looked like pretty well all of them had knives. They had two pistols. Those two that had pistols also had knives, because one of them held a knife on me. He put the pistol in his pocket or did something with it after he threw me down in the car. I was very much excited at the time. Six of them had intercourse with me. I know which one had intercourse with me first; I know the second one that had intercourse with me. None of the boys had intercourse with me twice. I have made no statement to the newspaper men or to the National Guardsmen or others that some of the men had intercourse with me two or three times; I have not made such a statement. They wanted to, but I did not say they did it; I said they wanted to and they would have if the train had not stopped, I guess. There were twelve of those boys and only six had intercourse with me. I did have intercourse with six of them, and six with the other girl.

I can tell you that all six had intercourse with me, but as far as picking out each one that came, one at a time, that is pretty hard to do; I could not undertake to pick them out from the first to the sixth one; I had seen some of these negroes before; I had seen two of them before in Huntsville but did not know them. I do not believe that I had ever seen this defendant before, not until that day. I have seen these defendants since I got off the train at Paint Rock; I have seen them once or twice over there at the jail. I have not talked to them; I had no business to talk with them. I don't associate with them. I was hurt, I was not well and was pretty sick. I was not torn. I have been married; I have been married twice. Both of my husbands are not now living; one of them is dead.

[Counsel for defendant asked]:
Q. Are you divorced?
The State objected to the question, which objection was sustained by the court, to which ruling the defendant duly and legally reserved an exception.

[Counsel for defendant asked]:
Q. Did you ever practice prostitution?
[The State objected to the question, which objection was sustained by the court, to which ruling the defendant duly and legally reserved an exception].

The witness (continuing): I don't know what you are talking about. I do not know what prostitution means. I have not made it a practice to have intercourse with other men.

[Counsel for defendant asked]:
Q. Never did?
[The State objected to the question, which objection was sustained by the court, to which ruling the defendant duly and legally reserved an exception].
The witness (continuing): I have not had intercourse with any other white man but my husband; I want you to distinctly understand that.

I went to Chattanooga looking for work. One of these white boys was in the gondola car when the train got to Paint Rock. I know which one that was; it as the Gilley boy. The other six white boys that were on the train when it left Stevenson were knocked off by the negroes. They were knocked off about five or ten minutes after the train left Stevenson; I could not say the exact place it was. When the negroes had intercourse with me, there was only one white boy on the gondola with me. He saw the whole thing. The negroes got these white boys off the train. They knocked two of the white boys in the head before they were put off. The white boys did not fight them. They did not have anything to fight them with. Eleven negroes had knives and guns. . . .

Ruby Bates, a witness for the State, being first duly sworn, testified:
My name is Ruby Bates; I am 17 years old. I was with Victoria Price on a freight train in this County running from Chattanooga to Huntsville. I was riding on that freight train between Stevenson and Paint Rock. On that train, I saw the defendant over there; I saw him there on the train. When I first saw him, the train was just this side of Stevenson, and at that time he was coming over a box car with the rest of the colored boys. I could not tell you just how many colored men I saw there; I saw more than the defendant; I saw more than one. When I first saw them, I was sitting down in the gondola. There was gravel in this car; it was not plumb full. I was in the end of the car next to where the negroes jumped into it. Mrs. Price and I were together. At the time the negroes jumped over in there, there were seven white boys in there with us. After the negroes jumped in there, they told the white boys to "unload" and hit two of them in the head with pistols, and then all of them got off but one; he stayed on there. All seven of the white boys got off but one. They had a fight with those negroes; they fought back with them. I saw two negroes with pistols; this defendant was one of them; I saw him with a pistol; he was one that had a pistol, and another one had a pistol and the rest had knives, and these knives were open.

I know what happened after these white boys got off the train. They threw us down in the gondola and they all ravished us. I saw some of them ravish Victoria Price. I saw the defendant. I saw him when he was having intercourse with her. When he had his hands on her or was on her, I saw other colored men around her. One of them had a knife holding it on her throat and the other was holding her legs, and that is when I saw this defendant over there (indicating), the one sitting next to Mr. Roddy (of counsel for defendant) on Victoria Price.

I got off the train at Paint Rock. These colored men were on the train when we reached Paint Rock or stopped there. When the train stopped there, the colored men ran toward the engine and the people down there surrounded the train and got them off. I got off the gondola car without anybody helping me off. When I got off the car, Victoria Price was unconscious at that time; she got nearly off the car and fell off and I picked her up and laid her on some grass and stayed there with her about ten minutes before the people brought a chair down there and put her in it and carried her to a store. Mrs. Price and I did not go anywhere until they brought us up here. Some doctors made an examination of Mrs. Price after she got to Scottsboro.

I have never traveled with Victoria Price; I had never been with her before. I had never ridden a freight train before. I had known Victoria Price a little over a year. I worked with her in the mill. I did not live in the same house with her; I have never lived with her. We are good friends. We go with each other.

I did not see any negroes coming across from the box car into the gondola after I left Chattanooga. When I saw them first, I climbed up on the gondola car and they were then fighting. I rode from Chattanooga down to Stevenson between the gondola the girls were in and the box car; I did not see any negroes from Chattanooga to Paint Rock climb from the box car over into the gondola; I was on the other end and they climbed on this end, I guess, but none of them climbed from back this way; I was on the front end of the gondola, and there was a box car on the front and next to the gondola and I was on that end. I did not see any negroes coming over the box car into the gondola from the back end. I could not see all right; I could not see any further than my head. I did not look into the gondola until I saw one of the white boys getting off and then I climbed up on the steps and saw the fight and I then got in the gondola and walked between the other box car and the gondola and got down between them. I did not see any girls in there where the fight was going on; I went from one end to the other and did not see a girl in there at all.

I was this side of Stevenson when I went through that car; that was while they were all fighting. I could not tell you who was doing the fighting; I did not know who they were. I was trying to get out of the way. I left the front end of the gondola and went to the back end of it because the white boys was getting off there; I just moved to give them room to get off. I did not have anything to do with this girl; I did not see the girls; I did not see anybody ravish her. I was riding there at one end of the gondola from Stevenson to Paint Rock; I was not looking in; I did not see inside until I crossed over and went across there and got down between there; I did not see inside then until I got to Paint Rock; I got up under that little, old flat and got up on the side of that. I did not have anything to do with the girls; I did not rape one of them myself.

I do not know a white boy named Gilley; I did not have my knife on a white boy's throat while the fighting was going on; I did not have a knife at all; I did not have anything to do with the fight. I did not see Olen Montgomery until we got to Paint Rock. I did not see the defendant until we got to Paint Rock; I did not see either one of the Wright boys; I saw a gang in the box car, but I could not tell who they were—not in a box car, but in the gondola where the fight was going on; I saw the fighting going on, but did not see any girls in there. I tell the jury I did not rape one of those girls. Here the defendant rested his case.

Victoria Price, a witness for the State, being called in rebuttal, testified:

I saw the two Wright boys that came around on the witness stand, and also Olen Montgomery, the defendant, and the last witness here, Powell. They were all in the gondola. I stated that this defendant is one that raped me. This one here (indicating) held the knife on Gilley while the defendant raped me; there were two back there holding him and he was one of them. I saw this negro Powell; he was in the car when this defendant raped me, I mean the defendant that is on trial.

Examination of Dr. Edward E. Reisman, a defense witness:

Q. This is what we call the vagina (indicating)?

A. Yes sir. . . .

Q. About how much semen does the average man deposit in the vagina during a normal act of intercourse?

A. That is variable, it is greater in youth than in old age.

Q. Let us say a youth, young man about 18 or 17.

A. I should say from a dram and a half to two drams. I will say a dram represents a tea spoon full; from a tea spoon and a half to two tea spoons.

Q. Six men, young men, would deposit about how much into the vagina?

A. More than an ounce, there are eight drams in an ounce, eight tea spoons full, and six times a dram and a half would be nearly an ounce and a half. To illustrate better, an ordinary drinking glass, small one, the standard tumbler, this is an ordinary drinking glass (indicating), that roughly holds five and one half ounces. In order to illustrate that there would be say a fifth of that, that much (indicating) where my thumb is, of semen in six normal intercourse deposits in the human vagina. That would be a considerable quantity of semen and it would be approximately one-fifth of a drinking glass.

Q. Suppose we assume this state of facts; suppose a young woman about 21 years of age were lying in a box car, lying in some place, and first one man got on top of her and had intercourse with her and he got off and right after that another one got on and he got off, until six men had had intercourse with her, suppose the woman didn't douche herself—explain to the jury what douching means?

A. Douching is the act of washing out this vagina.

Q. With a syringe or bulb?

A. Yes sir, or using some liquid to wash it out.

Q. If she didn't use a towel, or stick her finger in the vagina with a towel, or do anything at all to clean it out in there, and suppose an hour and a half later she was taken to a physician's office and placed on a table, and the physician in his scientific way examined her privates with a speculum, a speculum is an instrument that opens up like forceps, as an expert gynecologist, a man that has had so many years experience, would you expect to find in that vagina—

Court: Ask him what he would expect to find.

Q. What would you expect to find with reasonable certainty?

Court: What would be found in your opinion.

A. I would expect to find on the folds of the vagina some of this thick viscid sticky semen, and I would expect to find under the microscope many spermatozoa, because they would be imbedded in the semen.

Q. Would you expect to find a large quantity of semen in the vagina?

A. I would expect to find a good quantity.

Q. Suppose upon an examination of this particular woman we have in mind, there was no semen in the vagina at all and in the canal zone, that in order to find even a semblance of semen the doctor was compelled to use a swab, that is a stick with a piece of cotton on it, and go way up to where the cervix was, where the mouth of the womb is, before he could get a trace of any semen, would you say that woman could have had intercourse with six different men; can you state with reasonable certainty as a medical man, an expert, whether a woman prior to such an examination could have had six intercourses one after another with six men within an hour or an hour and a half before the examination?

Q. Explain it in a way so the jury can understand it, Doctor.

A. To my mind it would be quite inconceivable that six men would have intercourse with one woman and not leave tell-tale traces of their presence in considerable quantities of semen in the vagina. To my mind that would be inconceivable.

Q. When you take those spermatozoa out of the vaginal canal and put them under the microscope immediately and the tails don't wiggle, they don't move, what does the physician call that?

A. Sterility.

Q. What does the phrase non-motile mean?

A. Dead, not moving, not alive.

Q. Suppose I told you this particular case we have been considering, the spermatozoa removed by the doctor from this particular woman was non-motile?

A. They were dead.

Q. How long in the normal woman would it take for the spermatozoa way up there to die? A. They would live a long time, I couldn't answer exactly, but in a period of hours. I would say they would live, well at least twelve hours roughly.

Q. In this particular case the spermatozoa was dead, non-motile, what significance has that, what significance has that from a medical standpoint?

A. They had been there for a long time, deposited for a considerable period.

Q. Of course if the woman is diseased, the disease might kill the germ immediately, is that right?

A. That is correct.

Q. What you call an acid womb?

A. Yes sir. . . .

Q. In the normal woman, where the woman hasn't got an acid vagina, where she is absolutely healthy, how long would the spermatozoa live?

A. We have demonstrated scientifically they live active for twenty-four hours at least.

Q. Suppose I told you doctor there was not even a spoon full, nor the considerable portion of a spoon full of semen in a woman's vagina, not even a portion of a spoon full, and she came along and claimed she had had intercourse with six men, one after the other, would you say with reasonable certainty as a physician, would you say that is possible.

Q. What amount in your opinion would be there?

A. Well as I said before I would expect a greater quantity if six men had intercourse with a woman an hour previous. I certainly would expect to find a great quantity of semen.

Q. You would expect a great quantity and you would also expect to find the spermatozoa alive?

A. Yes sir.

Cross examination by Attorney General Knight:

Q. Suppose the intercourse was entirely unwilling, would that have any effect on the spermatozoa?

A. Well only in this way; if in the struggles or resistance the semen was not discharged in the vagina, which would be possible of course, then naturally there would not be any semen to be obtained from the vagina, but if intercourse or entrance in the vagina was made there is bound to be great quantities of semen in the vaginal tract.

Q. Does the spermatozoa become immediately active, or does it live there, you said twenty-four hours?

A. They may not become immediately active, but they are in the vagina and active for twenty-four hours.

On January 23, 1933, the International Labor Defense asked that a letter written by Ruby Bates be entered in court as evidence for the defense. Miss Bates had written a letter to a sweetheart, saying the Negro youths did not touch her and the police had forced her to lie. The defense introduced the following.

Jan. 5, 1933
Huntsville, Ala.
215 Connelly Ave.

Dearest Earl,

I want to make a statement too you Mary Sanders is a goddam lie about those Negroes jazzing me those policemen made me tell a lie that is my statement because I want to clear myself that is all too if you want to believe me OK. If not that is okay. You will be sorry some day if you had too stay in jail with eight Negroes you would tell a lie two those Negroes did not touch me or those white boys I hope you will believe me the law dont, i love you better than Mary does or anybody else in the world that is why I am telling you of this thing. i was drunk at the time and did not know what i was doing i know it was wrong too let those Negroes die on account of me i hope you will believe my statement because it is the gods truth i hope you will believe me i was jazzed but those white boys jazzed me i wish those Negroes are not Burnt on account of me it is those white boys fault that is my statement, and that is all I know i hope you tell the law hope you will answer

Ruby Bates

Huntsville Ala
215 Connelly Ave.
P.S. This is one time that I might tell a lie But it is the truth so God help me.

On June 22, 1933, Judge James E. Horton of the Alabama Circuit Court granted a motion for a new trial in the case of Haywood Patterson on the ground that the conviction was against the weight of the evidence. Horton was defeated in the subsequent election for Circuit Court judge.

His decision follows:

The defendant in this case has been tried and convicted for the crime of rape with the death penalty inflicted. He is one of the nine charged with a similar crime at the same time.

The case is now submitted for hearing on a motion of a new trial. As human life is at stake, not only of this defendant, but of eight others, the Court does and should approach a consideration of this motion with a feeling of deep responsibility, and shall endeavor to give it that thought and study it deserves.

The vital ground of this motion, as the Court sees it, is whether or not the verdict of the jury is contrary to the evidence. Is there sufficient credible evidence upon which to base a verdict? . . .

The claim of the State is that this defendant raped Victoria Price; that is the charge. The circumstances under which the crime was claimed to have been committed appear as follows:

On March 25th, 1931, the prosecutrix, Victoria Price, and Ruby Bates, her companion, boarded a freight train at Chattanooga, Tennessee, for the purpose of going to Huntsville, Alabama. On the same train were seven white boys, and twelve negroes, who it appears participated or are charged with participating in the occurrences on such train. All were tramps or "hoboing" their way upon this same freight train.

About Stevenson, Alabama, a fight occurred between the negroes and the white boys and all the white boys, except one named Gilley, got off the train, or were thrown off the train, a short time after the train left Stevenson, Alabama. The distance from Stevenson to Paint Rock is thirty-eight miles. Some of the white boys who were thrown off the train returned to Stevenson, Alabama, and the operator telegraphed to Paint Rock, a place down the line, reporting the fight, causing a posse and a large crowd to form at Paint Rock, and they surrounded the train as it pulled into Paint Rock and took therefrom nine negroes, one of whom was this defendant, the two white girls, and their white companion, Gilley. The negroes were arrested and lodged in the Scottsboro jail as well as the two women and the seven white boys. The two women were forthwith carried to the office of a physician in Scottsboro, arriving there from one hour to one and one-half hours after they claimed a rape was committed upon them, and were examined by two skilled physicians. Drs. Bridges and Lynch. It was while the train was travelling between Stevenson and Paint Rock shortly after noon and three o'clock that the alleged rape was committed.

There have been two trials in this case; one at Scottsboro and the other the recent trial at Decatur. The trial at Scottsboro was reversed by the Supreme Court of the United States, who declared the defendants did not have the assistance of counsel. The motion in this case is upon the result of the trial at Decatur. The evidence at the trial at Decatur was vastly more extensive and differed in many important respects from the evidence at Scottsboro. . . .

As stated, the State relies on the evidence of the prosecutrix, Victoria Price, as to the fact of the crime itself, necessarily claiming that her relation is true. The defense insists that her evidence is a fabrication—fabricated for the purpose of saving herself from a prosecution for vagrancy and some other charge.

The Court will therefore first set out the substantial facts testified to by Victoria Price and test it as the law requires as to its reliability or probability, and as to whether it is contradicted by other evidence.

She states that on March 25, 1931, she was on a freight train travelling through Jackson County from Stevenson to Paint Rock; that Ruby Bates was with her on the train; that she had boarded the train at Chattanooga, Tennessee; that when she had boarded the train she got on an oil-tank car. That at Stevenson, she and Ruby Bates walked down the train and got on a gondola car—a car without a top. That the train was filled with chert, lacking about one and one-half or two feet of being full; that the chert was sharp, broken rock with jagged ends.

That as the train proceeded from Stevenson seven white boys got in the car with them and that they all sat down in one end of the car, next to a box car; that in about five or ten minutes twelve colored boys jumped from the box car into the gondola, jumping over their heads. That the defendant was one of them. That the colored boys had seven knives and two pistols; that they engaged in a fight with the white boys, ejecting all from the train except one, Orville Gilley; that this white boy stayed on the gondola, remained there and was still on the car when Paint Rock was reached, and saw the whole thing that thereafter occurred on this car.

That one of the negroes picked her up by the legs and held her over the gondola, and said he was going to throw her off; that she was pulled back in the car and one of the negroes hit her on the side of the head with a pistol causing her head to bleed; that the negroes then pulled off the overalls she was wearing and tore her step-ins apart. That they then threw her down on the chert and with some of the negroes holding her legs and with a knife at her throat, six negroes raped her, one of whom was the defendant; that she lay there for almost an hour on that jagged rock, with the negroes lying on top of her, some of whom were pretty heavy; that the last one finished just five minutes before reaching Paint Rock and that her overalls had just been pulled on when the train stopped at Paint Rock with the posse surrounding it.

That she got up and climbed over the side of the gondola and as she alighted she became unconscious for a while, and that she didn't remember anything until she came to herself in a grocery store and she was then taken to Scottsboro, as the evidence shows. . . .

None of the seven white boys were put on the stand, except Lester Carter, and he contradicted her.

Next, was Victoria Price hit in the head with a pistol? For this we must turn to Dr. Bridges. It was agreed in open court that Dr. Lynch who in company with Dr. Bridges at Scottsboro examined the two girls, would testify in all substantial particulars as Dr. Bridges, and Dr. Lynch was excused with that understanding when Dr. Bridges completed his examination. In considering Dr. Bridges' testimony we observe he was a witness placed on the stand by the State. His intelligence, his fair testimony, his honesty, and his high professional attainments impressed the Court and certainly all that heard him. He was frank and unevasive in his answers. The Court's opinion is that he should be given full faith and credit. In further considering his testimony it was shown that he was examining these women with the most particular care to find evidence of a rape upon them, and that the women were accusing the negroes, and were being required to cooperate and exhibit whatever indicated they had been abused.

Returning to the pistol lick on the head. The doctor testifies: "I did not sew up any wound on this girl's head; I did not see any blood on her scalp. I don't remember my attention being called to any blood or blow on the scalp." And this was the blow that the woman claimed helped force her into submission.

Next, was she thrown and abused, as she states she was, upon the chert—the sharp jagged rock?

Dr. Bridges states as to physical hurts;—we found some small scratches on the back part of the wrist; she had some blue places in the small of her back, low down in the soft part, three or four bruises about like the joint of your thumb, small as a pecan, and then on the shoulders a blue place about the same size—and we put them on the table, and an examination showed no lacerations.

The evidence of other witnesses as well as the prosecutrix will show that the women had travelled from Huntsville to Chattanooga and were on the way back. There is other evidence tending to show they had spent the night in a hobo dive; that they were having intercourse with men shortly before that time. These few blue spots and this scratch would be the natural consequence of such living; vastly greater physical signs would have been expected from the forcible intercourse of six men under such circumstances.

Victoria Price testified that as the negroes had repeated intercourse with her she became wetter and wetter around her private parts; that they finished just as they entered Paint Rock, and that she was taken in an automobile immediately to the doctors' office. There Dr. Bridges and Dr. Lynch, as has been shown, examined her. They looked for semen around her private parts; they found on the inside of her thighs some dirty places. The dirty places were hardly dry, and were infiltrated with dust, about what one would get from riding trains. It was dark dirt or dust. While the doctor did not know what this drying fluid was, his opinion was that it was semen, but whatever it was, it was covered with heavy dust and dirt.

He next examines the vagina to see whether or not any semen was in the vagina. In order to do this he takes a cotton mop and with the aid of a speculum and headlight inserts the cotton mop into the woman's vagina and swabs around the cervix, which is the mouth of the uterus or womb. He extracts from this vagina the substance adhering to the cotton after he has swabbed around the cervix, and places this substance under the microscope. He examines this substance to see if spermatozoa are to be found, and what is the condition of the spermatozoa. Upon the examination under the microscope he finds that there are spermatozoa in the vagina. This spermatozoa he ascertains to be non-motile. He says to the best of his judgment that non-motile means the spermatozoa were dead.

For any fluid escaping from the vagina to become infiltrated with coal dust and dirt, this dirt under the circumstances in this case must have gradually sifted upon the drying fluid, and necessarily a considerable period of time would be required for such an infiltration. The fresh semen emitted by so many negroes would have had a tendency rather to wash off any dirty places around the vagina, and it must have remained there for a considerable period for it to become thus infiltrated with dust and coal dust. Around the cervix the spermatozoa live under the most favorable conditions. While the life of the spermatozoa may be variable, still it appears from the evidence in such a place as this it would have taken at least several hours for the spermatozoa to have become non-motile or dead.

When we consider, as the facts hereafter detailed will show, that this woman had slept side by side with a man the night before in Chattanooga, and had intercourse at Huntsville with Tiller on the night before she went to Chattanooga; when we further take into consideration that the semen being emitted, if her testimony were true, was covering the area surrounding the private parts, the conclusion becomes clearer and clearer that this woman was not forced into intercourse with all of these negroes upon that train, but that her condition was clearly due to the intercourse that she had had on the nights previous to this time.

Is there any other corroboration? There was a large crowd at Paint Rock when the freight arrived there. While they differed in many details as to the make-up of the train and the exact car from which the different persons were taken, all of which is apparently unimportant, all agreed upon the main fact—that the nine negroes, the two women, and the white boy were all taken from the train. This undisputed fact constitutes about the whole extent of their evidence except a statement by Ruby Bates that she had been raped, which experience the said Ruby Bates now repudiates.

This statement by Ruby Bates appears to have been made under the following circumstances. There were three witnesses who testified to having seen the women at Paint Rock. One of the witnesses first saw them after they had gotten off the car and were both standing. Another witness did not see them for some time, he having first rounded up all the negroes. The third witness saw them as they were getting off the car. He states they first started to run toward the engine and as they approached a crowd of men they turned and ran back in the opposite direction, and met a part of the posse who stopped them. Mr. Hill, the station agent, then came up to the women and asked them if the negroes had bothered them. Thereupon Ruby Bates stated that they had been raped. The facts appearing that the women instead of seeking the protection of the white men they saw were at first frightened, and the question propounded was in itself suggestive of an answer. Mr. Hill also states that the negroes were in a coal car; that he saw the heads of the negroes over the top of the car and they were trying to climb over the sides, were pulling themselves up, trying to get off. This clearly indicates that the negroes were not in the car filled with chert, as the prosecutrix claims.

For any other corroboration in the evidence we now return to the freight train as it passes along the track just after leaving Stevenson. The witness, Lee Adams, at a point about one quarter of a mile from the train, sees a fight between a number of white and colored boys; this is an admitted fact in the case.

The evidence of Ory Dobbins was admitted in corroboration of Victoria Price. When his evidence is studied it is found it does not corroborate her, or if so very slightly. The good faith of this witness need not be the slightest questioned, only the lack of correspondence of his testimony with hers. He stated that he lived three miles from Stevenson near the railroad as it ran toward Scottsboro; that as he walked to his barn he saw a freight train; that as it passed his house he saw a white woman sitting on the side of a gondola and a negro put his arm around her waist and throw her back in the car; that he saw the car as it passed; that it was in his line of vision for a few feet, pointing out a door in the court room as the distance. His reason for stating it was a woman is as follows:

Q. You know it was a woman, don't you?
A. She had on women's clothes.
COURT: She had on women's clothes?
Q. What kind of clothes, overalls?
A. No, sir, dress.

The very basis of this statement that she was a woman because she had on a dress does not apply to the women in this case, who were dressed in overalls.

He said she was in a coal car and there were five or six people in the car. Victoria Price says when they took hold of her that it occurred in a car filled with chert, and there were fifteen people in the car. The witness Dobbins said the gondola was between two box cars, while the evidence shows the gondola in which the woman was, was the fifth of a string of eight gondolas.

The witness further stated that the car upon which he saw this occurrence was back toward the caboose. On the other hand the official make-up of the train shows the freight train consisted of forty cars; that the women were in the eleventh or twelfth car from the engine and there were twenty-eight or twenty-nine cars between this car and the caboose. In view of the fact that it was along in this vicinity that the fight was occurring between the negroes and the white boys, and as his reason for saying it was a woman was on account of the dress, and all agree these women had on overalls, this can at best be only slight corroboration.

This is the State's evidence. It corroborates Victoria Price, slightly, if at all, and her evidence is contradictory to the evidence of the doctors who examined her that it has been impossible for the Court to reconcile their evidence with hers.

Next, was the evidence of Victoria Price reasonable or probable? Were the facts stated reasonable? This is one of the tests the law applies.

Rape is a crime usually committed in secrecy. A secluded place or a place where one ordinarily would not be observed is the natural selection for the scene of such a crime. The time and place and stage of this alleged act are such to make one wonder and question did such an act occur under such circumstances. The day is a sunshiny day the latter part in March; the time of day is shortly after the noon hour. The place is upon a gondola or car without a top. This gondola according to the evidence of Mr. Turner the conductor, was filled to within six inches to twelve or fourteen inches of the top with chert [rocks of chalcedony, quartz, and silica], and according to Victoria Price up to one and one half feet or two feet of the top. The whole performance necessarily being in plain view of any one observing the train as it passed. Open gondolas on each side.

On top of this chert twelve negroes rape two white women; they undress them while they are standing up on this chert; the prosecuting witness is then thrown down and with one negro continuously kneeling over her with a knife at her throat, and one or more holding her legs, six negroes successively have intercourse with her on top of that chert; as one arises off of her person, another lies down upon her; those not engaged are standing or sitting around; this continues without intermission although that freight train travels for some forty miles through the heart of Jackson County; through Fackler, Hollywood, Scottsboro, Larkinsville, Lin Rock and Woodville, slowing up at several of these places until it is halted at Paint Rock; Gilley, a white boy, pulled back on the train by the negroes, and sitting off, according to Victoria Price, in one end of the gondola, a witness to the whole scene; yet he stays on the train, and he does not attempt to get off of the car at any of the places where it slows up to call for help; he does not go back to the caboose to report to the conductor or to the engineer in the engine, although no compulsion is being exercised upon him, and instead of there being any threat of danger to him from the negroes, they themselves have pulled him back on the train to prevent his being injured from jumping off the train after it had increased its speed; and in the end by a fortuitous circumstance just before the train pulls into Paint Rock, the rapists cease and just in the nick of time the overalls are drawn up and fastened and the women appear clothed as the posse sight them. The natural inclination of the mind is to doubt and to seek further search.

The Court will next consider her credibility, and in doing so, some of the evidence offered for the defendant will also come in for consideration. . . .

Victoria Price said that she and Ruby Bates went to Chattanooga seeking work; that they went alone and spent the night at Mrs. Callie Brochie's, a friend of hers formerly living in Huntsville, but who had moved to Chattanooga. Was this true? The Chattanooga directory was introduced in evidence; residents of Chattanooga both white and colored, took the stand stating that no such woman as Callie Brochie lived in Chattanooga and had not ever lived there as far as they knew. Though Victoria Price first made this statement more than two years ago at Scottsboro, no witness was offered either from Chattanooga or Huntsville showing any such woman had ever lived in either such place.

Victoria Price said the negroes jumped off a box car over their heads into the gondola, where she, Ruby Bates and the seven white boys were riding, with seven knives and two pistols and engaged in a fight with the white boys. The conductor of the train who had the official make-up of the train stated there were eight gondola cars together on the train; that the women were in one of the middle cars, and that there were three gondola cars between the car in which they were riding and the nearest box car. Lester Carter stated that he was one of the seven boys engaged in the fight with the negroes; that he did not see a single knife or pistol in the hands of the negroes. And although these seven white boys were kept in jail at Scottsboro until after the first trial no one testified to any knife or pistol wounds on any of them.

Further there was evidence of trouble between Victoria Price and the white boys in the jail at Scottsboro because one or more of them refused to go on the witness-stand and testify as she did concerning the rape; that Victoria Price indicated that by so doing they would all get off lighter.

The defendant and five of the other negroes charged with participating in this crime at the same time went on the stand and denied any participation in the rape; denied that they knew anything about it, and denied that they saw any white women on the train. Four of them did state that they took part in a fight with the white boys which occurred on the train. Two of them testified that they knew nothing of the fight nor of the girls, and [were] on an entirely different part of the train. Each of these two testified as to physical infirmities. One testified he was so diseased he could hardly walk, and he was examined at Scottsboro according to the evidence and was found to be diseased. The other testified that one eye was entirely out and that he could only see sufficiently out of the other to walk unattended. The physical condition of this prisoner indicates apparently great defect of vision. He testified, and the testimony so shows that he was in the same condition at Scottsboro and at the time of the rape. He further testified that he was on an oil-tank near the rear of the train, about the seventh car from the rear; that he stayed on this oil-tank all the time and that he was taken from off of this oil-tank.

The evidence of one of the trainmen tends to show that one of the negroes was taken off an oil-tank toward the rear of the train. This near-blind negro was among those whom Victoria Price testified was in the fight and in the party which raped her and Ruby Bates. The facts strongly contradict any such statement.

Conclusion

History, sacred and profane, and the common experience of mankind teach us that women of the character shown in this case are prone for selfish reasons to make false accusations both of rape and insult upon the slightest provocation, or even without provocation for ulterior purposes. These women are shown, by the great weight of the evidence, on this very day before leaving Chattanooga, to have falsely accused two negroes of insulting them, and of almost precipitating a fight between one of the white boys they were in company with and these two negroes. This tendency on the part of the women shows that they are pre-disposed to make false accusations upon any occasion whereby their selfish ends may be gained.

The Court will not pursue the evidence any further.

As heretofore stated the law declares that a defendant should not be convicted without corroboration where the testimony of the prosecutrix bears on its face indications of unreliability or improbability and particularly when it is contradicted by other evidence.

The testimony of the prosecutrix in this case is not only uncorroborated, but it also bears on its face indications of improbability and is contradicted by other evidence, and in addition thereto the evidence greatly preponderates in favor of the defendant. It therefore becomes the duty of the Court under the law to grant the motion made in this case.

It is therefore ordered and adjudged by the Court that the motion be granted; that the verdict of the jury in this case and the judgment of the Court sentencing this defendant to death be, and the same hereby set aside and that a new trial be and the same is hereby ordered.

JAMES E. HORTON
Circuit Judge

This June 22nd, 1933

10
Red Scare
The Army-McCarthy Hearings
1954

America's painful adjustment to the Cold War will be forever memorialized by the era to which Joseph McCarthy gave his name. When people do not understand what is happening or what is required of them, when their best instincts and their worst fears are somehow tangled together, then men like Joseph McCarthy have their chance. In the early 1950's there was such a thing as subversion; the problem of disloyalty was real if limited; some spies were discovered in government (although not by Senator McCarthy). But a limited security problem in the hands of an oily demagogue proved to have virtually unlimited political use. McCarthy became a prime agent in the Republican drive to oust the Democrats from a twenty-year hold on the federal government. Through accusation or insinuation he retired people from public careers and damaged the reputation of many innocent men and women in private lives.

Buoyed by these successes, McCarthy took on establishment institutions such as the church and—in the case before you—the army.

McCarthy should have selected his victims with more care. Six months after his bout with the army he had been censured by his colleagues in the Senate and his national influence was over. McCarthy had believed that he represented a massive national sentiment which could do battle with every constituted power; and many commentators and politicians, liberal and conservative, had taken him at his word. They were all wrong: when powerful men decided to stop him, he was quickly demolished, and with few political aftereffects.

The Army-McCarthy hearings were on television for 188 hours during their thirty-six day run from April 22 to June 16, 1954. In David T. Bazelon's description it was "the greatest political show on earth." Amid the welter of names, the confusion of charges and countercharges, the points of order and other interruptions, millions of viewers nevertheless got the message. As Richard Nixon's Checkers speech showed the way television could save a political career, these hearings showed how it could pitilessly destroy one. The show was unforgettable. McCarthy's sarcasm and disparaging tone of voice lost their customary effectiveness; he went from fame to an alcoholic's death. His flinty adversary, Joseph E.

SUGGESTIONS FOR FURTHER READING: Robert Griffith, *The Politics of Fear: Joseph R. McCarthy and the Senate*, 2nd ed. (Amherst, MA: University of Massachusetts Press 1987); David Oshinsky, *A Conspiracy So Immense: The World of Joe McCarthy* (New York: The Free Press, 1985).

Welch, whose capacity for wit as well as for righteous indignation had thrilled twenty million viewers, was able in his retirement to play a star role on television as a movie lawyer. The age of television politics was upon us.

The Army-McCarthy Hearings

Cast of principal characters:

Robert T. Stevens	Secretary of the Army
Senator Joseph R. McCarthy	U.S. Senator, Wisconsin (Rep.) Chairman, Senate subcommittee
John G. Adams	Counselor for the Army
Joseph N. Welch	Special Counsel for the Army
Senator Karl E. Mundt	U.S. Senator, Kansas (Rep.) Chairman of hearings
Ray H. Jenkins	Chief Counsel, Senate subcommittee
John L. McClellan	U.S. Senator, Arkansas (Dem.) Subcommittee member
Stuart Symington	U.S. Senator, Missouri (Dem.) Subcommittee member
Pvt. G. David Schine	U.S. Army private and former McCarthy aide
Roy M. Cohn	Chief Counsel for Sen. McCarthy

Secretary STEVENS. Gentlemen of the committee, I am here today at the request of this committee. You have my assurance of the fullest cooperation.

In order that we may all be quite clear as to just why this hearing has come about, it is necessary for me to refer at the outset to Pvt. G. David Schine, a former consultant of this committee. David Schine was eligible for the draft. Efforts were made by the chairman of this committee, Senator Joseph R. McCarthy, and the subcommittee's chief counsel, Mr. Roy M. Cohn, to secure a commission for him. Mr. Schine was not qualified, and he was not commissioned. Selective service then drafted him. Subsequent efforts were made to seek preferential treatment for him after he was inducted.

* * *

Before getting into the Schine story I want to make two general comments.

First, it is my responsibility to speak for the Army. The Army is about a million and a half men and women, in posts across this country and around the world, on active duty and in the National Guard and Organized Reserves, plus hundreds of thousands of loyal and faithful civil servants.

Senator MCCARTHY. Mr. Chairman, a point of order.

Senator MUNDT. Senator McCarthy has a point of order.

Senator MCCARTHY. Mr. Stevens is not speaking for the Army. He is speaking for Mr. Stevens, for Mr. Adams, and Mr. Hensel. The committee did not make the Army a party to this controversy, and I think it is highly improper to try to make the Army a party. Mr. Stevens can only speak for himself. . . .

May I say that, regardless of what the Chair and Mr. McClellan decided, when Mr. Stevens says, "It is my responsibility to speak for the Army," he is not speaking for the Army here. All we were investigating has been some Communists in the Army, a very small percentage, I would say much less than 1 percent. And when the Secretary says that, in effect "I am speaking for the Army," he is putting the 99.9 percent of good, honorable, loyal men in the Army into the position of trying to oppose the exposure of Communists in the Army.

I think it should be made clear at the outset, so we need not waste time on it, hour after hour, that Mr. Stevens is speaking for Mr. Stevens and those who are speaking through him; when Mr. Adams speaks, he is speaking for Mr. Adams and those who are speaking through him, and likewise Mr. Hensel.

I may say I resent very, very much this attempt to connect the great American Army with this attempt to sabotage the efforts of this committee's investigation into communism.

Mr. JENKINS. I again say, Mr. Chairman, there is nothing in this statement from which an inference can be drawn that the Army has become a party in interest to this controversy. We are in accord with the Senator, that the parties in interest are Mr. Stevens, Mr. Adams, and Mr. Hensel.

Senator MCCARTHY. If that is understood, then I have no objection. . . .

I speak for the Army today out of a pride and confidence that grows greater every day I spend on the job. There are personal reasons, too, for my pride in the Army and for my resentment of any slur against it or any of the armed services. The 2 oldest of our 4 sons enlisted in the Navy during World War II. Our third son enlisted in 1952 as a private and is now a corporal with the Seventh Army in Europe. He has been overseas 21 months.

Second, I want to affirm here my full belief in the right of Congress to investigate—and that means scrutinizing the activities of the Army or any other department of the executive branch of the Government. The conscientious exercise of this obligation is one of the checks, contemplated by the Constitution, against the possibility of unlimited executive authority by the executive branch of the Government.

As a member of the executive branch, it is my duty to do everything I properly can to help this and other committees of Congress. I have such a profound regard for elective office in this country that it comes very easily for me to cooperate with the Senators, the Representatives, and the committees of Congress.

Let me now turn to the point at issue and first summarize the Schine story. I have been informed that—

1. From mid-July of last year until March 1 of this year, David Schine was discussed between one branch or other of the Department of the Army and Senator McCarthy or members of his staff in more than 65 telephone calls.

2. During the same period, this matter was discussed at approximately 19 meetings between Army personnel and Senator McCarthy or members of his staff.

3. Requests made on Schine's behalf ranged from several for a direct commission before he was inducted into the Army to many for special assignments, relief from routine duties such as KP, extra time off, and special visitor privileges.

4. From November 10, 1953, to January 16, 1954, Schine, by then a private in the Army, obtained 15 passes from the post. By way of comparison, the majority of other newly inducted personnel obtained three passes during the same period. . . .

About that time these two friends left, and because I wanted Senator McCarthy to restate before Mr. Cohn what he had told me on the courthouse steps, I said, "Let's talk about Schine."

That started a chain of events, an experience similar to none which I have had in my life.

Mr. Cohn became extremely agitated, became extremely abusive. He cursed me and then Senator McCarthy. The abuse went in waves. He would be very abusive and then it would kind of abate and things would be friendly for a few moments. Everybody would eat a little bit more, and then it would start in again. It just kept on.

I was trying to catch a 1:30 train, but Mr. Cohn was so violent by then that I felt I had better not do it and leave him that angry with me and that angry with Senator McCarthy because of a remark I had made. So I stayed and missed my 1:30 train. I thought surely I would be able to get out of there by 2:30. The luncheon concluded

Mr. JENKINS. You say you were afraid to leave Senator McCarthy alone there with him? Mr. ADAMS, what did he say? You say he was very abusive.

Mr. ADAMS. He was extremely abusive.

Mr. JENKINS. Was or not any obscene language used?

Mr. ADAMS. Yes.

Mr. JENKINS. Just omit that and tell what he did say which constituted abuse, in your opinion.

Mr. ADAMS. I have stated before, sir, the tone of voice has as much to do with abuse as words. I do not remember the phrases, I do not remember the sentences, but I do remember the violence.

Mr. JENKINS. Do you remember the subject?

Mr. ADAMS. The subject was Schine. The subject was the fact—the thing that Cohn was angry about, the thing that he was so violent about, was the fact that, (1), the Army was not agreeing to an assignment for Schine and, (2), that Senator McCarthy was not supporting his staff in its efforts to get Schine assigned to New York. So his abuse was directed partly to me and partly to Senator McCarthy.

As I say, it kind of came in waves. There would be a period of extreme abuse, and then there would be a period where it would get almost back to normal, and ice cream would be ordered, and then about halfway through that a little more of the same. I missed the 2:30 train, also.

This violence continued. It was a remarkable thing. At first Senator McCarthy seemed to be trying to conciliate. He seemed to be trying to conciliate Cohn and not to state anything contrary to what he had stated to me in the morning. But then he more or less lapsed into silence. Finally, at about 3 o'clock or 10 minutes to 3 we left the restaurant and got in Cohn's car, which was directly in front of the restaurant. Mr. Cohn stated that he was going to give me a ride to the station, which is directly uptown from the courthouse. I had proposed going by subway, but he said, "No, I can get you there quicker."

So we began riding up Fourth Avenue in New York and Cohn's anger erupted again. As it erupted it was directed more on this occasion toward Senator McCarthy than it was to me. As we were riding uptown Senator McCarthy turned around to me and on 2 or 3 occasions during the ride uptown, which took about 15 minutes, he asked me if I could not when I got back to Washington talk to Mr. Stevens and arrange an assignment in New York for Schine.

When we got to 34th Street, which is where——

Mr. JENKINS. What was your reply to that request of the Senator, Mr. Adams?

Mr. ADAMS. My recollection is that I made no reply. I didn't say much on the ride uptown. It was a little difficult.

Mr. JENKINS. YOU mean that both you and the Senator had been completely subdued?

Mr. ADAMS. I had been.

Mr. JENKINS. All right. You were riding uptown in Mr. Cohn's car, being driven by Mr. Cohn, as a matter of fact?

Mr. ADAMS. Yes sir.

Mr. JENKINS. YOU were being taken to the station?

Mr. ADAMS. That is right.

Mr. JENKINS. I will ask you to tell the committee the events of that trip.

Mr. ADAMS. As I stated, Senator McCarthy said to me 2 or 3 times, or asked me on 2 or 3 occasions if I wouldn't go back to Washington and ask Mr. Stevens to arrange for Schine's assignment in New York. When we got to 34th Street, which is where the turn must be made if you are going to go over to Penn Station, which is on 7th Avenue, we attempted a left turn which was not permitted and a policeman would not permit it and ordered us to go on ahead, which took us under a long tunnel, the tunnel which goes under the Grand Central Station, and we came out about 45th Street or thereabouts going away from the station and I had then 10 or 12 minutes to make the 3:30 train. I complained to Mr. Cohn. I said, "You are just taking me away from the station," and in a final fit of violence he stopped the car in the middle of four lanes of traffic and said, "Get there however you can." So I climbed out of the car in the middle of four lanes of traffic between 46th and 47th Street on Park Avenue, ran across the street and jumped into a cab to try to make the 3:30 train.

Mr. JENKINS. Senator Potter directs me to ask you whether or not you made the train. [Laughter.]

Mr. ADAMS. The 3:30 train was 10 minutes late, so I made it.

Mr. Carr told me a few days later that he didn't think that I should feel badly about the way I was put out of the car because he said I should have been there to see the way Senator McCarthy left the car a few blocks later.

*　　*　　*

Mr. JENKINS. Mr. ADAMS, when did you finally tell Mr. Cohn, if you did so, that Schine in all probability was scheduled for overseas duty?

Mr. ADAMS. On January 13. I was at the Capitol with Mr. Stevens. He was coming up on another appointment. I often use that means of talking to him. He is a very busy man. I jump in his car and ride to his appointment with him. I did it on this occasion. When I got here to the Senate Office Building, instead of going back to the Pentagon as I had originally planned, I told Mr. Stevens that I thought I would go down and see if I could not get back in good with Mr. Cohn and conciliate him because we had been having so much difficulty over Schine.

So I went down to room 101. Mr. Cohn was there and Mr. Carr was there. As I remember, we lunched together in the Senate cafeteria, and everything was peaceful. When we returned to room 101, toward the latter part of the conversation I asked Cohn—I knew that 90 percent of all inductees ultimately face overseas duty and I knew that one day we were going to face that problem with Mr. Cohn as to Schine.

So I thought I would lay a little groundwork for future trouble I guess. I asked him what would happen if Schine got overseas duty.

Mr. JENKINS. You mean you were breaking the news gently, Mr. Adams?

Mr. ADAMS. Yes, sir; that is right. I asked him what would happen if Schine got overseas duty. He responded with vigor and force, "Stevens is through as Secretary of the Army."

I said, "Oh, Roy," something to this effect, "Oh, Roy, don't say that. Come on. Really, what is going to happen if Schine gets overseas duty?"

He responded with even more force, "We will wreck the Army."

Then he said, "The first thing we are going to do is get General Ryan for the way he has treated Dave at Fort Dix. Dave gets through at Fort Dix tomorrow or this week, and as soon as he is gone we are going to get General Ryan for the obscene way in which he has permitted Schine to be treated up there."

He said, "We are not going to do it ourselves. We have another committee of the Congress interested in it."

Then he said, "I wouldn't put it past you to do this. We will start investigations. We have enough stuff on the Army to keep investigations going indefinitely, and if anything like such-and-such doublecross occurs, that is what we will do."

This remark was not to be taken lightly in the context in which it was given to me. . . .

Senator SYMINGTON. Have you the written instructions that you were going to deliver to the committee?

Mr. ADAMS. It is a letter to the Secretary of Defense from the President of the United States.

This is a letter signed Dwight D. Eisenhower addressed the Honorable, the Secretary of Defense, Washington, D. C.:

> DEAR MR. SECRETARY: It has long been recognized that to assist the
> Congress in achieving its legislative purposes every Executive Department

or Agency must, upon the request of a Congressional Committee, expeditiously furnish information relating to any matter within the jurisdiction of the Committee, with certain historical exceptions—some of which are pointed out in the attached memorandum from the Attorney General. This Administration has been and will continue to be diligent in following the principle. However, it is essential for the successful working of our system that the persons entrusted with power over any one of the three great branches of Government shall not encroach upon the authority confided to the others. The ultimate responsibility for the conduct of the Executive Branch rests with the President.

Within this Constitutional framework each branch should cooperate fully with each other for the common good. However, throughout our history the President has withheld information whenever he found that what was sought was confidential or its disclosure would be incompatible with the public interest or jeopardize the safety of the Nation.

Because it is essential to efficient and effective administration that employees of the Executive Branch be in a position to be completely candid in advising with each other on official matters, and because it is not in the public interest that any of their conversations or communications, or any documents or reproductions, concerning such advice be disclosed, you will instruct employees of your Department that in all of their appearances before the Subcommittee of the Senate Committee on Government Operations regarding the inquiry now before it they are not to testify to any such conversations or communications or to produce any such documents or reproductions. This principle must be maintained regardless of who would benefit by such disclosures.

I direct this action so as to maintain the proper separation of powers between the Executive and Legislative Branches of the Government in accordance with my responsibilities and duties under the Constitution. This separation is vital to preclude the exercise of arbitrary power by any branch of the Government. By this action I am not in any way restricting the testimony of such witnesses to what occurred regarding any matters where the communication was directly between any of the principals in the controversy within the Executive Branch on the one hand and a member of the Subcommittee or its staff on the other.

Sincerely,
/S/ DWIGHT D. EISENHOWER

To the letter, sir, is attached a 10-page memorandum from the Attorney General to the President. . . .

Senator MCCARTHY. Mr. Chairman, I must admit that I am somewhat at a loss as to know what to do at the moment. One of the subjects of this inquiry is to find out who was responsible for succeeding and calling off the hearing of Communist infiltration in Government. That the hearings have been called off, no one can question. I fear that maybe in my mind I was doing an injustice, possibly, to Mr. Adams and Mr. Hensel.

I strongly felt all along that they were the men responsible for it. At this point,

I find out there is no way of ever getting at the truth, because we do find that the charges were conceived, instigated, at a meeting which was testified to by Mr. Adams.

Now for some fantastically strange reason, the iron curtain is pulled down so we can't tell what happened at that meeting. I don't think the President is responsible for this. I don't think his judgment is that bad, Mr. Chairman.

There is no reason why any one should be afraid of the facts, of the truth, that came out of that meeting. It is a very important meeting. It doesn't have to do with security matters. It doesn't have to do with national security. It merely has to do with why these charges were filed. . . .

The question is how far can—I am not talking about the present occupant in the White House. But we have a tremendously important question here, Mr. Chairman. That is, how far can the President go? Who all can he order not to testify? If he can order the Ambassador to the U. N. not to testify about something having nothing to do with the U. N., but a deliberate smear against my staff, then any President—and we don't know who will be President in 1956, 1960, 1964—but any President [laughter]—I won't repeat that. Any President can, by an Executive order, keep the facts from the American people. . . .

Now we are getting down to the meat of the case, Mr. Chairman, and that is, who was responsible for the issuance of the smear that has held this committee up for weeks and weeks and weeks, and has allowed Communists to continue in our defense plants, Mr. Chairman, handling top-secret material, as I said before, with a razor poised over the jugular vein of this Nation? Who is responsible for keeping all these Army officers down here and all the Senators tied up while the world is going up in flames?

I do think, Mr. Chairman, that we should go into executive session. I must have a ruling as to what will be behind an iron curtain and what facts we can bring out before I can intelligently question the witnesses. I do think that someone, for his own benefit, should contact the President immediately and point out to him, perhaps, that he and I and many of us campaigned and promised the American people that if they would remove our Democrat friends from the control of this Government, then we would no longer engage in Government by secrecy, whitewash and coverup.

Mr. JENKINS. You will recall, Mr. Cohn, that he testified that you said that if Schine went overseas, Stevens was through as Secretary of the Army?

Mr. COHN. I heard him say that, sir.

Mr. JENKINS. Did you or not?

Mr. COHN. No, sir.

Mr. JENKINS. Did you say anything like that, Mr. Cohn?

Mr. COHN. No, sir, and my recollection is that I did not. I have talked to Mr. Carr who was sitting there the whole time, and he says I did not. . . .

Mr. JENKINS. All right, now you are saying you did not say it, Mr. Cohn?

Mr. COHN. Yes, sir. I am saying I am sure I did not make that statement, and I am sure that Mr. Adams and anybody else with any sense, and Mr. Adams has a lot of sense, could ever believe that I was threatening to wreck the Army or that I could wreck the Army. I say, sir, that the statement is ridiculous.

Mr. JENKINS. I am talking about Stevens being through as Secretary of the Army.

Mr. COHN. That is equally ridiculous, sir.

Mr. JENKINS. And untrue?

Mr. COHN. Yes, sir, equally ridiculous and untrue, I could not cause the President of the United States to remove Stevens as Secretary of the Army.

*   *   *

Senator McCARTHY. Let me ask you this, Mr. Cohn: Had you something to do with the Hiss case, I believe, also; is that right?

Mr. COHN. I had. What I had to do with the Hiss case is not important enough to mention here, sir.

Senator McCARTHY. Enough to do with it so that you are aware of the facts in the case. Let me ask you this: Are you convinced if it had not been for a congressional committee having exposed the facts in the Hiss case, that Alger Hiss today would be free?

Mr. COHN. Yes, sir. . . .

Senator McCARTHY. Just this one question: Mr. Cohn, do you agree with me that, No. 1, the administration is certainly heading in the right direction so far as getting rid of Communists are concerned, and, No. 2, that it is ridiculous, a complete waste of time to have these exchanges of statements between the White House and this committee, that there is no reason on earth why there should be any contest between the executive department and this committee insofar as exposing Communists, graft, and corruption is concerned, that we all should be heading the same way, there should be none of this silly bickering, fighting about this exposure, that we should be getting the complete cooperation from the executive and that should be flowing both ways, of course?

Senator MUNDT. The Senator's time has expired. You can answer the question.

Senator McCARTHY. Let me finish the question. And if that could be accomplished, a great service could be performed for the country?

Mr. COHN. I am sure of that, sir.

Senator MUNDT. Mr. Welch, you have 10 minutes. After your 10 minutes, we will recess.

Mr. WELCH. Mr. Chairman, ordinarily, with the clock as late as it is I would call attention to it, but not tonight.

Mr. COHN, what is the exact number of Communists or subversives that are loose today in these defense plants?

Mr. COHN. The exact number that is loose, sir?

Mr. WELCH. Yes, sir.

Mr. COHN. I don't know.

Mr. WELCH. Roughly how many?

Mr. COHN. I can only tell you, sir, what we know about it.

Mr. WELCH. That is 130, is that right?

Mr. COHN. Yes, sir. I am going to try to particularize for you, if I can.

Mr. WELCH. I am in a hurry. I don't want the sun to go down while they are still in there, if we can get them out.

Mr. COHN. I am afraid we won't be able to work that fast, sir.

Mr. WELCH. I have a suggestion about it, sir. How many are there?

Mr. COHN. I believe the figure is approximately 130.

Mr. WELCH. Approximately one-two-three?

Mr. COHN. Yes, sir. Those are people, Mr. Welch—

Mr. WELCH. I don't care. You told us who they are. In how many plants are they?

Mr. COHN. How many plants?

Mr. WELCH. How many plants.

Mr. COHN. Yes, sir; just 1 minute, sir. I see 16 offhand, sir.

Mr. WELCH. Sixteen plants?

Mr. COHN. Yes, sir.

Mr. WELCH. Where are they, sir?

Mr. COHN. Senator McCarthy——

Mr. WELCH. Reel off the cities.

Mr. COHN. Would you stop me if I am going too far?

Mr. WELCH. You can't go too far revealing Communists, Mr. Cohn. Reel off the cities for us.

Mr. COHN. Schenectady, N .Y.; Syracuse, N. Y.; Rome, N. Y.; Quincy, Mass.; Fitchburg, Mass.; Buffalo, N. Y.; Dunkirk, N. Y.; another at Buffalo, N. Y.; Cambridge, Mass.; New Bedford, Mass.; Boston, Mass.; Quincy, Mass.; Lynn, Mass.; Pittsfield, Mass.; Boston, Mass.

Mr. WELCH. Mr. Cohn, you not only frighten me, you make me ashamed when there are so many in Massachusetts. [Laughter.] This is not a laughing matter, believe me. Are you alarmed at that situation, Mr. Cohn?

Mr. COHN. Yes, sir; I am.

Mr. WELCH. Nothing could be more alarming, could it?

Mr. COHN. It certainly is a very alarming thing.

Mr. WELCH. Will you not, before the sun goes down, give those names to the FBI and at least have those men put under surveillance.

Mr. COHN. Mr. WELCH, the FBI——

Senator MCCARTHY. Mr. Chairman.

Mr. WELCH. That is a fair question.

Senator MCCARTHY. Mr. Chairman, let's not be ridiculous. Mr. Welch knows, as I have told him a dozen times, that the FBI has all of this information. The defense plants have the information. The only thing we can do is to try and publicly expose these individuals and hope that they will be gotten rid of. And you know that, Mr. Welch.

Mr. WELCH I do not know that.

Mr. COHN do you mean to tell us that J. Edgar Hoover and the FBI know the names of these men and are doing nothing about them?

Mr. COHN. NO, sir. I mean to say—

Mr. WELCH. Do you mean to tell us they are doing something about them?

Mr. COHN. Yes, sir.

Mr. WELCH. What are they doing about them?

Mr. COHN. Here is what they do about them. They notify the Defense Department and the appropriate security——

Mr. WELCH. Don't they put them under surveillance?

Mr. COHN. Appropriate security agencies involved. The FBI gives them full information. It is then up to them, the places where the information goes, to decide whether or not they will act on the FBI information. All the FBI can do is give the information. Their power ends right there.

Mr. WELCH. Cannot the FBI put these 130 men under surveillance before sundown tomorrow?

Mr. COHN. Sir, if there is need for surveillance in the case of espionage or anything like that, I can well assure you that Mr. John Edgar Hoover and his men know a lot better than I, and I quite respectfully suggest, sir, than probably a lot of us, just who should be put under surveillance. I do not propose to tell the FBI how to run its shop. It does it very well.

Mr. WELCH. And they do it, don't they, Mr. Cohn?

Mr. COHN. When the need arises, of course.

Mr. WELCH. And will you tell them tonight, Mr. Cohn, that here is a case where the need has arisen, so that it can be done by sundown tomorrow night?

Mr. COHN. No, sir; there is no need for my telling the FBI what to do about this or anything else.

Mr. WELCH. Are you sure they know every one of them?

Mr. COHN. I would take an oath on it, sir. I think the FBI has complete information about the Communist movement in this country and that would include information about these people.

Mr. WELCH. That being true, Mr. Cohn, can you and I both rest easy tonight?

Mr. COHN. Sir, I certainly agree with you, it is a very disturbing situation.

Mr. WELCH. Well, if the FBI has got a firm grasp on these 130 men, I will go to sleep.

Do you assure me that is so?

Mr. COHN. Sir, I am sure that the FBI does its job well, that it knows all about these people, that it has told the appropriate agencies about these people, and that the failure to act goes elsewhere than in the hands of the FBI.

Mr. WELCH. Just for the purpose of safety, for fear something could be missed somewhere, would you mind, as a patriotic American citizen, sending the 130 names over to the FBI tonight? Let's be sure we are not taking any chances. Mr. Cohn. I wouldn't mind it at all, sir. Mr. Welch. Would you do it, sir? Senator McCarthy. Would you yield? Mr. Welch. No; I won't yield. I want to find out if he will do it and if he won't, will you do it?

Senator MCCARTHY. You asked a question. Will you let me answer

Mr. WELCH. I asked it of the witness, sir.

Senator MCCARTHY. I want you to know that the FBI has complete access to any files we have, any information we have, at any time.

Mr. WELCH knows, I am sure you do, Mr. Welch, that the FBI has no power to order anyone fired. You know that, for example, in the Alger Hiss case, the FBI had furnished all the information and he still rose to be a top man in the State Department. You know, Mr. Welch, that the FBI furnished all the information on the spy Harry Dexter White. You know that despite that fact, Mr. Welch, despite the fact that the FBI had given all of the information, and sent over reports day after day after day, Harry Dexter White, the Communist spy, got to be a top Treasury official. So let's not deceive the American people by blaming the FBI for Communists being in defense plants. . . .

Mr. WELCH. Well, Mr. Chairman, my confidence in the FBI is simply limitless, and I think Mr. Cohn's confidence is similar; is that right, sir?

Mr. COHN. Yes, sir; that is right.

Mr. WELCH. All I am suggesting is that we just nudge them a little and be sure they are busy on these 130.

Would you mind helping nudge them?

Mr. COHN. Sir, you do not have to nudge the FBI about this or about anything else.

Mr. WELCH Then they have got the whole 130, have they, Mr. Cohn?

Mr. COHN. I am sure of it, sir, and a lot more.

*   *   *

Mr. WELCH. Then, as a second line of defense, let's send the 130 names to the Department of Defense tonight. Would you mind doing that?

Mr. COHN. Whatever the committee directs on that, sir.

Mr. WELCH. I wish the committee would direct that all the names be sent both to the FBI and to the Department of Defense with extreme suddenness.

Mr. WELCH. Mr. Cohn, tell me once more: Every time you learn of a Communist or a spy anywhere, is it your policy to get them out as fast as possible?

Mr. COHN. Surely, we want them out as fast as possible, sir.

Mr. WELCH And whenever you learn of one from now on, Mr. Cohn, I beg of you, will you tell somebody about them quick?

Mr. COHN. Mr. WELCH, with great respect, I work for the committee here. They know how we go about handling situations of Communist infiltration and failure to act on FBI information about Communist infiltration. If they are displeased with the speed with which I and the group of men who work with me proceed, if they are displeased with the order in which we move, I am sure they will give me appropriate instructions along those lines, and I will follow any which they give me.

Mr. WELCH. May I add my small voice, sir, and say whenever you know about a subversive or a Communist spy, please hurry. Will you remember those words?

Senator MCCARTHY. Mr. Chairman.

Mr. COHN Mr. WELCH, I can assure you, sir, as far as I am concerned, and certainly as far as the chairman of this committee and the members, and the members of the staff, are concerned, we are a small group, but we proceed as expeditiously as is humanly possible to get out Communists and traitors and to bring to light the mechanism by which they have been permitted to remain where they were for so long a period of time.

Senator MCCARTHY. Mr. Chairman, in view of that question—

Senator MUNDT. Have you a point of order?

Senator MCCARTHY Not exactly, Mr. Chairman, but in view of Mr. Welch's request that the information be given once we know of anyone who might be performing any work for the Communist Party, I think we should tell him that he has in his law firm a young man named Fisher whom he recommended, incidentally, to do work on this committee, who has been for a number of years a member of an organization which was named, oh, years and years ago, as the legal bulwark of the Communist Party, an organization which always swings to the defense of anyone who dares to expose Communists. I certainly assume that Mr. Welch did not know of this young man at the time he recommended him as the assistant counsel for this committee, but he has such terror and such a great desire to know where anyone is located who may be serving the Communist cause, Mr. Welch, that I thought we should just call to your attention the fact that your Mr. Fisher, who is still in your law firm today, whom you asked to have down here looking over the secret and classified material, is a member of an organization, not named by me but named by various committees, named by the Attorney General, as I recall, and I think I quote this verbatim, as "the legal bulwark of the Communist Party." He belonged to that for a sizable number of years, according to his own admission, and he belonged to it long after it had been exposed as the legal arm of the Communist Party.

Knowing that, Mr. Welch, I just felt that I had a duty to respond to your urgent request that before sundown, when we know of anyone serving the Communist cause, we let the agency know. We are now letting you know that your man did belong to this organization for, either 3 or 4 years, belonged to it long after he was out of law school.

I don't think you can find anyplace, anywhere, an organization which has done more to defend Communists—I am again quoting the report—to defend Communists, to defend espionage agents, and to aid the Communist cause, than the man whom you originally wanted down here at your right hand instead of Mr. St. Clair.

I have hesitated bringing that up, but I have been rather bored with your phony requests to Mr. Cohn here that he personally get every Communist out of government before sundown. Therefore, we will give you information about the young man in your own organization.

I am not asking you at this time to explain why you tried to foist him on this committee. Whether you knew he was a member of that Communist organization or not, I don't know. I assume you did not, Mr. Welch, because I get the impression that, while you are quite an actor, you play for a laugh, I don't think you have any conception of the danger of the Communist Party. I don't think you yourself would ever knowingly aid the Communist cause. I think you are unknowingly aiding it when you try to burlesque this hearing in which we are attempting to bring out the facts, however.

Mr. WELCH. Mr. Chairman.

Senator MUNDT. Mr. Welch, the Chair should say he has no recognition or no memory of Mr. Welch's recommending either Mr. Fisher or anybody else as counsel for this committee.

I will recognize Mr. Welch.

Senator MCCARTHY. Mr. Chairman, I will give you the news story on that.

Mr. WELCH. Mr. Chairman, under these circumstances I must have something approaching a personal privilege.

Senator MUNDT. You may have it, sir. It will not be taken out of your time.

Mr. WELCH. Senator McCarthy, I did not know—Senator, sometimes you say "May I have your attention?"

Senator MCCARTHY. I am listening to you. I can listen with one ear.

Mr. WELCH. This time I want you to listen with both.

Senator MCCARTHY. Yes.

Mr. WELCH. Senator McCarthy, I think until this moment—

Senator MCCARTHY. Jim, will you get the news story to the effect that this man belonged to this Communist-front organization? Will you get the citations showing that this was the legal arm of the Communist Party, and the length of time that he belonged, and the fact that he was recommended by Mr. Welch? I think that should be in the record.

Mr. WELCH. You won't need anything in the record when I have finished telling you this.

Until this moment, Senator, I think I never really gaged your cruelty or your recklessness. Fred Fisher is a young man who went to the Harvard Law School and came into my firm and is starting what looks to be a brilliant career with us.

When I decided to work for this committee I asked Jim St. Clair, who sits on my right, to be my first assistant. I said to Jim, "Pick somebody in the firm who works under you that you would like." He chose Fred Fisher and they came down on an afternoon plane. That night, when he had taken a little stab at trying to see what the case was about, Fred Fisher and Jim St. Clair and I went to dinner together. I then said to these two young men, "Boys, I don't know anything about you except I have always liked you, but if there is anything funny in the life of either one of you that would hurt anybody in this case you speak up quick."

Fred Fisher said, "Mr. Welch, when I was in law school and for a period of months after, I belonged to the Lawyers Guild," as you have suggested, Senator. He went on to say, "I am secretary of the Young Republicans League in Newton with the son of Massachusetts' Governor, and I have the respect and admiration of the 25 lawyers or so in Hale & Dorr."

I said, "Fred, I just don't think I am going to ask you to work on the case. If I do, one of these days that will come out and go over national television and it will just hurt like the dickens."

So, Senator, I asked him to go back to Boston.

Little did I dream you could be so reckless and so cruel as to do an injury to that lad. It is true he is still with Hale & Dorr. It is true that he will continue to be with Hale & Dorr. It is, I regret to say, equally true that I fear he shall always bear a scar needlessly inflicted by you. If it were in my power to forgive you for your reckless cruelty, I will do so. I like to think I am a gentleman, but your forgiveness will have to come from someone other than me.

Senator McCARTHY. Mr. Chairman.

Senator MUNDT. Senator McCarthy?

Senator McCARTHY. May I say that Mr. Welch talks about this being cruel and reckless. He was just baiting; he has been baiting Mr. Cohn here for hours, requesting that Mr. Cohn, before sundown, get out of any department of Government anyone who is serving the Communist cause.

I just give this man's record, and I want to say, Mr. Welch, that it has been labeled long before he became a member, as early as 1944—

Mr. WELCH. Senator, may we not drop this? We know he belonged to the Lawyers Guild, and Mr. Cohn nods his head at me. I did you, I think, no personal injury, Mr. Cohn.

Mr. COHN. No, sir.

Mr. WELCH. I meant to do you no personal injury, and if I did, beg your pardon.

Let us not assassinate this lad further, Senator. You have done enough. Have you no sense of decency sir, at long last? Have you left no sense of decency?

Senator McCARTHY. I know this hurts you, Mr. Welch. But I may say, Mr. Chairman, on a point of personal privilege, and I would like to finish it—

Mr. WELCH. Senator, I think it hurts you, too, sir.

Senator McCARTHY. I would like to finish this.

Mr. Welch has been filibustering this hearing, he has been talking day after day about how he wants to get anyone tainted with communism out before sundown. I know Mr. Cohn would rather not have me go into this. I intend to, however, Mr. Welch talks about any sense of decency. If I say anything which is not the truth, then I would like to know about it.

The foremost legal bulwark of the Communist Party, its front organizations, and controlled unions, and which, since its inception, has never failed to rally to the legal defense of the Communist Party, and individual members thereof, including known espionage agents.

Now, that is not the language of Senator McCarthy. That is the language of the Un-American Activities Committee. And I can go on with many more citations. It seems that Mr. Welch is pained so deeply he thinks it is improper for me to give the record, the Communist front record, of the man whom he wanted to foist upon this committee. But it doesn't pain him at all—there is no pain in his chest about the unfounded charges against Mr. Frank Carr; there is no pain there about the attempt to destroy the reputation and take the jobs away from the young men who were working in my committee.

And, Mr. Welch, if I have said anything here which is untrue, then tell me. I have heard you and every one else talk so much about laying the truth upon the table that when I hear—and it is completely phony, Mr. Welch, I have listened to you for a long time—when you say "Now, before sundown, you must get these people out of Government," I want to have it very clear, very clear that you were not so serious about that when you tried to recommend this man for this committee.

And may I say, Mr. Welch, in fairness to you, I have reason to believe that you did not know about his Communist-front record at the time you recommended him. I don't think you would have recommended him to the committee, if you knew that.

I think it is entirely possible you learned that after you recommended him.

Senator MUNDT. The Chair would like to say again that he does not believe that Mr. Welch recommended Mr. Fisher as counsel for this committee, because he has through his office all the recommendations that were made. He does not recall any that came from Mr. Welch, and that would include Mr. Fisher.

Senator MCCARTHY. Let me ask Mr. Welch. You brought him down, did you not, to act as your assistant?

Mr. WELCH. Mr. McCarthy, I will not discuss this with you further. You have sat within 6 feet of me, and could have asked me about Fred Fisher. You have brought it out. If there is a God in heaven, it will do neither you nor your cause any good. I will not discuss it further. I will not ask Mr. Cohn any more questions. You, Mr. Chairman, may, if you will, call the next witness.

Senator MUNDT. Are there any questions?

Mr. JENKINS. No further questions, Mr. Chairman.

Mr. JENKINS. Senator McCarthy, how do you regard the communistic threat to our Government as compared with other threats with which it is confronted?

* * *

Mr. Jenkins, the thing that I think we must remember is that this is a war which a brutalitarian force has won to a greater extent than any brutalitarian force has won a war in the history of the world before.

For example, Christianity, which has been in existence for 2,000 years, has not converted, convinced nearly as many people as this Communist brutalitarianism has enslaved in 106 years, and they are not going to stop.

I know that many of my good friends seem to feel that this is a sort of a game you can play, that you can talk about communism as though it is something 10,000 miles away.

Mr. Jenkins, in answer to your question, let me say it is right here with us now. Unless we make sure that there is no infiltration of our Government, then just as certain as you sit there, in the period of our lives you will see a red world. There is no question about that, Mr. Jenkins. . . .

11

Outlawing Segregation
Brown v. Board of Education
1954

The Brown case, perhaps the most celebrated in the history of the United States, began as four separate cases brought by the NAACP Legal Defense Fund. The goal was to overturn the doctrine announced in 1896 in Plessy v. Ferguson *that the Fourteenth Amendment permits segregation so long as each race is provided with equal facilities. Building on earlier successes in desegregating law and graduate schools, the Fund in 1951, under the direction of the African American attorney and later Supreme Court justice Thurgood Marshall, brought actions against school boards in Topeka, Kansas, Clarendon County, South Carolina, Prince Edward County, Virginia, and New Castle County, Delaware, arguing that segregated schools, even if equal in facilities and curriculum, violated the Fourteenth Amendment's guarantee of equal protection of the laws. The cases ground through the lower federal courts, then were argued before the Supreme Court in 1952 and sent back for reargument in 1953. Between the two sessions, Earl Warren replaced Fred M. Vinson as Chief Justice. The Court, noting that "a common legal question justifies their consideration together in this consolidated opinion," joined the four cases in its unanimous decision, read on May 17, 1954. Because Oliver Brown's last name fell early in the alphabet, the case has entered history as* Brown v. Board of Education of Topeka, *honoring beyond other equally worthy defendants the Topeka father who objected to his eight-year-old daughter Linda's traveling by bus to a black school when the family lived three blocks from an all-white one.*

The social reality facing the Court appears most starkly in the South Carolina case—presented here—for in that district black pupils outnumbered whites by a ratio of about ten to one. The arguments ranged over the history and meaning of the Fourteenth Amendment and the interpretation of expert testimony. But the justices' concern over the practical implications of overturning segregation—emphasized by the school board's attorney—was evident throughout the hearings.

In the Brown *decision, the Court was unequivocal in its interpretation of the Constitution: "in the field of public education the doctrine of 'separate but equal' has no place. Separate educational facilities are inherently unequal." But imple-*

SUGGESTIONS FOR FURTHER READING: Richard Kluger, *Simple Justice: The History of* Brown v. Board of Education, *Black America's Struggle for Equality,* New York: Alfred A. Knopf, 1976; Harvard Sitkoff, *The Struggle for Black Equality, 1954–1992,* revised edition, New York: Hill & Wang, 1993.

*mentation in places like Clarendon County remained a puzzle. "The formulation
of decrees in these cases," the decision acknowledged, "presents problems of considerable complexity." The Court requested further arguments from the attorneys
in the cases as well as from the "Attorneys General of the states requiring or permitting segregation in public education." Over a year later, on May 31, 1955, the
Court issued its decree. Rejecting the position of the NAACP that it should require instant and total school desegregation, the Court ordered the states to proceed "with all deliberate speed" to make a "prompt and reasonable start toward
full compliance." uncertain about the response to its decision from other institutions and from the American people, the Court had spoken and American life
had been changed in a fundamental way.*

Opening Argument of Thurgood Marshall Esq.

MR. MARSHALL: May it please the Court:

This case is here on direct appeal from the United States District Court for the
Eastern District of South Carolina. The issue raised in this case was clearly raised
in the pleadings, and was clearly raised throughout the first hearing. After the first
hearing, on appeal to this Court, it was raised prior to the second hearing. It was
raised on motion for judgment, and there can be no question that from the beginning of this case, the filing of the initial complaint, up until the present time, the
appellants have raised and have preserved their attack on the validity of the provision of the South Carolina Constitution and the South Carolina statute.

The specific provision of the South Carolina Code is set forth in our brief at
page ten, and it appears in appellees' brief at page fourteen, and reads as follows:

It shall be unlawful for pupils of one race to attend the schools provided by
boards of trustees for persons of another race.

That is the Code provision.

The constitutional provision is, again, on page ten of our brief, and is:

Separate school shall be provided for children of the white and black races—

This is the significant language:

. . . and no child of either race shall ever be permitted to attend a school provided for children of the other race.

Those are the two provisions of the law of the State of South Carolina under
attack in this particular case.

At the first hearing, before the trial got under way, counsel for the appellees
in open court read a statement in which he admitted that, although prior to that
time they had decided that the physical facilities of the separate schools were
equal, they had concluded finally that they were not equal, and they admitted in

open court that they did not have equality; and at the suggestion of senior Judge Parker this was made as an amendment to the answer, and the question as to physical facilities from that stage on was not in dispute.

At that time, counsel for the appellants, however, made the position clear that the attack was not being made on the "separate but equal" basis as to physical facilities, but the position we were taking was that these statutes were unconstitutional in their enforcement because they not only produced these inevitable inequalities in physical facilities, but that evidence would be produced by expert witnesses to show that the governmentally imposed racial segregation in and of itself was also a denial of equality.

I want to point out that our position is not that we are denied equality in these cases. I think there has been a considerable misunderstanding on that point. We are saying that there is a denial of equal protection of the laws, the legal phraseology of the clause in the Fourteenth Amendment, and not just this point as to equality, and I say that because I think most of the cases in the past have gone off on the point of whether or not you have substantial equality. It is a type of provision that, we think, tends to get us into trouble.

So, pursuing that line, we produced expert witnesses, who had surveyed the school situation, to show the full extent of the physical inequalities, and then we produced expert witnesses. Appellees in their brief comment say that they do not think too much of them. I do not think that the district court thought too much of them. But they stand in the record as unchallenged as experts in their field, and I think we have arrived at the stage where the courts do give credence to the testimony of people who are experts in their fields.

On the question that was raised a minute ago in the other case about whether or not there is any relevancy to this classification on a racial basis or not, in the case of the testimony of [the anthropologist] Dr. Robert Redfield—I am sure the Court will remember his testimony in *Sweatt v. Painter* [one of the graduate school cases]—the district court was unwilling to carry the case over an extra day. Dr. Redfield was stuck with the usual air travel from one city to another. And by agreement of counsel and with approval of the court, we placed into the record Dr. Redfield's testimony.

If you will remember, Dr. Redfield's testimony was to this effect: that there were no recognizable differences from a racial standpoint between children, and that if there could be such a difference that would be recognizable and connected with education, it would be so insignificant as to be unworthy of anybody's consideration. . . .

He has considerable testimony along the lines. But we produced testimony to show what we considered to be the normal attack on a classification statute, that this Court has laid down the rule in many cases set out in our brief, that in the case of the object or persons being classified, it must be shown: one, that there is a difference in the two; two, that the state must show that the difference has a significance with the subject matter being legislated; and the state has made no effort up to this date to show any basis for that classification other than that it would be unwise to do otherwise.

Witnesses testified that segregation deterred the development of the personalities of these children. Two witnesses testified that it deprives them of equal status in the school community, that it destroys their self-respect. Two other witnesses testified that it denies them full opportunity for democratic social development. Another witness said that it stamps him with a badge of inferiority. The summation of that testimony is that the Negro children have road blocks put up in their minds as a result of this segregation, so that the amount of education that they take in is much less than other students take in.

The other significant point is that one witness, [the African American psychologist] Dr. Kenneth Clark, examined the appellants in this very case and found that they were injured as a result of this segregation. The court completely disregarded that.

I do not know what clearer testimony we could produce in an attack on a specific statute as applied to a specific group of appellants.

The only evidence produced by the appellees in this case was one witness who testified as to, in general, the running of the school system and the difference between rural schools and consolidated schools, which had no basis whatsoever on the constitutional question.

Another witness, the South Carolina educator, E. R. Crow, was produced to testify as to the new bond issue that was to go into effect after the hearing in this case, at which time they would build more schools as a result of that money. That testimony was admitted into the record over objection of the appellants. The appellants took the position that anything that was to be talked about in the future was irrelevant to a constitutional issue where a personal and present right was asserted. However, the court overruled the objection. Mr. Crow testified.

Then he was asked as to whether or not it would not be "unwise" to break down segregation in South Carolina. Then Mr. Crow proceeded to testify as an expert. He had six years of experience, I think, as superintendent of schools, and prior to that time he was principal of a high school in Columbia. He testified that it would be unwise. He also testified that he did not know but what the legislature would not appropriate the money.

On cross-examination he was asked as to whether or not he meant by the first statement that if relief was granted as prayed, the appellees might not conform to the relief, and Judge Parker made a very significant statement which appears in the record, that, "If we issue an order in this case, it will be obeyed, and I do not think there is any question about it."

On this second question on examination, when he was asked, who did he use as the basis for his information that this thing would not work in the South, he said he talked to gangs of people, white and colored, and he was giving the sum total of their testimony, or rather their statements to him. And again on cross-examination he was asked to name at least one of the Negroes he talked to, and he could not recall the name of a single Negro he had ever talked to. I think the basis of his testimony on that point should be weighed by that statement on cross-examination.

He also said that there was a difference between what happened in northern states, because they had a larger number of Negroes in the South, and they had a larger problem because the percentage of Negroes was so high. And again on cross-examination, he was asked the specific question:

Well, assuming that in South Carolina the population was 95 percent white and five percent colored, would your answer be any different?

And he said, no, he would make the same answer regardless.

That is the only evidence in the record for the appellees here. They wanted to put on the speech of Professor Howard Odom, and they were refused the right to put the speech in, because, after all, Professor Odom was right across in North Carolina and could have been called as a witness.

So here we have a record that has made no effort whatsoever—no effort whatsoever—to support the legislative determinations of the State of South Carolina. And this Court is being asked to uphold those statute, the statute and the constitutional provision, because of two reasons. One is that these matters are legislative matters, as to whether or not we are going to have segregation. For example, the majority of the court in the first hearing said, speaking of equality under the Fourteenth Amendment:

How this shall be done is a matter for the school authorities and not for the court, so long as it is done in good faith and equality of facilities is offered.

Again the court said, in Chief Judge Parker's opinion:

We think, however, that segregation of the races in the public schools, so long as equality of rights is preserved, is a matter of legislative policy for the several states, with which the Federal courts are powerless to interfere.

So here we have the unique situation of an asserted federal right which has been declared several times by this Court to be personal and present, being set aside on the theory that it is a matter for the state legislature to decide, and it is not for this Court. And that is directly contrary to every opinion of this Court. . . .

MR. JUSTICE FRANKFURTER: May I call your attention to what Mr. Justice Holmes said about the Fourteenth Amendment:

The Fourteenth Amendment itself as an historical product did not destroy history for the state and substitute mechanical departments of law . . .

MR. MARSHALL: I agree, sir.

MR. JUSTICE FRANKFURTER: Then you have to face the fact that this is not a question to be decided by an abstract starting point of natural law, that you cannot have segregation. If we start with that, of course, we will end with that.

MR. MARSHALL: I do not know of any other proposition, sir, that we could consider that would say that because a person who is as white as snow with blue eyes and blond hair has to be set aside.

MR. JUSTICE FRANKFURTER: Do you think that is the case?

MR. MARSHALL: Yes, sir. The law of South Carolina applies that way.

MR. JUSTICE FRANKFURTER: Do you think that this law was passed for the same reason that a law would be passed prohibiting blue-eyed children from attending public schools? You would permit all blue-eyed children to go to separate schools? You think that this is the case?

MR. MARSHALL: No, sir, because the blue-eyed people in the United States never had the badge of slavery which was perpetuated in the statutes.

MR. JUSTICE FRANKFURTER: If it is perpetuated as slavery, then the Thirteenth Amendment would apply.

MR. MARSHALL: But at the time—

MR. JUSTICE FRANKFURTER: Do you really think it helps us not to recognize that behind this are certain facts of life, and the question is whether a legislature can address itself to those facts of life in spite of or within the Fourteenth Amendment, or whether, whatever the facts of life might be, where there is a vast congregation of Negro population as against the states where there is not, whether that is an irrelevant consideration? Can you escape facing those sociological facts, Mr. Marshall?

MR. MARSHALL: No, I cannot escape it. But if I did fail to escape it, I would have to throw completely aside the personal and present rights of those individuals.

MR. JUSTICE FRANKFURTER: No, you would not. It does not follow because you cannot make certain classifications, you cannot make some classifications.

MR. MARSHALL: But the personal and present right that I have to consider, like any other citizen of Clarendon County, South Carolina, is a right that has been recognized by this Court over and over again. And so far as the appellants in this case are concerned, I cannot consider it sufficient to be relegated to the legislature of South Carolina where the record in this Court shows their consideration of Negroes, and I speak specifically of the primary cases.

MR. JUSTICE FRANKFURTER: If you would refer to the record of the case, there they said that the doctrine of classification is not excluded by the Fourteenth Amendment, but its employment by state legislatures has no justifiable foundation.

MR. MARSHALL: I think that when an attack is made on a statute on the ground that it is an unreasonable classification, and competent, recognized testimony is produced, I think then the least that the state has to do is to produce something to defend their statutes.

MR. JUSTICE FRANKFURTER: I follow you when you talk that way.

MR. MARSHALL: But Mr. Justice Frankfurter, I was trying to make three different points. I said that the first one was peculiarly narrow, under the *McLaurin* and the *Sweatt* decision [the graduate school cases]. The second point was that on a classification basis, these statutes were bad. The third point was the broader point, that racial distinctions in and of themselves are invidious. I consider it as a three-pronged attack. Any one of the three would be sufficient for reversal.

MR. JUSTICE FRANKFURTER: You may recall that this Court not so many years ago decided that the legislature of Louisiana could restrict the calling of pilots on the Mississippi to the question of who your father was.

MR. MARSHALL: Yes, sir.

MR. JUSTICE FRANKFURTER: And there were those of us who sustained that legislation, not because we thought it was admirable or because we thought it comported with human notions or because we believed in primogeniture, but for different reasons, that it was so imbedded in the conflict of the history of that problem in Louisiana that we thought on the whole that was an allowable justification.

MR. MARSHALL: But Mr. Justice Frankfurter, I do not think that segregation in public schools is any more ingrained in the South than segregation in transportation, and this Court upset it in the *Morgan* case. I do not think it is any more ingrained.

MR. JUSTICE FRANKFURTER: It upset it in the *Morgan* case on the ground that it was none of the business of the state; it was an interstate problem.

MR. MARSHALL: That is a different problem. But a minute ago the very question was raised that we have to deal with realities, and it did upset that. Take the primary case. There is no more ingrained rule than there were in the cases of *McLaurin* and *Sweatt*, the graduate school cases.

But I say, sir, that most of my time is spent down in the South, and despite all these predictions as to what might happen, I do not think that anything is going to happen any more except on the graduate and professional level. And this Court can take notice of the reports that have been in papers such as *The New York Times*. But it seems to me on that question, this Court should go back to the case of *Buchanan* v. *Warley*, where on the question as to whether or not there was this great problem, this Court in *Buchanan* v. *Warley* said:

That there exists a serious and difficult problem arising from a feeling of race hostility which the law is powerless to control, and to which it must give a measure of consideration, may be freely admitted. But its solution cannot be promoted by depriving citizens of their constitutional rights and privileges.

In this case, granting that there is a feeling of race hostility in South Carolina, if there be such a thing, or granting that there is that problem, we cannot have the individual rights subjected to this consideration of what the groups might do. . . .

So what do we have in the record? We have testimony of physical inequality. It is admitted. We have the testimony of experts as to the exact harm which is inherent in segregation wherever it occurs. That I would assume is too broad for the immediate decision, because after all, the only point before this Court is the statute as it was applied in Clarendon County. But if this Court would reverse and the case would be sent back, we are not asking for affirmative relief. That will not put anybody in any school. The only thing that we ask for is that the state-imposed racial segregation be taken off, and to leave the county school board, the county people, the district people, to work out their own solution of the problem, to assign children on any reasonable basis they want to assign them on.

MR. JUSTICE FRANKFURTER: You mean, if we reverse, it will not entitle every mother to have her child go to a nonsegregated school in Clarendon County?

MR. MARSHALL: No, sir.

MR. JUSTICE FRANKFURTER: What will it do? Would you mind spelling this out? What would happen?

MR. MARSHALL: Yes, sir. The school board, I assume, would find some other method of distributing the children, a recognizable method, by drawing district lines.

MR. JUSTICE FRANKFURTER: What would that mean?

MR. MARSHALL: The usual procedure—

MR. JUSTICE FRANKFURTER: You mean that geographically the colored people all live in one district?

MR. MARSHALL: No, sir, they do not. They are mixed up somewhat.

MR. JUSTICE FRANKFURTER: Then why would not the children be mixed?

MR. MARSHALL: If they are in the district, they would be. But there might possibly be areas—

MR. JUSTICE FRANKFURTER: You mean we would have gerrymandering of school districts?

MR. MARSHALL: Not gerrymandering, sir. The lines could be equal.

MR. JUSTICE FRANKFURTER: I think that nothing would be worse than for this Court—I am expressing my own opinion—nothing would be worse, from my point of view, than for this Court to make an abstract declaration that segregation is bad and then have it evaded by tricks.

MR. MARSHALL: No, sir. As a matter of fact, sir, we have had cases where we have taken care of that. But the point is that it is my assumption that where this is done, it will work out, if I might leave the record, by statute in some states.

MR. JUSTICE FRANKFURTER: It would be more important information in my mind to have you spell out in concrete what would happen if this Court reverses and the case goes back to the district court for the entry of a decree.

MR. MARSHALL: I think, sir, that the decree would be entered which would enjoin the school officials from, one, enforcing the statute; two, from segregating on the basis of race or color. Then I think whatever district lines they draw, if it can be shown that those lines are drawn on the basis of race or color, then I think they would violate the injunction. If the lines are drawn on a natural basis, without regard to race or color, then I think that nobody would have any complaint.

For example, the colored child that is over here in this school would not be able to go to that school. But the only thing that would come down would be the decision that whatever rule you set in, if you set in, it shall not be on race, either actually or by any other way. It would violate the injunction, in my opinion.

MR. JUSTICE FRANKFURTER: There is a thing that I do not understand. Why would not that inevitably involve—unless you have Negro ghettoes, or if you find that language offensive, unless you have concentrations of Negroes, so that only Negro children would go there, and there would be no white children mixed with them, or vice versa—why would it not involve Negro children saying, "I want to go to this school instead of that school"?

MR. MARSHALL: That is the interesting thing in this procedure. They could move over into that district, if necessary. Even if you get stuck in one district, there is always an out, as long as this statute is gone.

There are several ways that can be done. But we have instances, if I might, sir, where they have been able to draw a line and to enclose—this is in the North—to enclose the Negroes, and in New York those lines have on every occasion been declared unreasonably drawn, because it is obvious that they were drawn for that purpose.

MR. JUSTICE FRANKFURTER: Gerrymandering?

MR. MARSHALL: Yes, sir. As a matter of fact, they used the word "gerrymander."

So in South Carolina, if the decree was entered as we have requested, then the school district would have to decide a means other than race, and if it ended up that the Negroes were all in one school, because of race, they would be violating the injunction just as bad as they are by violating what we consider to be the Fourteenth Amendment now.

MR. JUSTICE FRANKFURTER: Now, I think it is important to know, before one starts, where he is going. As to available schools, how would that cut across this problem? If everything was done that you wanted done, would there be physical facilities within such drawing of lines as you would regard as not evasive of the decree?

MR. MARSHALL: Most of the school buildings are now assigned to Negroes, so that the Negro buildings are scattered around in that county. Now, as to whether or not lines could be properly drawn, I say quite frankly, sir, I do not know. But I do know that in most of the southern areas—it might be news to the Court—there are very few areas that are predominantly one race or the other.

The point would come up as to, if a decree in this case should happen to be issued by the district court, or in a case similar to this, as to whether or not there would be a time given for the actual enrollment of the children, etcetera, and changing of children from school to school. It would be my position in a case like that, which is very much in answer to the brief filed by the United States in this case—it would be my position that the important thing is to get the principle established and if a decree were entered saying that facilities are declared to be unequal and that the appellants are entitled to an injunction, and then the district court issues the injunction, it would seem to me that it would go without saying that the local school board had the time to do it. But obviously it could not do it overnight, and it might take six months to do it one place and two months to do it another place.

Again, I say it is not a matter for judicial determination. That would be a matter for legislative determination.

Arguments of John W. Davis, Esq., on Behalf of the Appellees

MR. DAVIS: May it please the Court:

I think if the appellants' construction of the Fourteenth Amendment should prevail here. . . . I am unable to see why a state would have any further right to segregate its pupils on the ground of sex or on the ground of age or on the ground of mental capacity. If it may classify it for one purpose on the basis of admitted facts, it may, according to my contention, classify it for other.

Now, I want to address myself during the course of this argument to three propositions, and I will utilize the remaining minutes of the afternoon to state them.

The first thing which I want to contend for before the Court is that the mandate of the court below, which I quote, required:

> . . . the defendants to proceed at once to furnish plaintiffs and other Negro pupils of said district educational facilities, equipment, curricula, and opportunities equal to those furnished white pupils.

That mandate has been fully complied with. We have been found to have obeyed the court's injunction. The question is no longer in the case, and the complaint which is made by the appellants in their brief, that the school doors should have been immediately thrown open instead of taking the time necessary to readjust the physical facilities, is a moot question at this stage of the case.

The second question to which I wish to address myself is that Article XIV, section 7, of the Constitution of South Carolina, and section 5377 of the Code, both making the separation of schools between white and colored mandatory, do not offend the Fourteenth Amendment of the Constitution of the United States or deny equal protection. The right of a state to classify the pupils in its public schools on the basis of sex or age or mental capacity, or race, is not impaired or affected by that Amendment.

Third, I want to say something about the evidence offered by the plaintiffs upon which counsel so confidently relied. I say that the evidence offered by the plaintiffs, be its merits what it may, deals entirely with legislative policy, and does not treat on constitutional right. Whether it does or not, it would be difficult for me to conceal my opinion that the evidence in and of itself is of slight weight and in conflict with the opinion of other and better informed sources.

When the first hearing was at an end, the court entered its decree, demanding us to proceed forthwith to furnish, not merely physical facilities, as my friend would have it, but educational facilities, equipment, curricula, and opportunities equal on the part of the state for the Negro as for the white pupil. . . .

The district . . . set it down for a hearing in March of 1952, at which time the defendants filed a supplemental report showing the progress up to that precise day and minute. Thereupon, the court declared that the defendants had made every possible effort to comply with the decree of the court, that they had done all that was humanly possible, and that by the month of September, 1952, equality between the races in this area would have been achieved. So the record reads.

What could be done immediately—and with this I shall close for the afternoon—what could be done immediately by this school board was done. Salaries of teachers were equalized. Curricula were made uniform, and the State of South Carolina appropriated money to furnish school buses for black and white. Of course, in these days, the schoolboy no longer walks. The figure of the schoolboy trudging four miles in the morning and back four in the afternoon swinging his books as he went is as much a figure of myth as the presidential candidate born in a log cabin. Both of these characters have disappeared.

I come, then, to what is really the crux of the case. That is the meaning and interpretation of the Fourteenth Amendment to the Constitution of the United States. We devote to that important subject but five pages of our brief. We trust the Court will not treat that summary disposition of it as due to any lack of earnestness on our part.

How should we approach it? I use the language of the Court: An Amendment to the Constitution should be read, you have said,

. . . in a sense most obvious to the common understanding at the time of its adoption. For it was for public adoption that it was proposed.

Still earlier you have said it is the duty of the interpreters,

. . . to place ourselves as nearly as possible in the condition of the men who framed the instrument.

What was the condition of those who framed the instrument? The resolution proposing the Fourteenth Amendment was proffered by Congress in June, 1866. In the succeeding month of July, the same Congress proceeded to establish or to continue separate schools in the District of Columbia, and from that good day to this Congress has not waivered in that policy. It has confronted the attack upon it repeatedly. During the life of Charles Sumner, over and over again, he undertook to amend the law of the District so as to provide for mixed and not for separate schools, and again and again he was defeated.

MR. JUSTICE BURTON: What is your answer, Mr. Davis, to the suggestion mentioned yesterday that at that time the conditions and relations between the two races were such that what might have been unconstitutional then would not be unconstitutional now?

MR. DAVIS: My answer to that is that changed conditions may affect policy, but changed conditions cannot broaden the terminology of the Constitution; the thought is an administrative or a political question, and not a judicial one.

MR. JUSTICE BURTON: But the Constitution is a living document that must be interpreted in relation to the facts of the time in which it is interpreted. Did we not go through with that in connection with child labor cases, and so forth?

MR. DAVIS: Oh, well, of course, changed conditions may bring things within the scope of the Constitution which were not originally contemplated, and of that perhaps the aptest illustration is the interstate commerce clause. Many things have been found to be interstate commerce which at the time of the writing of the Constitution were not contemplated at all. Many of them did not even exist. But when they come within the field of interstate commerce, then they become subject to congressional power, which is defined in terms of the Constitution itself. So circumstances may bring new facts within the purview of the constitutional provision, but they do not alter, expand or change the language that the framers of the Constitution have employed.

MR. JUSTICE FRANKFURTER: Mr. Davis, do you think that "equal" is a less fluid term than "commerce between the states"?

MR. DAVIS: Less fluid?

MR. JUSTICE FRANKFURTER: Yes.

MR. DAVIS: I have not compared the two on the point of fluidity.

MR. JUSTICE FRANKFURTER: Suppose you do it now.

MR. DAVIS: I am not sure that I can approach it in just that sense.

MR. JUSTICE FRANKFURTER: The problem behind my question is whatever the phrasing of it would be.

MR. DAVIS: That what is unequal today may be equal tomorrow or vice versa?

MR. JUSTICE FRANKFURTER: That is it.

MR. DAVIS: That might be. I should not philosophize about it. But the effort in which I am now engaged is to show how those who submitted this Fourteenth Amendment and those who adopted it conceded it to be, and what their conduct by way of interpretation has been since its ratification in 1868.
MR. JUSTICE FRANKFURTER: What you are saying is, that as a matter of history, history puts a gloss upon "equal" which does not permit elimination or admixture of white and colored in this aspect to be introduced?
MR. DAVIS: Yes, I am saying that. I am saying that equal protection in the minds of Congress of the United States did not contemplate mixed schools as a necessity.
What did the states think about this at the time of the ratification? At the time the Amendment was submitted, there were 37 states in the Union. Thirty of them had ratified the Amendment at the time it was proclaimed in 1868. Of those thirty ratifying states, 23 either then had, or immediately installed, separate schools for white and colored children under their public school systems. Were they violating the Amendment which they had solemnly accepted? Were they conceiving of it in any other sense than that it did not touch their power over their public schools?

How do they stand today? Seventeen states in the Union today provide for separate schools for white and colored children, and four others make it permissive with their school boards. Those four are Wyoming, Kansas, of which we heard yesterday, New Mexico, and Arizona; so that you have 21 states today which conceive it their power and right to maintain separate schools if it suits their policy. . . .

It would be an interesting, though perhaps entirely useless, undertaking to enumerate the numbers of men charged with official duty in the legislative and the judicial branches of the Government who have declared that segregation is not per se unlawful. The members of Congress, year after year, and session after session, the members of state constitutional conventions, the members of state legislatures, year after year and session after session, the members of the higher courts of the states, the members of the inferior federal judiciary, and the members of this tribunal—what their number may be, I do not know, but I think it reasonably certain that it must mount well into the thousands, and to this I stress for Your Honors that every one of that vast group was bound by oath to support the Constitution of the United States and any of its Amendments. Is it conceivable that all that body of concurrent opinion was recreant to its duty or misunderstood the constitutional mandate, or was ignorant of the history which gave to the mandate its scope and meaning? I submit not.

Now, what are we told here that has made all that body of activity and learning of no consequence? Says counsel for the plaintiffs, or appellants, we have the uncontradicted testimony of expert witnesses that segregation is hurtful. And in their opinion hurtful to the children of both races, both colored and white. These witnesses severally described themselves as professors, associate professors, assistant professors, and one describes herself as a lecturer and adviser on curricula. I am not sure exactly what that means.

I did not impugn the sincerity of these learned gentlemen and lady. I am quite sure that they believe that they are expressing valid opinions on their subject. But there are two things notable about them. Not a one of them is under any official duty in the premises whatever; not a one of them has had to consider the welfare of the people for whom they are legislating or whose rights they were called on to adjudicate. And only one of them professes to have the slightest knowledge of conditions in the states where separate schools are now being maintained. Only one of them professes any knowledge of the condition within the 17 segregating states.

I want to refer just a moment to that particular witness, Dr. Clark. Dr. Clark professed to speak as an expert and an informed investigator on this subject. His investigating consisted of visits to the Scott's Branch primary and secondary school at Scott's Branch, which he undertook at the request of counsel for the plaintiffs. He called for the presentation to himself of some 16 pupils between the ages of six and nine years, and he applied to them what he devised and what he was pleased to cal an objective test. That consisted of offering to them sixteen white and colored dolls, and inviting them to select the doll they would prefer, the doll they thought was nice, the doll that looked bad, or the doll that looked most like themselves. He ascertained that ten out of his battery of sixteen preferred the white doll. Nine thought the white doll was nice, and seven thought it looked most like themselves. Eleven said that the colored doll was bad, and one that the white doll was bad. And out of that intensive investigation and that application of that thoroughly scientific test, he deduced the sound conclusion that segregation there had produced confusion in the individuals—and I use his language—"and their concepts about themselves conflicting in their personalities, that they have been definitely harmed in the development of their personalities."

That is a sad result, and we are invited to accept it as a scientific conclusion. But I am reminded of the scriptural saying, "Oh, that mine adversary had written a book." And Professor Clark, with the assistance of his wife, has written on this subject and has described a similar test which he submitted to colored pupils in the northern and nonsegregated schools. He found that 62 percent of the colored children in the South chose a white doll; 72 percent in the North chose the white doll; 52 percent of the children in the South thought the white doll was nice; 68 percent of the children in the North thought the white doll was nice; 49 percent of the children in the South thought the colored doll was bad; 71 percent of the children in the North thought the colored doll was bad.

Now, these latter scientific tests were conducted in nonsegregating states, and with those results compared, what becomes of the blasting influence of segregation to which Dr. Clark so eloquently testifies? . . .

It seems to me that much of that which is handed around under the name of social science is an effort on the part of the scientist to rationalize his own preconceptions. They find usually, in my limited observation, what they go out to find.

Once more, Your Honors, I might say: What underlies this whole question? What is the great national and federal policy on this matter? Is it not a fact that the very strength and fiber of our federal system is local self-government in those matters for which local action is competent? Is it not, of all the activities of government, the one which most nearly approaches the hearts and minds of people, the question of the education of their young?

Is it not the height of wisdom that the matter in which that shall be conducted should be left to those most immediately affected by it, and that the wishes of the parents, both white and colored, should be ascertained before their children are forced into what may be an unwelcome contact?

I respectfully submit to the Court, there is no reason assigned here why this Court or any other should reverse the findings of ninety years.

MR. CHIEF JUSTICE VINSON: Mr. Marshall.

Rebuttal argument of Thurgood Marshall, Esq., of behalf of appellants

MR. MARSHALL: May it please the Court:

So far as the appellants are concerned in this case, at this point it seems to me that the significant factor running through all these arguments up to this point is that for some reason, which is still unexplained, Negroes are taken out of the main stream of American life in these states. There is nothing involved in this case other than race and color, and I do not need to go to the background of the statutes or anything else. I just read the statutes, and they say, "white and colored."

While we are talking about the feeling of the people in South Carolina, I think we must once again emphasize that under our form of government, these individual rights of minority people are not to be left to even the most mature judgment of the majority of the people, and that the only testing ground as to whether or not individual rights are concerned is in this Court.

If I might digress just for a moment, on this question of the will of the people of South Carolina, if Ralph Bunche[1] were assigned to South Carolina, his children would have to go to a Jim Crow school. No matter how great anyone becomes, if he happens to have been born a Negro, regardless of his color, he is relegated to that school.

Now, when we talk of the reasonableness of this legislation, the reasonableness, the reasonableness of the Constitution of South Carolina, and when we talk about the large body of judicial opinion in this case, I respectfully remind the Court that the exact same argument was made in the *Sweatt* case, and the brief in the *Sweatt* case contained, not only the same form, but the exact same type of appendix showing all the ramifications of the several decisions which had repeatedly upheld segregated education.

I also respectfully remind the Court that in the *Sweatt* case, as the public policy of the State of Texas, they also filed a public opinion poll of Texas showing that by far the majority of the people of Texas at this late date wanted segregation.

I do not believe that that body of law has any more place in this case than it had in the *Sweatt* case.

I think we should also point out in this regard that when we talk about reasonableness, what I think the appellees mean is reasonable insofar as the legislature of South Carolina decided it to be reasonable, and reasonable to the people of South Carolina. But what we are arguing in this case is as to whether or not it is reasonableness within the decided cases of this Court on the Fourteenth Amendment.

Insofar as the argument about the states having a right to classify students on the basis of sex, learning ability, etcetera, I do not know whether they do or not, but I do believe that if it could be shown that they were unreasonable, they would feel, too, that any of the actions of the state administrative officials that affect any classification must be tested by the regular rules set up by this Court.

So we in truth and in fact have what I consider to be the main issue in this case. They claim that our expert witnesses and all that we have produced are a legislative argument at best; that the witnesses were not too accurate, and were the run-of-the-mill scientific witnesses. But I think if it is true that there is a large body of scientific evidence on the other side, the place to have produced that was in the

---

1. African American United Nations official, winner of the Nobel Peace Prize in 1950.

district court, and I do not believe that the State of South Carolina is unable to produce witnesses for financial or other reasons.

MR. JUSTICE FRANKFURTER: Can we not take judicial notice of writings by people who competently deal with these problems? Can I not take judicial notice of Myrdal's[2] book without having him called as a witness?

MR. MARSHALL: Yes, sir. But I think when you take judicial notice of Gunnar Myrdal's book, we have to read the matter, and not take portions out of context. Gunnar's Myrdal's whole book is against the argument.

MR. JUSTICE FRANKFURTER: That is a different point. I am merely going to the point that in these matters this Court takes judicial notice of accredited writings, and it does not have to call the writers as witnesses. How to inform the judicial mind, as you know, is one of the most complicated problems. It is better to have witnesses, but I did not know that we could not read the works of competent writers.

MR. MARSHALL: Mr. Justice Frankfurter, I did not say that it was bad. I said that it would have been better if they had produced the witnesses so that we would have had an opportunity to cross-examine and test their conclusions. For example, the authority of Hodding Carter, the particular article quoted, was a magazine article of a newspaperman answering another newspaperman, and I know of nothing further removed from scientific work than one newspaperman answering another.

I am not trying—

MR. JUSTICE FRANKFURTER: I am not going to take issue with you on that.

MR. MARSHALL: You would, sir, but I do not believe that there are any experts in the country who would so testify. And the body of law is that—even the witnesses, for example, who testified in the next case coming up, the Virginia case, all of them, admitted that segregation in and of itself was harmful. They said that the relief would not be to break down segregation. But I know of no scientist that has made any study, whether he be anthropologist or sociologist, who does not admit that segregation harms the child.

MR. JUSTICE FRANKFURTER: What the consequences of the proposed remedy are is relevant to the problem.

MR. MARSHALL: I think, sir, that the consequences of the removal of the remedy are a legislative and not a judicial argument, sir. I rely on *Buchanan v. Warley*, where this Court said that insofar as this is a tough problem, it was tough, but the solution was not to deprive people of their constitutional rights.

---

2. Gunnar Myrdal, a Swedish economist who wrote an influential book on American race relations, *An American Dilemma* (1944).

MR. JUSTICE FRANKFURTER: Then the testimony is irrelevant to the question.

MR. MARSHALL: I think the testimony is relevant as to whether or not it is a valid classification. That is on the classification point.

MR. JUSTICE FRANKFURTER: But the consequences of how you remedy a conceded wrong bear on the question of whether it is a fair classification.

MR. MARSHALL: I do not know. But it seems to me that the only way that we as lawyers could argue before this Court, and the only way that this Court could take judicial notice of what would happen, would be that the Attorney General or some responsible individual officer of the State of South Carolina would come to this Court and say that they could not control their own State.

MR. JUSTICE FRANKFURTER: No, that is not what I have in mind. I want to know from you whether I am entitled to take into account, in finally striking this judgment, whether I am entitled to make into account the reservation that Dr. Frank Graham[3] and two others, I believe, made in their report to the President. May I take that into account?

MR. MARSHALL: Yes, sir.

MR. JUSTICE FRANKFURTER: May I weigh that?

MR. MARSHALL: Yes, sir.

MR. JUSTICE FRANKFURTER: Then you have competent consideration without any testimony.

MR. MARSHALL: Yes, sir. But it is a policy matter. And that type of information, I do not believe, is more than persuasive when we consider constitutionally protected rights.

MR. JUSTICE FRANKFURTER: Of course, if it is written into the Constitution, then I do not care about the evidence. If it is in the Constitution, then all the testimony that you introduce is beside the point, in general.

MR. MARSHALL: I think, sir, that so far as the decisions of this Court, this Court has repeatedly said that you cannot use race as a basis of classification.

MR. JUSTICE FRANKFURTER: Very well. If that is a settled constitutional doctrine, then I do not care what any associate or full professor in sociology tells me. If it is

---

3. President of the University of North Carolina.

in the Constitution, I do not care about what they say. But the question is: Is it in the Constitution?

MR. MARSHALL: This Court has said just that on other occasions. They said it in the Fifth Amendment cases, and they also said it in some of the Fourteenth Amendment cases, going back to Mr. Justice Holmes. And I also think—I have no doubt in my mind—that this Court has said that these rights are present, and if all of the people in the State of South Carolina and most of the Negroes still wanted segregated schools, I understand the decision of this Court to be that any individual Negro has a right, if it is a constitutional right, to assert it, and he has a right to relief at the time he asserts that right.

MR. JUSTICE FRANKFURTER: Certainly. Any single individual, just one, if his constitutional rights are interfered with, can come to the bar of this Court and claim it.

MR. MARSHALL: Yes, sir.

12

The Abortion Controversy
Roe v. Wade
1973

Before the mid-nineteenth century, abortions performed before the "quickening," the first perception of fetal movement usually in the fifth month of pregnancy, were widely accepted in American society. Birthrates fell sharply in the early nineteenth century and the use of abortion apparently increased considerably. Abortionists openly advertised their services in the newspapers. State legislatures began to restrict abortion and access to information on birth control. In this, they were strongly encouraged by doctors, newly organized in the American Medical Association, who sought to protect women from health care providers they considered unqualified. Abortion, as a result, became a clandestine activity. Many nineteenth-century feminists opposed abortion as an invitation to unbridled male sexuality.

In the mid-twentieth century, attitudes shifted. A few dramatic incidents generated public support for liberalized abortion laws. In 1962, an epidemic of rubella—which can cause birth defects—generated sympathy for women struck with the disease who sought means of terminating their pregnancies. In the same year, Sherri Finkbine, a married woman with children who hosted a children's television program, discovered that she was likely to have a deformed child as a result of having taken thalidomide during her pregnancy. The national press gave extensive coverage to her struggle to obtain a legal abortion, which ended dramatically with a plane flight to Sweden, where abortion was legal.

Both physicians and feminists, whose predecessors in the nineteenth century had been opponents of abortion, were now on the other side. Doctors sought more liberal legislation. Properly performed abortions had become as safe as delivering a child. And many grew uncomfortable as hospitals frequently performed "therapeutic" abortions on private patients while poorer women desperately scrambled to find service from questionable providers. Even before the Supreme Court spoke on the issue in 1973, an abortion reform movement in the 1960s succeeded in liberalizing the statutes in seventeen states.

SUGGESTIONS FOR FURTHER READING: David J. Garrow, *Liberty and Sexuality: The Right to Privacy and the Making of Roe v. Wade*, New York: Macmillan, 1994; Linda Gordon, *Woman's Body, Woman's Right, Birth Control in America*, New York: Viking Penguin, 1990.

The "Roe" of Roe v. Wade *was a Texas woman, Norma McGorvey, who sued that state for denying her right to an abortion. Sarah Weddington, the attorney who presented the case to the Supreme Court in 1972, was arguing her very first case (Texas law firms were then reluctant to employ women lawyers). She had to argue it twice: only seven justices were sitting so the case was reargued in the next term when two new justices, Lewis Powell and William Rehnquist, joined the court. The arguments ranged over most of the issues that have since dominated the abortion debate: When does life begin? When does a fetus become a person? What is the balance between a woman's right to choose and the state's interest in maternal health and fetal life? Does the Constitution include a right to privacy? Is abortion included in that right?*

Associate Justice Harry Blackmun, speaking for a seven-to-two majority, supported "Roe" based on a right to privacy enunciated in an important 1965 case, Griswold v. Connecticut, *where the court voided a state law forbidding married couples from using contraceptives. Blackmun found the right to privacy assumed in many parts of the Constitution rather than elaborated in any single section. Nor was that right absolute. It had to be balanced against the state's interest in maternal health and "potential life." Blackmun, who had spent a decade as counsel for the famous Mayo Clinic, set this balance not through the traditional standard of "quickening," but by the physician's technical division of pregnancy into trimesters. In the first trimester, the woman's right to privacy was absolute; in the second the state could regulate in favor of maternal health; in the third, both maternal health and "potential life" were issues the state could consider. Justices William Rehnquist and Byron White wrote strong dissents.*

Making abortion legal brought to the surface of American life a profound disagreement. Public opinion polls have consistently shown that a majority of Americans want to see fewer abortions and a different *majority of Americans want to see abortion remain a legal right. While abortion supporters initially won an important victory for reproductive freedom, the decision galvanized opponents of the practice into a large and effective movement that has sharply limited the case's effect. Both the states and the federal government have continued to struggle with law and regulations that express shifting public opinion while remaining constitutional under the Court's complex decision. Political parties remain divided internally over abortion and for millions of voters it remains a crucial political test. The Court has heard a number of subsequent cases modifying* Roe v. Wade *in major ways, but not overturning it. Abortion remains one of the most divisive issue in American public life and* Roe v. Wade *continues to provoke fierce controversy.*

PROCEEDINGS

MR. CHIEF JUSTICE WARREN BURGER: We will hear arguments in No. 18, *Roe* against *Wade.*

Oral Argument of Mrs. Sarah Weddington, on Behalf of the Appellants

MRS. WEDDINGTON: Mr. Chief Justice, and may it please the court:

The instant case is a direct appeal from a decision of the United States District Court for the Northern District of Texas. The court declared the Texas abortion law to be unconstitutional . . . it violated a woman's right to continue or terminate a pregnancy. . . . The Texas law in question permits abortions to be performed only in instances where it is for the purpose of saving the life of the woman. . . .

In Texas, we tell the doctor that unless he can decide whether it's necessary for the purpose of saving her life, and for no other reason, that he is subject to criminal sanctions.

I think it's important to note the range of problems that could be presented to a doctor. The court, for example, cited the instance of suicide—if a woman comes in alleging that she will commit suicide. Is it then necessary for him to do—or can he do—an abortion for the purpose of saving her life? Or, is that a situation where he has to have something more? I think all of those questions cannot be answered, at this point. . . .

In Texas, the woman is the victim. The State cannot deny the effect that this law has on the women of Texas. Certainly there are problems regarding even the use of contraception. Abortion now, for a woman, is safer than childbirth. In the absence of abortions—or, legal, medically safe abortions—women often resort to the illegal abortions, which certainly carry risks of death, all the side effects such as severe infections, permanent sterility, all the complications that result. And, in fact, if the woman is unable to get either a legal abortion or an illegal abortion in our State, she can do a self-abortion, which is certainly, perhaps, by far the most dangerous. And that is no crime. . . .

Texas, for example, it appears to us, would not allow any relief at all, even in situations where the mother would suffer perhaps serious physical and mental harm. There is certainly a great question about it. If the pregnancy would result in the birth of a deformed or defective child, she has no relief. Regardless of the circumstances of conception, whether it was because of rape, incest, whether she is extremely immature, she has no relief.

I think it's without question that pregnancy to a woman can completely disrupt her life. Whether she's unmarried; whether she's pursuing an education; whether she's pursuing a career; whether she has family problems; all of the problems of personal and family life, for a woman, are bound up in the problem of abortion.

For example, in our State there are many schools where a woman is forced to quit if she becomes pregnant. In the City of Austin that is true. A woman, if she becomes pregnant, and if in high school, must drop out of regular education process. And that's true of some colleges in our State. In the matter of employment, she often is forced to quit at an early point in her pregnancy. She has no provision for maternity leave. She has—she cannot get unemployment compensation under our laws, because the laws hold that she is not eligible for employment, being pregnant, and therefore is eligible for no unemployment compensation. At the same time, she can get no welfare to help her at a time when she has no unemployment compensation and she's not eligible for any help in getting a job to provide for herself.

There is no duty for employers to rehire women if they must drop out to carry a pregnancy to term. And, of course, this is especially hard on the many women in Texas who are heads of their own households and must provide for their already existing children. And, obviously, the responsibility of raising a child is a most serious one, and at times an emotional investment that must be made, cannot be denied.

So, a pregnancy to a woman is perhaps one of the most determinative aspects of her life. It disrupts her body. It disrupts her education. It disrupts her employment. And it often disrupts her entire family life. And we feel that, because of the impact on the woman, this certainly—in as far as there are any rights which are fundamental—is a matter which is of such fundamental and basic concern to the woman involved that she should be allowed to make the choice as to whether to continue or to terminate her pregnancy.

Oral Argument of Mr. Jay Floyd, Esq., on Behalf of the State of Texas

MR. FLOYD: Mr. Chief Justice, may it please the Court:

It's an old joke, but when a man argues against two beautiful ladies like this, they are going to have the last word.

MR. FLOYD: I think that the original purpose [of the Texas legislation] Mr. Justice, and the present prevailing purpose, may be the same in this respect. There have been statistics furnished to this Court in various briefs from various groups, and from medical societies of different groups of physicians and gynecologists, or whatever it may be. These statistics have not shown me, for instance—for example, that abortion is safer than normal childbirth. They have not shown me that there are not emotional problems that are very important, resulting from an abortion.

The protection of the mother, at one time, may still be the primary—but the policy considerations, Mr. Justice, would seem to me to be for the State legislature to make a decision.

THE COURT [JUSTICE BURGER]: Certainly that's true. Policy questions are for legislative and executive bodies, both in the State and Federal Governments. But we have here a constitutional question. And, in deciding it, it's important to know what the asserted interest of the State is in the enactment of this legislation.

MR. FLOYD: I am—and this is just from my—I speak personally, if I may—I would think that even when this statute was first passed, there was some concern for the unborn fetus.

THE COURT: When was it enacted?

MR. FLOYD: 1859 was the original statute. This, I believe, was around 1900, 1907.

THE COURT: It goes back—

MR. FLOYD: It goes back—

THE COURT:—to the middle of the nineteenth century?

MR. FLOYD: Yes, sir.

THE COURT: Before that there were no criminal abortion laws in Texas?

MR. FLOYD: As far as I know there were not, no. I think this is, maybe, set out in some of the briefs.

THE COURT: Well, in any event, MR. FLOYD, apart from your personal attitude, your court has spoken on the intent of the statute, has it not?

MR. FLOYD: Yes.

THE COURT: Well, I can't quite square that most recent pronouncement with the earlier decisions of the Texas Court, that refer to the mother as the victim. Can you?

MR. FLOYD: Well, as I say, Your Honor, the—I don't think the courts have come to the conclusion that the unborn has full juristic rights—not yet. Maybe they will. I don't know. I just don't feel like they have, at the present time.

THE COURT: In the first few weeks of pregnancy?

MR. FLOYD: Sir?

THE COURT: In the first few weeks of pregnancy?

MR. FLOYD: At any time, Mr. Justice. We make no distinctions in our statute.

THE COURT: You make no distinctions whether there's life there or not?

MR. FLOYD: We say there is life from the moment of impregnation.

THE COURT: And do you have any scientific data to support that?

MR. FLOYD: Well we begin, Mr. Justice, in our brief, with the development of the human embryo, carrying it through the development of the fetus from about seven to nine days after conception.

THE COURT: Well, what about six days?

MR. FLOYD: We don't know.

THE COURT: But the statute goes all the way back to one hour?

MR. FLOYD: I don't—Mr. Justice, there are unanswerable questions in this field. I—

[*Laughter*]

THE COURT: I appreciate it.

MR. FLOYD: This is an artless statement on my part.

THE COURT: I withdraw the question.

MR. FLOYD: Thank you.

When does the soul come into the unborn—if a person believes in a soul—I don't know.

I assume the appellants now are operating under the Ninth Amendment rights. There are allegations of First Amendment rights being violated. However, I feel there is no merit—this statute does not establish any religion; nor does it prohibit anyone from practicing of any part of any religious group. I see no merit in their contentions that it could possibly be under freedom of speech, or press. In fact, there have been some articles recently in this City's newspaper—yesterday, for instance—about it.

The other constitutional rights that the appellant speaks of, I think, are expressed in two manners: The individual, or marital right of privacy; and, secondly—or the right to choose whether or not to abort a child. Now, if the Does are out of the case, the marital privacy is out of the case. But be that as it may, neither individual nor marital privacy has been held to be absolute. We have legal search and seizure. We have the possession of illegal drugs; the practice of polygamy, and other matters. A parent, I do not believe—or parents, cannot refuse to give their child some form of education.

As far as the freedom over one's body is concerned, this is not absolute—the use of illicit drugs; the indecent exposure legislation; and, as Mr. Goldberg stated in the *Griswold* case, that adultery and fornication are constitutional beyond doubt.

THE COURT: "Are constitutional"? Or do you mean laws against them are constitutional?

MR. FLOYD: The laws against them are constitutional.

Now there is nothing in the United States Constitution concerning birth, contraception, or abortion. Now, the appellee does not disagree with the appellants' statement that a woman has a choice. But, as we have previously mentioned, we feel that this choice is left up to the woman prior to the time she becomes pregnant. . . .

THE COURT: Texas doesn't grant any exemption in the case of a rape, where the woman's pregnancy has resulted from rape—either statutory or otherwise—does it?

MR. FLOYD: There is nothing in our statute about that.

Now, the procedure—

THE COURT: And such a woman wouldn't have had a choice, would she?

MR. FLOYD: The procedure—and now I'm telling the Court something that's outside the record—as I understand, the procedure when a woman is brought in after a rape, is to try to stop whatever has occurred, immediately, by the proper procedure in the hospital. Immediately, she's taken there, if she reports it immediately. But, no, there is nothing in the statute.

Now as I previously informed the Court, the statistics—or the people who prepare the statistics, and the different statistics are not in conformity in connection with the medical aspects of abortion; that is, whether or not it's safer. There are statistics that say it is, and statistics that say it's not. It has been provided to this Court, the common law and the legislative history of abortion; and that the morality of abortion has been injected in various cases by various groups. We think these matters are matters of policy which can be properly addressed by the State legislature. We think that the consideration should be given to the unborn, and in some instances, a consideration should be given for the father, if he would be objective to abortion.

MRS. WEDDINGTON: We are once again before this Court to ask relief against the continued enforcement of the Texas abortion statute. And I ask that you affirm the ruling of the three judge court below which held our statute unconstitutional for two reasons: The first, that it was vague; and the second, that it interfered with the Ninth Amendment rights of a woman to determine whether or not she would continue or terminate a pregnancy.

As you will recall, there are three plaintiffs and one intervenor involved here. The first plaintiff was Jane Roe, an unmarried, pregnant girl who had sought an abortion in the State of Texas and was denied it because of the Texas abortion statute, which provides an abortion is lawful only for the purpose of saving the life of the woman.

In the original action she was joined by a married couple, John and Mary Doe. Mrs. Doe had a medical condition. Her doctor had recommended, first, that she not get pregnant; and, second, that she not take the pill.

After this cause was instituted, and after, in fact, the three judge court had been granted, those three plaintiffs were joined by an intervenor, Dr. Hallford, who was, at the time he intervened, under a pending State criminal prosecution under the statute.

He did not ask that his prosecution be stopped by the court, but rather joined in the original request for a declaratory judgment and injunctive relief against future prosecution. As a matter of fact, he has not—his prosecution has not been continued. But the District Attorney against whom we filed the suit has taken a position that, because there was no injunction, he is still free to institute prosecutions. There is a letter from his office in the Appendix stating that he will continue prosecution. And, in fact, there have been a very limited number of prosecutions in the State of Texas since the three judge court entered its declaratory judgment.

THE COURT: Prosecutions of doctors, you're speaking of?

MRS. WEDDINGTON: Prosecutions of doctors, yes, sir.

The problem that we face in Texas is that even though we were granted a declaratory judgment ruling the law unconstitutional, even though we've been before this Court once in the past, in Texas women still are not able to receive abortions from licensed doctors, because doctors still fear that they will be prosecuted under the statute.

So, if the declaratory judgment was any relief at all, it was an almost meaningful relief, because the women of Texas still must either travel to other states—if they are that sophisticated and can afford it—or they must resort to some other less—some other very undesirable alternatives.

THE COURT: You said "meaningful." You meant "meaningless," didn't you?

MRS. WEDDINGTON: Yes

It's just—in fact, we pointed out in our supplemental brief filed here that there have been something like 1,600 Texas women who have gone to New York City alone for abortions in the first nine months of 1971. In addition, I think the Court would recognize there are many other women going to other parts of the country.

One of the objections that our opponents have raised—the same in this Court—"It's moot because, of course, the woman is no longer pregnant. It's been almost three years since we instituted the original action." And yet we can certainly show that it is a continuing problem to Texas women. There still are unwanted pregnancies. There are still women who, for various reasons, do not wish to continue the pregnancy—whether because of personal health considerations; whether because of their family situation; whether because of financial situations, education, working situations; some of the many things we discussed at the last hearing.

Since the last hearing before this Court, there have been a few cases decided that we wanted to draw the Court's attention to, and are covered in our supplemental brief. In addition, there is a supplemental brief filed by an *amicus* party, Harriet Pilpel, on behalf of Planned Parenthood of New York, that seeks to point out to the Court, at pages 6 and 7 and subsequent pages, some of the changing medical statistics available regarding the procedure of abortion.

For example, that brief points out that the overall maternal death rate from legal abortion in New York dropped to 3.7 per 100,000 abortions in the last half of 1971. And that, in fact, is less than half the death rate associated with live delivery for women. That, in fact, the maternal mortality rate has decreased by about two-thirds to a record low in New York in 1971. That now, in 1971, New York recorded the lowest infant mortality rate ever in that State. That during the first 18 months of—well, from July·1st, 1970, to December 31st, 1971, out-of-wedlock pregnancies have dropped by 14 percent.

We now have other statistics coming from California, and other states, that show that not only has the overall birth rate declined, but the welfare birth rate has also declined accordingly.

As to the women, this is their only forum. They are in a very unique situation for several reasons. First, because of the very nature of the interest involved, their primary interest being the interest associated with the question of whether or not they will be forced by the State to continue an unwanted pregnancy.

In our original brief we alleged a number of constitutional grounds. The main ones that we are relying on before this Court are the Fifth, the Ninth, and the Fourteenth Amendments. There is a great body of precedents. Certainly we cannot say that there is in the Constitution—so stated—the right to an abortion. Neither is there stated the right to travel, or some of the other very basic rights that this Court has held are under the United States Constitution.

The Court has in the past, for example, held that it is the right of the parents, and of the individual, to determine whether or not they will send their child to private school; whether or not their children will be taught foreign languages; whether or not they will have offspring—the *Skinner* case; whether—the right to determine for themselves whom they will marry—the *Loving* case; and even in *Boddie v. Connecticut*, the choice of saying that marriage itself is so important that the State cannot interfere with termination of a marriage, just because the woman is unable to pay the cost. *Griswold*, of course, is the primary case, holding that the State could not interfere in the question of whether or not a married couple would use birth control. And, since then, this Court, of course, has held that the individual has the right to determine—whether they are married or single—whether they will use birth control.

So there is a great body of cases decided in the past by this Court in the areas of marriage, sex, contraception, procreation, child-bearing, and education of children, which say that there are certain things that are so much a part of the individual concern that they should be left to the determination of the individual.

THE COURT: Well, is it critical to your case that the fetus not be a person under the due process clause?

MRS. WEDDINGTON: It seems too me that it is critical, first, that we prove this is a fundamental interest on behalf of the woman, that it is a constitutional right. And, second—

THE COURT: Well, yes. But about the fetus?

MRS. WEDDINGTON: Okay.

And, second, that the State has no compelling State interest. And the State is alleging a compelling State interest in—

THE COURT: Yes. But I'm just asking you, under the Federal Constitution, is the fetus a person, for the protection of due process?

MRS. WEDDINGTON: All of the cases—the prior history of this statute—the common law history would indicate that it is not. The State has shown no—

THE COURT: Well, what about—would you lose your case if the fetus was a person?

MRS. WEDDINGTON: Then you would have a balancing of interest.

THE COURT: Well, you say you have anyway, don't you?

MRS. WEDDINGTON: Excuse me?

THE COURT: You have anyway, don't you? You're going to be balancing the rights of the mother against the rights of the fetus.

MRS.WEDDINGTON: It seems to me that you do not balance constitutional rights of one person against mere statutory rights of another.

THE COURT: You think a State interest, if it's only a statutory interest, or a constitutional interest under the State law, can never outweigh a constitutional right?

MRS. WEDDINGTON: I think—it would seem to me that—

THE COURT: So all talk of compelling State interest is beside the point. It can never be compelling enough.

MRS. WEDDINGTON: If the State could show that the fetus was a person under the Fourteenth Amendment, or under some other Amendment, or part of the Constitution, then you would have the situation of trying—you would have a State compelling interest which, in some instances, can outweigh a fundamental right. This is not the case in this particular situation.

THE COURT: Do you make any distinction between the first month, and ninth month of gestation?

MRS. WEDDINGTON: Our statute does not.

THE COURT: Do you, in your position in this case?

MRS. WEDDINGTON: We are asking, in this case, that the Court declare the statute unconstitutional; the State having proved no compelling interest at all.

There are some states that now have adopted time limits. Those have not yet been challenged. And, perhaps that question will be before this Court. Even those statutes, though, allow exceptions. Well New York, for example, says an abortion is lawful up to 24 weeks. But, even after the 24 weeks it is still lawful where there's rape or incest; where the mother's mental or physical health is involved. In other words, even after that period, it's not a hard and fast cutoff.

Oral Argument of Mr. Flowers for the State of Texas

MR. FLOWERS: It is the position of the State of Texas that, upon conception, we have a human being; a person, within the concept of the Constitution of the United States, and that of Texas, also.

THE COURT: Now how should that question be decided? Is it a legal question? A constitutional question? A medical question? A philosophical question? Or, a religious question? Or what is it?

MR. FLOWERS: Your Honor, we feel that it could be best decided by a legislature, in view of the fact that they can bring before it the medical testimony—the actual people who do the research. But we do have—

THE COURT: So then it's basically a medical question?

MR. FLOWERS: From a constitutional standpoint, no, sir. I think it's fairly and squarely before this Court. We don't envy the Court for having to make this decision.

THE COURT: Do you know of any case, anywhere, that's held that an unborn fetus is a person within the meaning of the Fourteenth Amendment?

MR. FLOWERS: No, sir. We can only go back to what the framers of our Constitution had in mind.

THE COURT: Well, these weren't the framers that wrote the Fourteenth Amendment. It came along much later.

MR. FLOWERS: No, sir. I understand. But the Fifth Amendment—under the Fifth Amendment, no one shall be deprived of the right to life, liberty, and property, without due process of law.

THE COURT: Yes. But then the Fourteenth Amendment defines "person" as somebody who's born, doesn't it?

MR. FLOWERS: I'm not sure about that, sir. I—

THE COURT: All right. Any person born, or naturalized in the United States.

MR. FLOWERS: Yes, sir.

THE COURT: It doesn't—that's not the definition of a "person," but that's the definition of a "citizen."

MR. FLOWERS: Your Honor, it's our position that the definition of a person is so basic, it's so fundamental, that the framers of the Constitution had not even set out to define it. We can only go to what the teachings were at the time the Constitution was framed. We have numerous listings in the brief by Mr. Joe Witherspoon—a professor at the University of Texas—that tries to trace back what was in their mind when they had the "person" concept, when they drew up the Constitution. He quoted Blackstone here in 1765, and he observed in his *Commentaries* that: "Life. This right is inherent by nature in every individual, and exists even before the child is born."

I submit to you that the Declaration of Independence, "We hold these"—

THE COURT: Mr. Flowers, when you quote Blackstone, is it not true that in Blackstone's time abortion was not a felony?

MR. FLOWERS: That's true, Your Honor. But my point there was to see the thinking of the framers of the Constitution, from the people they learned from, and the general attitudes of the times.

THE COURT: Well, I think—I'm just wondering if there isn't basic inconsistency there. And let me go back to something else that you said. Is it not true—or is it true, that the medical profession itself is not in agreement as to when life begins?

MR. FLOWERS: I think that's true, sir. But, from a layman's standpoint, medically speaking, we would say that at the moment of conception from the chromosomes, every potential that anybody in this room has is present—from the moment of conception.

THE COURT: But then you're speaking of potential of right.

MR. FLOWERS: Yes, sir.

THE COURT: With which everyone can agree.

MR. FLOWERS: On the seventh day, I think that the heart, in some form, starts beating. On the 20th day, practically all the facilities are there that you and I have, Your Honor. I think that—

THE COURT: Well, if you're correct that the fetus is a person, then I don't suppose you'd have—the State would have great trouble permitting an abortion, would it?

MR. FLOWERS: Yes, sir.

THE COURT: In any circumstances?

MR. FLOWERS: It would, yes, sir.

THE COURT: To save the life of a mother, or her health, or anything else?

MR. FLOWERS: Well, there would be the balancing of the two lives, and I think that—

THE COURT: Well, what would you choose? Would you choose to kill the innocent one, or what?

MR. FLOWERS: Well, in our statute, the State did choose that way, Your Honor.

THE COURT: Well—

MR. FLOWERS: The protection of the mother.

THE COURT: Well, did the State of Texas say that if it is for the benefit of the health of the wife to kill the husband—

[*Laughter*]

MR. FLOWERS: I'm sorry, I didn't understand your question.

THE COURT: Could Texas say, if it confronts the situation, for the benefit of the health of the wife, that the husband has to die? Could they kill him?

MR. FLOWERS: I wouldn't think so, sir.

THE COURT: Is there any statute in Texas that prohibits the doctor from performing any operation, other than an abortion?

MR. FLOWERS: I don't—I don't think so, sir. And there is another thrust of our argument. If we declare, as the appellees in this case have asked this Court to declare, that an embryo or a fetus is a mass of protoplasm similar to a tumor, then of course the State has no compelling interest whatsoever.

THE COURT: But there is no—the only operation that a doctor can possibly commit that will bring on a criminal penalty is an abortion?

MR. FLOWERS: Yes, sir.

THE COURT: Why?

MR. FLOWERS: As far as—

THE COURT: Well, why don't you limit some other operations?

MR. FLOWERS: Because this is the only type of operation that would take another human life.

THE COURT: Well, a brain operation could.

MR. FLOWERS: Well, there again that would be—I think that in every feat that a doctor performs that he is constantly making this judgment.

THE COURT: Well, if a doctor performs a brain operation and does it improperly, he could be guilty of manslaughter, couldn't he?

MR. FLOWERS: I would think so, if he was negligent.

THE COURT: Well, why wouldn't you charge him with manslaughter if he commits an abortion?

MR. FLOWERS: In effect, Your Honor, we did, in the Statute 1195 that has been very carefully avoided all throughout these proceedings. It's not attacked as unconstitutional, for some reason.

If you will permit me to—

THE COURT: But is it in issue here?

MR. FLOWERS: No, sir. You asked the question about whether we had made manslaughter—or an abortion manslaughter.

THE COURT: Maybe the reason is: Why have two statutes?

MR. FLOWERS: Well, this was in context with—this is 1195. They are attacking 1191 through 1196, but omitted 1195. Here's what 1195 says—provides: "Whoever shall, during the parturition of the mother, destroy the vitality or life in a child in a state of being born, before actual birth—and before actual birth—which child would have otherwise been born alive, which—shall be confined to the penitentiary for life, or not less than five years."

THE COURT: What does the statute mean?

MR. FLOWERS: Sir?

THE COURT: What does it mean?

MR. FLOWERS: I would think that—

THE COURT: That it is an offense to kill a child in the process of childbirth?

MR. FLOWERS: Yes, sir. It would be immediately before childbirth, or right in the proximity of the child being born.

THE COURT: Which is not an abortion.

MR. FLOWERS: Which is not—would not be an abortion, yes, sir. You're correct, sir. It would be homicide.

Gentlemen, we feel that the concept of a fetus being within the concept of a person, within the framework of the United States Constitution and the Texas Constitution, is an extremely fundamental thing.

THE COURT: Of course, if you're right about that, you can sit down, you've won your case.

MR. FLOWERS: Your Honor—

THE COURT: Except insofar as, maybe, the Texas abortion law presently goes too far in allowing abortions.

MR. FLOWERS: Yes, sir. That's exactly right. We feel that this is the only question, really, that this Court has to answer. We have a—

THE COURT: Do you think the case is over for you? You've lost your case, then, if the fetus or the embryo is not a person? Is that it?

MR. FLOWERS: Yes, sir, I would say so.

THE COURT: You mean the State has no interest of its own that it can assert, and—

MR. FLOWERS: Oh, we have interests, Your Honor—preventing promiscuity, say, . . .

THE COURT: Is there any medical testimony of any kind that says that a fetus is a person at the time of inception?

MR. FLOWERS: Your Honor, I would like to call the Court's attention, in answering that question, to what I feel to believe was one of the better culminations of the medical research, and that was Senior Judge Campbell's dissenting opinion in *Doe* v. *Scott*, which is very similar to the case we have before us. He goes in chronological order of what the medical research has determined, from the chromosome structure at the time of conception; what the potential is; down through each day of life, until it's born.

THE COURT: But I understood you to say that the State of Texas says it extends from the date of inception until the child is born.

MR. FLOWERS: The date of conception until the day of—yes, sir.

THE COURT: And that's it?

MR. FLOWERS: Yes, sir.

THE COURT: Now, you're now quoting the judge. I want you to give me a medical, recognizable medical writing of any kind that says that at the time of conception the fetus is a person.

MR. FLOWERS: I do not believe that I could give that to you, without researching through the briefs that have been filed in this case, Your Honor. I'm not sure that I could give it to you after research.

THE COURT: Mr. Flowers—

MR. FLOWERS: Yes, sir?

THE COURT: —did Judge Campbell rely on medical authorities in that statement you're summarizing?

MR. FLOWERS: Yes, sir, he did. . . .

I find no way that I know that any court or any legislature or any doctor anywhere can say that here is the dividing line. Here is not a life; and here is a life, after conception. Perhaps it would be better left to that legislature. There they have the facilities to have some type of medical testimony brought before them, and the opinion of the people who are being governed by it.

THE COURT: Well, if you're right that an unborn fetus is a person, then you can't leave it to the legislature to play fast and loose dealing with that person. In other words, if you're correct, in your basic submission that an unborn fetus is a person, then abortion laws such as that which New York has are grossly unconstitutional, isn't it?

MR. FLOWERS: That's right, yes.

THE COURT: Allowing the killing of people.

MR. FLOWERS: Yes, sir.

THE COURT: A person.

MR. FLOWERS: Your Honor, in Massachusetts, I might point out—

THE COURT: Definitely it isn't up to the legislature. It's a constitutional problem, isn't it?

MR. FLOWERS: Well, if there would be any exceptions within this—

THE COURT: The basic constitutional question, initially, is whether or not an unborn fetus is a person, isn't it?

MR. FLOWERS: Yes, sir, and entitled to the constitutional protection.

THE COURT: And that's critical to this case, is it not?

MR. FLOWERS: Yes, sir, it is. And we feel that the treatment that the courts have given unborn children in descent, in distribution of property rights, tort laws, have all pointed out that they have, in the past, have given credence to this concept.

THE COURT: Mr. Flowers, doesn't the fact that so many of the state abortion statutes do provide for exceptional situations in which an abortion may be performed—and presumably these date back a great number of years, following Mr. Justice Stewart's comment—suggest that the absolute proposition that a fetus from the time of conception is a person, just is at least against the weight of historical legal approach to the question?

MR. FLOWERS: Yes, sir. I would think, possibly, that that would indicate that. However, Your Honor, in this whole field of abortion here, we have on the one hand great clamoring for this liberalization of it. Perhaps this is good. Population explosion. We have just so many things that are arriving on the scene in the past few years that might have some effect on producing this type of legislation, rather than facing the facts squarely. I don't think anyone has faced the fact, in making a decision, whether this is a life, in a person concept.

Thank you, Your Honors.

THE COURT: Mr. Flowers, when was the first abortion statute adopted in your State?

MR. FLOWERS: Your Honor, in 1854.

THE COURT: Prior to 1854, what was the situation in Texas?

MR. FLOWERS: I do not think it was an offense, Your Honor. I think it was silent—the State was silent.

THE COURT: So, on your theory, destruction of the person in the form of a fetus was legal?

MR. FLOWERS: Yes, sir. Well, at least the legislature hadn't spoken on it, Your Honor.

THE COURT: Then it was legal.

MR. FLOWERS: Yes, sir.

THE COURT: Mr. Flowers, did Texas have an abortion statute on the books at the time—at least in the eyes of the North—when it was readmitted to the Union after the Civil War?

MR. FLOWERS: No, sir. The State was admitted to the Union in 1845, Your Honor, and—

THE COURT: Well, at the time that it was—passed muster with the—

MR. FLOWERS: When it was a republic?

THE COURT: Well, my historical impression is that following the Civil War Congress went through the procedure, at any rate, of readmitting the states which had seceded. And passing on their constitutional provisions, and that sort of thing. Did Texas have an abortion statute at that time?

MR. FLOWERS: Yes, sir. It was passed in 1854, Your Honor.

THE COURT: Do you know, as a matter of historical fact, when most of these abortion statutes came on the books?

MR. FLOWERS: I think it was—most of them were in the mid-1800s, Your Honor.

THE COURT: In fact, the latter half of the Nineteenth Century?

MR. FLOWERS: Yes, sir.

THE COURT: Do you know why they all came on at that time?

MR. FLOWERS: No, sir, I surely don't.

THE COURT: So that the materials indicate that, during that period, they were enacted to protect the health and lives of pregnant women, because of the danger of operative procedures generally around that time?

MR. FLOWERS: I'm sure that was a great factor, Your Honor.

THE COURT: Well, isn't it historically pretty well accepted as a fact that in the early period of the history of this country there was a general reliance upon religious disciplines to preclude this kind of activity—abortions—and when that didn't seem to cover it, then the states began to enact the statutes?

MR. FLOWERS: Yes, sir.

THE COURT: As had been done in England.

MR. FLOWERS: Also in the exploration and the Indian days, if you wish, frontier days, I don't imagine that too many abortions—intentional abortions—were created in this, these United States. People were of such a necessity to develop the United States.

Thank you, Your Honor.

Rebuttal Argument of Mrs. Sarah R. Weddington, on Behalf of the Appellants

MRS. WEDDINGTON: Thank you, Your Honor.

I think Mr. Flowers well made the point when he said that no one can say "here is the dividing line; here is where life begins; life is here; and life is not over here."

In a situation where no one can prove where life begins, where no one can show that the Constitution was adopted—that it was meant to protect fetal life, in those situations where it is shown that that kind of decision is so fundamentally a part of individual life of the family, of such fundamental impact on the person—

THE COURT: Well, I gather your argument is that a state may not protect the life of the fetus or prevent an abortion even at any time during pregnancy?

Right up until the moment of birth?

MRS. WEDDINGTON: At this time my point is that this particular statute is unconstitutional. . . .

As to the Hippocratic oath, it seems to me that the oath was adopted at a time when abortion was extremely dangerous to the health of the woman. And, second, that the oath is to protect life. And here the question is: What does life mean in this particular context? It's the same vagueness. . . .

In this case, this Court is faced with a situation where there have been 14 three judge courts that have ruled on the constitutionality of abortion statutes. Nine courts have favored the women, five have gone against her; 25 judges have favored the woman, 17 have gone against her; 9 circuit judges have favored the woman, 5 have gone against her; 16 district court judges have favored the woman, 10 have gone against her.

No one is more keenly aware of the gravity of the issues or the moral implications of this case, that it is a case that must be decided on the Constitution. We do not disagree that there is a progression of fetal development. It is the conclusion to be drawn from that upon which we disagree.

We are not here to advocate abortion. We do not ask this Court to rule that abortion is good, or desirable in any particular situation. We are here to advocate that the decision as to whether or not a particular woman will continue to carry or will terminate a pregnancy is a decision that should be made by that individual; that, in fact, she has a constitutional right to make that decision for herself; and that the State has shown no interest in interfering with that decision.

THE COURT: But any doctor, I suppose you would say, may refuse her?

MRS. WEDDINGTON: Certainly, Your Honor. He may refuse any kind of medical procedure whatsoever.

THE COURT: But the State may not—yes.

MRS. WEDDINGTON: Here it's the question of whether or not the State, by the statute, will force the woman to continue. The woman should be given that freedom, just as the doctor has the freedom to decide what procedures he will carry out, and what he will refuse to his patients.

THE COURT: To be sure that I get your argument in focus, I take it from your recent remarks that you are urging upon us abortion on demand of the woman alone, not in conjunction with her physician?

MRS. WEDDINGTON: I am urging that, in this particular context, this statute is unconstitutional. That in the *Baird* v. *Eisenstadt* case this Court said, "If the right of privacy is to mean anything, it is the right of the individual, whether married or single, to make determinations for themselves."

It seems to me that you cannot say this is a woman of this particular doctor, and this particular woman. It is, it seems to me—

THE COURT: Well, doesn't it follow from that, then, that a woman can come into a doctor's office and say, "I want an abortion"?

MRS. WEDDINGTON: And he can say, "I'm sorry, I don't perform them."

THE COURT: And then what does she do?

MRS. WEDDINGTON: She goes elsewhere, if she so chooses. If she stays with that—you know, that's an impossible question. Certainly I don't think the State could say the first doctor a woman goes to shall make that determination, and she cannot go elsewhere.

MR. CHIEF JUSTICE BURGER: Your time is up now, Mrs. Weddington.

MRS. WEDDINGTON: Thank you.

MR. CHIEF JUSTICE BURGER: Thank you, Mrs. Weddington. Thank you, Mr. Flowers.

The case is submitted.

13

Life and Death
In the Matter of Karen Ann Quinlan
1976

As late as 1950, most Americans died at home surrounded—if they were fortunate—by people, not by expensive high-technology life-preserving machinery. But in the next twenty-five years rapid advances in medicine revolutionized the way Americans died. The overwhelming majority of deaths now occurred in institutions such as hospitals and nursing homes where new devices could keep comatose patients alive, often for years. Many of the ethical, legal, and practical implications of this stunning change first drew public notice and debate in 1975 when the parents of a young New Jersey woman, Karen Ann Quinlan, reduced to a "persistent vegetative state" by ingesting alcohol and tranquilizers requested that their daughter be removed from the respirator which assisted her breathing and be allowed to die "with grace and dignity."

The parents, Thomas and Julia Quinlan, filed suit after their daughter's physicians refused to disconnect the respirator fearing that doing so might constitute malpractice or even homicide. The first hearing went against the Quinlans, but on appeal the New Jersey Supreme Court in 1976 ruled in their favor. That decision set several important precedents. Once medical authorities saw "no reasonable possibility" of recovery, the patient's right to privacy exceeded the state's interest in preserving life. The final decision, the court announced, rested with the family, not with doctors or courts. And no one would be held criminally liable for removing life support: death at that point was considered to be "from existing natural causes."

Just as the case had stirred national debate on the ethical dilemma raised by artificial life supports, so the decision influenced policy in many states and led to a Presidential Commission in 1981 which recommended a legal definition of death as the cessation of brain function in place of the previous standard of a discernible heartbeat. The director of that commission, Alexander M. Capron, remarking on the importance of the case asserted that: "Karen Quinlan in her mute, comatose condition became one of the world's great teachers." She re-

---

SUGGESTIONS FOR FURTHER READING: *New York Times*, June 12, 1985 (Obituary); Joseph and Julia Quinlan, with Phyllis Battelle, *Karen Ann: The Quinlans Tell Their Story*, Garden City, New York: Doubleday and Company, 1977; *The Complete Legal Briefs, Court Proceedings, and Decision in the Superior Court of New Jersey*, vol. I (Trenton, NJ: 1989), *passim*.

mained alive for nine years after the respirator was removed, dying in 1985 at age thirty-one.

The Plaintiff, Joseph Thomas Quinlan, [residing at 510 Ryerson Road, Landing, New Jersey, says]:

He, and his wife, Julia Ann Quinlan, are the adoptive parents of Karen Ann Quinlan who was born on the 29th day of March, 1954, is domiciled at 510 Ryerson Road, Landing, New Jersey, and is presently confined to the Intensive Care Unit at Saint Clare's Hospital in Denville, New Jersey, where her vital processes are artificially sustained via the extraordinary means of a mechanical MA-1 Respirator.

He has the care and custody of the said Karen Ann Quinlan.

The said Karen Ann Quinlan is an incompetent as a result of unsoundness of mind, as appears from the Affidavits of the Physicians annexed hereto. She is unable to govern herself and manage her affairs and has been in this state for approximately six months.

On April 15, 1975, the said Karen Ann Quinlan was admitted to the Intensive Care Unit of the Newton Memorial Hospital, 75 High Street, Newton, New Jersey, in a coma of unknown etiology. A Tracheotomy was performed and she was transferred to the Intensive Care Unit of Saint Clare's Hospital on April 24, 1975, where her vital processes are artificially sustained via the extraordinary means of a mechanical MA-1 Respirator.

After consultation with his Religious, Medical and Legal counsellors, with the support of his wife, Julia, his son, John, and his daughter, Mary Ellen, and in concert with the tenets and teachings of their shared Catholic faith and the expressed desires of his daughter, Karen Ann Quinlan, the Plaintiff, Joseph Thomas Quinlan therefore, with awe, sets before the Court the following prayer:

WHEREFORE, the Plaintiff, Joseph Thomas Quinlan, respectfully prays that this Honorable Court enter a judgment adjudicating Karen Ann Quinlan to be mentally incompetent as a result of unsoundness of mind and granting to the Plaintiff letters of guardianship with the express power of authorizing the discontinuance of all extraordinary means of sustaining the vital processes of his daughter, Karen Ann Quinlan.

DATED: This 10th day of September, 1975.

Affidavit of Physician

ROBERT J. MORSE: Being duly sworn, says:

I am a permanent resident of this State and a physician licensed to practice medicine in the State of New Jersey. I am and have been in the actual practice of medicine and surgery for 6 years. I was given the degree of D.O. from the Chicago College of Osteopathic Medicine.

I am not a relative either through blood or marriage of Karen Quinlan, the alleged incompetent. I am not the proprietor, director or chief executive of any institution for the care and treatment of the insane in which the said Karen Quinlan is living or in which it is proposed to place her; nor am I professionally employed by the management thereof as a resident physician; nor am I financially interested therein.

On 4/25, 1975, Karen Quinlan was admitted to Saint Clare's Hospital, at Denville, New Jersey.

In my opinion, the said Karen Quinlan is unfit and unable to govern herself and to manage her affairs.

My opinion is based upon the circumstances and present condition of said Karen Quinlan and a history of her condition, as set forth below:

This 21 year old female is presently confined to the Intensive Care Unit at St. Clare's Hospital at Denville, New Jersey where she manifests decorticate posturing, oculopharangeal movements, and requires an MA-1 Respirator to maintain life. Because of this patient's neurological condition she is unable to communicate by verbal or auditory or written communications. I do not feel that this patient is capable of handling her own affairs.

I have examined the said Karen Quinlan personally from time to time over a period of 5 months, the last examination having been made on 8/28/75.

Affidavit of Physician

ARSHAD JAVED: being duly sworn, says:

I am a permanent resident of this State and a physician licensed to practice medicine in the State of New Jersey. I am and have been in the actual practice of medicine and surgery for 2 years. I was given the degree of M.D. from the Nishtarr Medical College, University of Punjab, Pakistan.

I am not a relative either through blood or marriage of Karen Quinlan, the alleged incompetent. I am not the proprietor, director or chief executive of any institution for the care and treatment of the insane in which the said Karen Quinlan is living or in which it is proposed to place her; nor am I professionally employed by the management thereof as a resident physician; nor am I financially interested therein.

On April 24, 1975, Karen Quinlan was admitted to Saint Clare's Hospital, at Denville, New Jersey.

In my opinion, the said Karen Quinlan is unfit and unable to govern herself and to manage her affairs.

My opinion is based upon the circumstances and present condition of said Karen Quinlan and a history of her condition, as set forth below:

Since admission to St. Clare's Hospital, patient has required assisted mechanical ventilation; has extensive cerebral damage. Patient is fed through nasogastric tube. Has been in this condition for more than four months, and there is no hope of improvement in patient's condition.

I have examined the said Karen Quinlan personally from time to time over a period of 4 months, the last examination having been made on August 28, 1975.

*　　*　　*

**In the
Superior Court of New Jersey
Chancery Division, Morris County**

*In the Matter of Karen Quinlan
an Alleged Incompetent*

ORDER APPOINTING GUARDIAN AD LITEM

The Court having determined, after consideration of the application and affidavits filed in the above matter and after consideration of the relief sought, that a Guardian ad Litem be appointed for Karen Quinlan.

It is on the 15th day of September 1975 ORDERED, pursuant to Rule 4:26-2(b)(4) that Daniel Coburn, Esq. be appointed Guardian ad Litem of Karen Quinlan to represent her in this action.

DANIEL R. COBURN, being duly sworn, says:

I am an Attorney-At-Law of the State of New Jersey;

On September 15, 1975, I was appointed Guardian ad Litem of Karen Quinlan for purposes of the above action;

Pursuant to the Order to Show Cause filed in this matter providing that affidavits of the various parties should be filed on or before September 19, 1975, I feel obligated to file this affidavit setting forth my position as it exists at the present time. It should be noted that this is certainly not a final position by myself as Guardian ad Litem of Karen Quinlan but rather my position based on the facts, medical opinions and law as I understand it today;

The application by Paul W. Armstrong, Esq. on behalf of Plaintiff Joseph Thomas Quinlan, father of Karen Quinlan, requests two particular forms of relief: First, a judgment by this Court that Karen Quinlan is mentally incompetent at the present time and, second, granting Joseph Quinlan "letters of guardianship with the express power of authorizing discontinuance of all extraordinary means of sustaining the vital processes of his daughter."

As a result of every effort possible on my part, I feel obligated to bring to the Court's attention a number of factors why the aforementioned request should be denied at least insofar as the present time is concerned:

On September 15, 1975 at approximately 8:00 p.m., I visited with Karen Quinlan in the Intensive Care Unit at St. Clare's Hospital, Denville, New Jersey. Her condition, as best I could determine, can be described as follows: She is presently being maintained on a mechanical respirator connected to her body apparently as a result of a tracheotomy; her eyes are open and move in a circular manner as she breathes; her eyes blink approximately three or four times per minute; her forehead evidenced very noticeable perspiration; her mouth is open while the respirator expands to ingest oxygen and while her mouth is open, her tongue appeared to be moving in a rather random manner; her mouth closes as the oxygen is ingested into her body through the tracheotomy and she appears to be slightly convulsing or gasping as the oxygen enters her windpipe; her hands are visible in emaciated form, facing in a praying position away from her body; her present weight would seem to be in the vicinity of 70/80 pounds and her legs appear to be tucked towards her body rather than extended in the normal extended position. There were no visible means of mechanical support attached to her other than the respirator but other mechanical devices apparently of a diagnostic nature were present near her bed. . . .

On the basis of all the foregoing resources that I have consulted, it would appear at this time that the definition of "brain death" given its most flexible interpretation requires the existence of four specific conditions to exist. Summarizing those conditions, it is first necessary that there must be a total unawareness to extraordinary applied stimuli and complete unresponsiveness. As I understand it, this would mean that a person would not respond to any stimuli. In Karen's situation, I was unable to make an objective determination that was helpful to the physicians I consulted from which they could formulate any opinion before examinations are conducted. The second factor is that there should be no spontaneous muscular movements or spontaneous respiration. As I understand it, the only way to determine whether there is spontaneous breathing is to turn off the respirator for approximately three minutes in order to determine whether the patient can breathe spontaneously. Obviously, I was in no position nor had I any intentions to attempt that at the time of my visit with Karen. However, insofar as no movements of the body is concerned, it appeared to me that as the oxygen was being ingested into her body, Karen moved slightly, her mouth definitely closed and her tongue seemed to be moving in a rather uncontrollable fashion. The significance of my observations certainly could have no substantial bearing on the ultimate medical decisions in this matter but the physicians I consulted indicated to me that the conditions I described are not totally consistent with any elimination of "brain death." The other factor is the absence of reflexes on the part of the patient. As I understand this criteria, certain body reflexes such as yawning, blinking of eyes, swallowing, and vocal sounds would be absent. There is absolutely no doubt that I witnessed Karen blinking, that she was attempting, at least, to swallow, and her eyes were moving. The physicians I consulted again indicated that the conditions as I described them also were not consistent with "brain death." The final factor to be considered is the presence of a flat electroencephalogram. My information insofar as this particular facet of the case is concerned is based primarily on the statement made publicly by the attorney for the Quinlan family and other press information from allegedly "informed sources," which indicates the existence of some minimal brain waves on the electroencephalogram conducted at St. Clare's Hospital. Assuming that such information is accurate, my physicians indicated to me that this would be another factor inconsistent of a finding of "brain death" insofar as Karen is concerned. More importantly, however, there is apparently a specific method of demonstrating an E.E.G. in cases where the determination is to be made as to whether a person is "brain dead." At this point, it would seem that no one is totally certain as how the E.E.G. conducted in this case was performed, nor in all frankness, does there appear to be any documentation of exactly what the results of the test conducted at St. Clare's Hospital are. I am in no way implying nor should it be intended that the E.E.G. referred to in the press does not, in fact, exist or that it was not conducted consistent with the highest medical standards or that there is any question as to the reliability of the informed sources involved. I merely state that my physicians have indicated to me that it would be well advised for me to obtain the volunteer services of a person who specializes in the administration of E.E.G.s for purposes of conducting specific type of E.E.G. necessary for any determination of "brain death." I am in the process of contacting such a specialist and will utilize his services at the earliest possible moment;

On the basis of all of the foregoing, it would seem that at least for the present time, there is substantial doubt on my part that Karen Quinlan is "brain dead" as that term is used in medical and legal treatises. . . .

Briefly stated, the results of my research indicate that no court has authorized the cessation of supportive mechanical devices necessary to sustain life such as the respirator in the present case regardless of whether "brain death" has occurred or not. Insofar as the question of "brain death" is concerned, this particular case would appear to be one of first impression. The argument pro and con concerning such an extraordinary situation involve theological, ethical, medical, practical, and most important to me as Karen's guardian, legal considerations. Quite obviously, there is no statute in the State of New Jersey authorizing the relief sought by Joseph Quinlan. That is not to say that such relief is therefore automatically barred. Analogies can certainly be drawn to heart transplant cases where removal of the heart from the body has apparently been authorized. However, in this case as previously stated, there is no substantial evidence to indicate the existence of "brain death." That fact standing alone compels me at this time as Karen's guardian to strenuously oppose the application filed on behalf of her father. Moreover, the lack of proof of "brain death" also would seem to raise serious problems insofar as the theological question of whether the Catholic Church condones the removal of the respirator in a situation such as this. In what little research on the subject I have been able to do and based on very few conversations with people of the Catholic faith whose opinions I respect, it would seem to me that there is a vast distinction between terminating supportive treatment in a situation involving a person whose death is imminent and whose brain death has occurred versus a person whose death is unpredictable and whose brain death is seriously disputed. In any event, that particular issue remains unsolved at this time.

Assuming that the allegations in the Order to Show Cause are not meant to indicate that Karen has suffered "brain death," then the only other interpretation that I can give to the request is that her life be terminated because her medical condition is hopeless, based on the words of Dr. Arshad Javed as set forth in his Affidavit supporting this application: "There is no hope of improvement in patient's condition." Without debating the moral, theological or practical considerations in such an application, it is absolutely certain in my mind that such a request is, in effect, asking that this Court authorize a "mercy killing." Without in any way intending to impugn the intentions or attitudes of any other party to this matter, it is my considered opinion as Karen's guardian and as an attorney-at-law of the State of New Jersey that such action is totally without precedent in the law and at this point would constitute a homicide. . . .

Joseph Thomas Quinlan.

Called as a witness on behalf of the plaintiffs, being duly sworn, testifies as follows:

Direct Examination

BY MR. ARMSTRONG [Quilan's attorney]

Q. Mr. Quinlan, will you please state your name?

A. Joseph Thomas Quinlan.

Q. Thank you, Joe.

You are the plaintiff in this case, are you not?

A. Yes, sir.

Q. Are you married?

A. Yes, I am.

Q. And to whom?

A. Julia Quinlan.

Q. And do you have any children?

A. Yes, I have three children.

Q. Three children?

A. Yes.

Q. And are you the father of Karen Ann Quinlan?

A. Yes, I am. . . .

Q. Mr. Quinlan, do you belong to an organized religion?

A. Yes, I do.

Q. Will you please tell the Court which faith this is?

A. Roman Catholic.

Q. Are you a member of a particular parish?

A. Yes, I am.

Q. Which parish is that, Mr. Quinlan?

A. Our Lady of the Lake Church in Mount Arlington.

Q. Have you raised your children as followers of this religion?

A. Yes, I have. . . .

Q. Mr. Quinlan, I show you this and ask you to identify it for the Court, please.

A. Yes. This is Karen, our daughter, Karen's baptismal certificate from Our Lady of the Lake parish. She was baptized at Our Lady of the Lake. . . .

Q. Is your daughter Karen Ann Quinlan a member of the Roman Catholic faith?

A. Yes, she is.

Q. Is she a member of Our Lady of the Lake parish?

A. She is. By "a member," you mean she has attended church?

Q. Is she considered to be a member of the parish?

A. She's a member. She doesn't ordinarily attend Mass there. She attends Christ House, different places with her own, you know, age group.

Q. I understand.

Mr. Quinlan, will you please explain how you, and to the Court, how you and your family arrived at your decision to seek the aid of this Court to resolve the tragic plight of your daughter?

A. It's going to be rather difficult. I'm afraid it will take time. If you'll bear with me. This decision took six months to arrive at. . . .

Q. When did you arrive at that decision?

A. I am terrible at dates.

Q. I am sorry. Go on.

A. I would say late August, early September, after the meetings that we had.

Q. What meetings were those?

A. With the doctors.

Q. What doctors?

A. Various medical meetings that we had with Dr. Javed and Dr. Morse.

Q. Could you explain to the Court what went on at these various medical meetings?

A. They would report to us Karen's medical condition, and they were very pessimistic, the reports that they had given us. I remember one time Dr. Morse, whom I love very much, and Dr. Javed both, I felt he didn't want me to get my hopes up, and at that time I had an awful lot of hope and I had an awful lot of faith, and I just felt this wasn't going to happen, but I wasn't ready for Dr. Morse at that time. But he had been telling me continuously not to get your hopes up, and at one time he had told me that, even if by some miracle Karen should survive, I would never take her home; she would spend the rest of her life in an institution. I thought on this and prayed on this all the way home in the car, and by the time I reached home, I had resolved my mind to the fact that, if this was God's will, I would accept it. I would take her under any conditions, as long as I had her.

Q. Mr. Quinlan, did you then seek the aid of your religion?

A. Not yet. I still wasn't convinced. As the reports got steadily worse, I was just told that there wasn't any hope, that Karen was going to die. It was just a matter of time. Dr. Morse couldn't tell me whether it would be six months, a year. The best estimate that he would give me is that he didn't think she would last a year. A year is a long time under those conditions.

Gradually, after all of these meetings, I finally became convinced that this had to be the Lord's will, that he was going to take Karen.

Q. Who was present at these meetings, Mr. Quinlan?

A. There were a number of meetings all along, and towards the end, I guess they became like official meetings, where, you know, Dr. Javed and Dr. Morse and Father Pat, a witness, in the room, and stuff like that; our whole family was there. These came pretty close to the end.

Q. Who is Father Pat?

A. Father Pat is the Chaplain at St. Clare's Hospital.

Q. Did you seek his aid and counsel at any time?

A. Yes, I did. I would say after I had arrived at my decision, and then, of course, I found out for the first time that my entire family had already arrived at this decision. . . . I realized that my decision was final, and that is when I had to seek the counsel of Father Tom. I realized I would have problems with this decision that I knew I had to make.

Q. Was it Father Tom, did you say?

A. Father Tom first.

Q. Who is Father Tom?

A. Father Tom is my pastor, Father Thomas Trapasso. I am sorry.

Q. Of what church is he pastor?

A. Our Lady of the Lake.

Q. Would you tell us what advice he had given you?

A. Well, I hadn't thought about it too much at that time, because it just seemed like a natural follow-up, you know, the fact that we had done everything possible for Karen, and now we had reached this point where there wasn't any hope. It just seemed like the natural step to go into, to consider, and then the artificial means.

This I spoke to Father Tom about, and the fact that I had a problem with the decision, realizing that I was the holdout. . . .

Q. Tell us how you felt after you received advice from Father Tom concerning this?

A. I felt a lot better, a lot better. He had enlightened me, helped me with my own conscience, and I felt a lot better about it.

Q. Were you able to make this decision?

A. Yes, I was. I think I had actually reached the decision before, but in talking with Father Tom, my pastor, it became definite.

Q. How did Doctors Morse and Javed advise you as to Karen's condition, Mr. Quinlan?

A. As to her condition, at that point they were both telling me that it was hopeless, and she just wouldn't survive.

Q. What advice did you receive from the physicians concerning this condition?

A. One of them advised, the advice of one of the physicians, was that we terminate it, that we turn the machine off.

Q. Who was that?

A. Dr. Javed. Dr. Morse was the doctor in charge of the case, and Dr. Morse, at that time, didn't advise any way, one way or the other. He simply stated the medical facts and more or less left the decision up to us; but he didn't advise us as to the machine at that time. That was one of the meetings near the end. There were several near the end; I guess they were about a week apart, approximately.

Q. Did there subsequently come a time when you requested of both physicians to remove this treatment?

A. Yes. After I had spoken to Father Tom, Father Pat, the whole family was in agreement at that time, and we felt it was the right and proper and moral thing to do. Then we asked for a meeting with Dr. Javed and Dr. Morse, and we had this meeting, and at the meeting—first of all, Father Pat spoke on the Church, how our own Church felt about this. He was able to quote—I guess I shouldn't be commenting on what he said—but anyway, he was able to quote, going back as far as Piux XII in 1958–1957—when he not only said that in certain cases extraordinary means are not required of a Roman Catholic, but in certain cases it is preferable not to use them. I remember those words well. . . .

I think it was the next day, or the same night, we had a paper drawn up, and there was a couple papers. I think the first one wasn't proper or something. And the hospital had another paper drawn up, a permission slip that my wife had to sign—

Q. A release?

A. —formally requesting the hospital and the doctors to turn the machine off, and releasing them of any and all responsibility. We signed the paper and we thought that was it. And that night we went home, and we were resolved that it was going to happen like the next day.

Cross-Examination

Q. Mr. Quinlan, in your testimony on direct examination by Mr. Armstrong, as I recall, you made no mention of exercising, on Karen's behalf, some right of religious belief that she had. Do you have any evidence to indicate that Karen's religious belief, that this is authorized by the Catholic Church, is the same as yours?

A. Karen had stated to the family that if they ever had to—

Q. Excuse me. Did she state it to you?

A. Not to me personally. I'm sorry. I said to the family. I never actually heard her say that. But I know she said it to my wife, because my wife told me, and I believe her. . . .

Q. Did Karen ever tell you those were her religious beliefs?

A. No, not to my knowledge. No, sir.

Q. When were you first aware, if at all, of your ability to enforce Karen's right of self-determination? If you don't understand what that is—

A. As her parent, I felt I had that right. She was incompetent. She was dying, I felt, and she wasn't able to act for herself. And I simply wanted, since I felt so strongly that this was the Lord's will, to give her back to the Lord. That was my only reason for this whole thing.

Q. But for the Catholic Church's authorization of what you feel would be removal of extraordinary means, would you ask the doctors to do this?

A. If I felt it was morally wrong, I couldn't. I'd have to leave her on the machine no matter how many years it took. I couldn't do anything that I felt was morally wrong.

Q. When did you first conclude that it was not morally wrong to authorize the doctors to do this?

A. After I had made up my decision, and I talked it over with Father Tom and

Father Pat. Then I realized that my decision was right in line with the Church's teachings and with moral law.

Q. Let me ask you this. At the time that you made the decision yourself, before you spoke to the priests, had you determined that it was not morally wrong to authorize this?

A. No, I just felt it was right. I felt it was the right thing to do. That was my own feelings.

Q. Was that regardless of what the Catholic Church position was?

A. You mean, would I have done it if the Catholic Church's position was against it?

Q. Yes.

A. I don't think so. I doubt that very much. That's my whole life.

Q. The Catholic Church?

A. Yes, sir . . .

Q. Is it safe to summarize your testimony that you have concluded that her death is a certainty, that there is no hope for recovery?

A. Yes, sir. That's it.

Q. And, of course, that is the Lord's will?

A. Yes, sir.

Q. And that, unless somebody convinces you otherwise, that will be your position?

A. Yes, sir.

Q. And, in order to effectuate that belief on your part, you feel that the life should be terminated at this point?

A. Not terminated—I don't like that word, too. There are certain words that irritate me. I want to put her back into a natural state, if she lives a day, if she lives a year or five years. This is the Lord's will. That is the way he works with the law of nature. He's the only one who can upset the law of nature. If He wants her to live in a natural state, He'll create a miracle and she'll live. If He wants her to die, she will be off all the artificial means, and she'll die whenever he calls her. This is what I want. It's very simple. I have nothing to gain in this. . . .

Q. Now, are you paying any of the bills in this case, the medical bills?

A. I'm not personally. Medicaid is going to pay it.

Q. Your intentions, if appointed guardian in this case, are, as you expressed them in the original petition, is that correct, to authorize the doctors to discontinue the use of the respirator?

A. Yes, sir. . . .

Q. Give antibiotics in the event infection sets in.

A. They've been doing this all along. She was given antibiotics all along. This is one of the hazards with the machine.

Cross-Examination

Q. At some point, Mr. Quinlan, you had a conversation with Dr. Morse and Dr. Javed, and they indicated they could not honor your request. Isn't that so?

A. That's what it amounted to, after we had signed the paper.

Q. Now, you mentioned a paper. What paper is this, do you know? What paper are you talking about?

A. It was like a formal permission slip or release from all responsibility to the hospital and doctors both, and requesting them formally in writing to turn the machine off.

Q. After you had signed this release, I gather you talked to them and you set forth the reasons why you wanted this. Am I right?

A. Yes.

Q. And they told you they couldn't do it. Am I right?

A. No. They were going to do it, to my knowledge. This was, I think it was on a Friday. It was going to take place on a Saturday, in a short period, anyway. I don't know. I'm terrible with time.

Q. That's okay.

A. I think it was on a Wednesday night, the meeting, and we felt it would take place on a weekend, Saturday.

Q. And, of course, it did not?

A. No, sir.

Q. Did you have any conversations with the two doctors as to why it was that this didn't happen?

A. Yes, sir.

Q. And they told you at that time that they didn't feel they could do it. Am I right?

A. Yes, sir. . . .

Cross-Examination

Q. Mr. Quinlan, when you went to that meeting, there were a number of hospital officials there, were there not?

A. Yes, sir.

Q. And there was Dr. Morse. Is that right?

A. Yes, sir.

Q. And there was Dr. Javed?

A. Yes.

Q. And there was Mrs. Quinlan?

A. Yes.

Q. Anybody else that you remember?

A. Mr. Khoury, Mrs. Rovinski, the assistant director.

Q. The assistant director of the hospital?

A. Yes. And Father Pat.

Q. And at that meeting, sir, did not the doctors take the position that they could not remove the respirator or other means, because it was contrary to medical tradition?

A. Yes, we knew that then.

Q. You knew that then. And at that time, was it not so that the point was raised that you would have to go to court or get an order?

A. That's right, sir.

Q. And at that meeting, Mr. Quinlan, was it not also stated by the doctors that, even if there was a court order, they would not remove the respirator or the other, what you call artificial means?

A. I don't remember that, sir, at all. . . .

Q. Now, Mr. Quinlan, there also came a time when you were talking to Dr. Morse, and I think you were pressing him about going ahead and doing this, and you mentioned to him that it was in conformity with your religious beliefs. Do you remember that?

A. I believe I did.

Q. And do you—

A. In that I had satisfied my own conscience.

Q. You had satisfied your own conscience?

A. Right.

Q. That is, you told that to Dr. Morse, did you not?

A. Yes, sir.

Q. And when you told him that, you were aware, were you not, that Dr. Morse is a devout member of the Roman Catholic Church, right?

A. Yes, sir; he told me that.

Q. Right. And at that time, did not Dr. Morse say to you, "Joe, look, there are no precedents for this. It would be against medical tradition?"

A. No, sir.

Q. Didn't he say that?

A. No, sir.

Q. Before this meeting with the hospital, you knew that he had called someone in New York, did you not? Didn't he mention that to you?

A. He asked for four days to—he wanted to have this Dr. Bender, Senior, to come in to examine Karen. The way he put it to me, he's sure of his diagnosis. He knows just what Dr. Bender is going to say. But to satisfy his own conscience, he wanted to hear him say it. This is why he asked for the additional time. He never said anything about any legal problem.

Q. Are you aware, or are you not aware, that in the hospital records Dr. Morse wrote the words, with reference to this subject that we are talking about now: "Subject to feasibility"; are you aware of that?

A. No, sir. What was subject to feasibility?

Q. All I want to know is if you're just aware of it or not?

A. No, sir. No, sir.

Q. Now, Mr. Quinlan, Dr. Javed was the man who was in charge of the respirator, was he not?

A. Yes.

Q. In your mind, all during these months he was not the attending physician, the chief physician, was he?

A. No. From what I understand, Dr. Morse, as the neurologist, was the doctor in charge.

Q. And you knew, did you not, at that time during those months, and even right down to today, that Dr. Morse is the man who makes the decisions, from the medical standpoint. Isn't that true?

A. Yes, sir.

Q. So I want you to think back a minute, please, and think about Dr. Javed and what you had mentioned before. Isn't it a fact, Mr. Quinlan, that Dr. Javed never said to you, "I'll turn off the machine," did he? I mean permanently.

A. When it came near the end, and not the last meeting or the meeting before, but possibly the third meeting near the end, Dr. Javed had advised us to turn the machine off.

Q. Well, now, Mr. Quinlan—

A. I hate this. I hate to give this bad reflection on these two men. I told you before I love them both. I really feel in my heart that they've done everything possible for my daughter, and I hate putting them on the spot, if I am. I'm just being honest and I hope they understand.

Q. Your recollections could be mistaken, could they not?

A. They could very well be.

Q. Now, Mr. Quinlan, just let me remind you of a statement that you made on direct examination. You said that there was a period of time when there was an effort made to get Karen off the respirator. Do you remember that?

A. Yes, sir, right.

Q. And you also said that Dr. Javed told you that that was rather risky. Do you remember that?

A. Before he did it?

No. He said he would try it, but he would watch it closely, and it would have to be with supervision, and things to that effect, but he was willing to do it. And that was enough, for me, to convince me that it wouldn't be risky, you know, under the circumstances that he had mentioned. Afterwards, he had mentioned that it would be risky to try it again, you know, after the first day. The second day he said it would be so risky that he just wouldn't do it again.

Q. Is it correct that they used the term, "trying to wean her off the machine"?

A. They had a machine at first. Well, they took her off the big machine, and they put her on this other machine that was intended to wean a person off, in that, when it didn't have that thing like an accordian that goes up and down and pumps the air. If she should breath, the machine would just stop, and it would just wait for her to breathe again for, I guess, so many seconds. And if she didn't then the machine would have to breathe for her. But it allowed her every benefit to breathe for herself.

Dr. Javed felt that this machine would be risky to put her on again, because it didn't have the alarms and all these other things that the big machine had.

Q. And Mr. Quinlan, he assured you that he would watch it closely, is that right?

A. Yes, sir.

Q. One more thing, Mr. Quinlan, before closing. Didn't Dr. Javed report to you that Karen couldn't come off the respirator? Didn't he report back to you?

A. Before the last meeting?

Q. Yes, before the last meeting.

A. That she couldn't come off?

Q. She couldn't come off the respirator. Didn't he report that to you?

A. No, he said that she would probable die.

Q. And that was a part of the decision, was it not, the ultimate decision, Mr. Quinlan, made by you that, after much prayer, that you wanted this to happen, and then that ultimately brought you to Father Trappaso, isn't that right?

A. I didn't want what I just said. I didn't want her to die. I just wanted to put her back in a natural state and leave it up to the Lord to decide.

Q. And there is one more thing that I want to clarify, and I think I'm trying to clarify it for your benefit. I notice some hesitancy on your part during the examination and during the cross-examination to use the words, "terminate life," or to use the word, "death." That's true, isn't it?

A. Not "death," no. "Terminate" is a word that I don't particularly like.

Q. So that it is consistent with your belief, Mr. Quinlan, and consistent with the belief in the Roman Catholic Church, that you really don't die; isn't that true, that what we in this world call death is really not death; isn't that so?

A. That it's just death to this world as we know it. There's a better world.

Q. Moving into another world; it's just a phase that we're in now?

A. Right.

Q. And then let's say, to use a kind word, it comes to an end, and we move into another world; isn't that right?

A. We go back to our permanent home.

Q. And what you, Mr. Quinlan, wanted for Karen was to get her back into a natural state; isn't that right?

A. Yes, sir.

Q. So that then, if it was the Lord's wish, she would then go into a better and more everlasting life; isn't that true?

A. Yes, sir. If it was the Lord's will.

Quinlan Decision

A death resulting from termination of treatment would not come within the scope of the homicide statutes proscribing only the unlawful killing of another. There is a real and in this case determinative distinction between the unlawful taking of the life of another and the ending of artificial life-support systems as a matter of self-determination.

Furthermore, the exercise of a constitutional right such as we have here found is protected from criminal prosecution. We do not question the State's undoubted power to punish the taking of human life, but that power does not encompass individuals terminating medical treatment pursuant to their right of privacy. The constitutional protection extends to third parties whose action is necessary to effectuate the exercise of that right where the individuals themselves would not be subject to prosecution or third parties are charged as accessories to an act which could not be a crime. And, under the circumstances of this case, these same principles would apply to and negate a valid prosecution for attempted suicide were there still such a crime in this State.

We thus arrive at the formulation of the declaratory relief which we have concluded is appropriate to this case. Some time has passed since Karen's physical and mental condition was described to the Court. At that time her continuing deterioration was plainly projected. Since the record has not been expanded we assume that she is now even more fragile and nearer to death than she was then. Since her present treating physicians may give reconsideration to her present posture in the light of this opinion, and since we are transferring to the plaintiff as guardian the choice of the attending physician and therefore other physicians may be in charge of the case who may take a different view from that of the present attending physicians, we herewith declare the following affirmative relief on behalf of the plaintiff. Upon the concurrence of the guardian and family of Karen, should the responsible attending physicians conclude that there is no reasonable possibility of Karen's ever emerging from her present comatose condition to a cognitive, sapient state and that the life-support apparatus now being administered to Karen should be discontinued, they shall consult with the hospital "Ethics Committee" or like body of the institution in which Karen is then hospitalized. If that consultative body agrees that there is no reasonable possibility of Karen's ever emerging from her present comatose condition to a cognitive, sapient state, the present life-support system may be withdrawn and said action shall be without any civil or criminal liability therefor on the part of any participant, whether guardian, physician, hospital or others. We herewith specifically so hold.

14
Race and Gender
The Clarence Thomas Confirmation Hearings
1991

Clarence Thomas and Anita Hill—whose testimony clashed before the Senate Judiciary Committee considering Thomas's proposed appointment to the U.S. Supreme Court—were both American success stories illustrating what the civil rights movement had accomplished. Each was born in rural poverty. Both attended integrated colleges, then Yale Law School, then quickly moved into positions in government directly concerned with civil rights. From there, Thomas had gone on to the federal bench and Hill to a professorship at a law school. In 1991 Thomas was about to be named an associate justice of the Supreme Court by Republican President George Bush, and Hill's career as a law professor appeared to be moving smoothly forward. Then came Hill's testimony against Thomas before the United States Senate, which had to confirm the nomination by a majority vote.

Unlike the precision of courtroom procedure, at a congressional hearing virtually anything goes. There are no set rules of evidence or settled forms of questioning witnesses. Questioners are free to ask about the most personal issues or about what was written in the newspaper the day before. Major questions can be pursued or they can be dropped. Charges and countercharges can be made and left unresolved. At the confirmation hearing, allegations that would never have been heard in a courtroom appeared on national television. Hill was questioned in uncomfortable detail while Thomas received far milder treatment. The two offered flatly contradictory sworn accounts of the relationship between them which were left unresolved at the hearings and since. "There were not the minimal protections that common criminals get," complained Senator John Danforth, one of Thomas's strongest supporters.

The hearings did not prevent Thomas's elevation to the Supreme Court—the vote was 52 to 48 in his favor—but they had substantial political consequences. Sexual harassment became a national issue. "Every time a man and a woman are at the water cooler," wrote an anthropologist, "Anita Hill's right there between them." What Senator Alan Simpson of Wyoming called on the Senate floor "this sexual harassment crap" was soon being called "the Anita Hill effect" on

---

SUGGESTIONS FOR FURTHER READING: Anita Hill, *Speaking Truth to Power* (New York: Doubleday, 1997) and David Brook, *The Real Anita Hill* (New York: Maxwell Macmillan International, 1993).

the 1992 elections. Forty-six women were elected to the House of Representatives and three to the Senate. Sexual harassment complaints before the Equal Employment Opportunity Commission increased over fifty percent in a year. Even the Senate, which "just didn't get it" according to a popular phrase describing the confirmation hearings, got it at last as sexual harassment charges helped end the careers of several senators.

Committee on the Judiciary

JOSEPH R. BIDEN, JR., Delaware, *Chairman*

EDWARD M. KENNEDY, Massachusetts	STROM THURMOND, South Carolina
HOWARD M. METZENBAUM, Ohio	ORRIN G. HATCH, Utah
DENNIS DECONCINI, Arizona	ALAN K. SIMPSON, Wyoming
PATRICK J. LEAHY, Vermont	CHARLES E. GRASSLEY, Iowa
HOWELL HEFLIN, Alabama	ARLEN SPECTER, Pennsylvania
PAUL SIMON, Illinois	HANK BROWN, Colorado
HERBERT KOHL, Wisconsin	

Dates of hearings:
Friday, October 11, 1991
Saturday, October 12, 1991
Sunday, October 13, 1991

Witnesses

Hill, Anita F., professor of law, University of Oklahoma, Norman, OK

Thomas, Judge Clarence, of Georgia, to be Associate Justice of the U.S. Supreme Court

Testimony of Anita F. Hill, Professor of Law, University of Oklahoma, Norman, Oklahoma

THE CHAIRMAN: Professor Hill, please make whatever statement you would wish to make to the committee.

MS. HILL: Mr. Chairman, Senator Thurmond, members of the committee, my name is Anita F. Hill, and I am a Professor of Law at the University of Oklahoma.

I was born on a farm in Okmulgee County, Oklahoma, in 1956. I am the youngest of thirteen children. I had my early education in Okmulgee County. My father, Albert Hill, is a farmer in that area. My mother's name is Erma Hill. She is also a farmer and a housewife.

My childhood was one of a lot of hard work and not much money, but it was one of solid family affection as represented by my parents. I was reared in a religious atmosphere in the Baptist faith, and I have been a member of the Antioch Baptist Church in Tulsa, Oklahoma, since 1983. It is a very warm part of my life at the present time.

For my undergraduate work, I went to Oklahoma State University, and graduated from there in 1977. . . .

I graduated from the university with academic honors and proceeded to the Yale Law School, where I received my J.D. degree in 1980.

Upon graduation from law school, I became a practicing lawyer with the Washington, DC firm of Wald, Harkrader & Ross. In 1981, I was introduced to now-Judge Thomas by a mutual friend. Judge Thomas told me that he was anticipating a political appointment and asked if I would be interested in working with him. He was, in fact, appointed as Assistant Secretary of Education for Civil Rights. After he had taken that post, he asked if I would become his assistant, and I accepted that position.

In my early period there, I had two major projects. First was an article I wrote for Judge Thomas's signature on the education of minority students. The second was the organization of a seminar on high-risk students, which was abandoned, because Judge Thomas transferred to the EEOC [Equal Employment Opportunity Commission], where he became the chairman of that office.

During this period at the Department of Education, my working relationship with Judge Thomas was positive. I had a good deal of responsibility and independence. I thought he respected my work and that he trusted my judgment.

After approximately three months of working there, he asked me to go out socially with him. What happened next and telling the world about it are the two most difficult things, experiences of my life. It is only after a great deal of agonizing consideration and a number of sleepless nights that I am able to talk of these unpleasant matters to anyone but my close friends.

I declined the invitation to go out socially with him, and explained to him that I thought it would jeopardize what at the time I considered to be a very good working relationship. I had a normal social life with other men outside of the office. I believed then, as now, that having a social relationship with a person who was supervising my work would be ill advised. I was very uncomfortable with the idea and told him so.

I thought that by saying "no" and explaining my reasons, my employer would abandon his social suggestions. However, to my regret, in the following few weeks he continued to ask me out on several occasions. He pressed me to justify my reasons for saying "no" to him. These incidents took place in his office or mine. They were in the form of private conversations which would not have been overheard by anyone else.

My working relationship became even more strained when Judge Thomas began to use work situations to discuss sex. On these occasions, he would call me into his office for reports on education issues and projects or he might suggest that because of the time pressures of his schedule, we go to lunch to a Government cafeteria. After a brief discussion of work, he would turn the conversation to a discussion of sexual matters. His conversations were very vivid.

He spoke about acts that he had seen in pornographic films involving such matters as women having sex with animals, and films showing group sex or rape scenes. He talked about pornographic materials depicting individuals with large penises, or large breasts involved in various sex acts.

On several occasions Thomas told me graphically of his own sexual prowess. Because I was extremely uncomfortable talking about sex with him at all, and particularly in such a graphic way, I told him that I did not want to talk about these subjects. I would also try to change the subject to education matters or to nonsexual personal matters, such as his background or his beliefs. My efforts to change the subject were rarely successful.

Throughout the period of these conversations, he also from time to time asked me for social engagements. My reactions to these conversations was to avoid them by limiting opportunities for us to engage in extended conversations. This was difficult because at the time, I was his only assistant at the Office of Education or Office for Civil Rights.

During the latter part of my time at the Department of Education, the social pressures and any conversation of his offensive behavior ended. I began both to believe and hope that our working relationship could be a proper, cordial, and professional one.

When Judge Thomas was made Chair of the EEOC, I needed to face the question of whether to go with him. I was asked to do so and I did. The work itself was interesting, and at that time, it appeared that the sexual overtures, which had so troubled me, had ended.

I also faced the realistic fact that I had no alternative job. While I might have gone back to private practice, perhaps in my old firm, or at another, I was dedicated to civil rights work and my first choice was to be in that field. Moreover, at that time the Department of Education, itself, was a dubious venture. President Reagan was seeking to abolish the entire department.

For my first months at the EEOC, where I continued to be an assistant to Judge Thomas, there were no sexual conversations or overtures. However, during the fall and winter of 1982, these began again. The comments were random, and ranged from pressing me about why I didn't go out with him, to remarks about my personal appearance. I remember him saying that some day I would have to tell him the real reason that I wouldn't go out with him.

He began to show displeasure in his tone and voice and his demeanor in his continued pressure for an explanation. He commented on what I was wearing in terms of whether it made me more or less sexually attractive. The incidents occurred in his inner office at the EEOC.

One of the oddest episodes I remember was an occasion in which Thomas was drinking a Coke in his office. He got up from the table, at which we were working, went over to his desk to get the Coke, looked at the can and asked, "Who has put pubic hair on my Coke?"

On other occasions he referred to the size of his own penis as being larger than normal and he also spoke on some occasions of the pleasures he had given to women with oral sex. At this point, late 1982, I began to feel severe stress on the job. I began to be concerned that Clarence Thomas might take out his anger with me by degrading me or not giving me important assignments. I also thought that he might find an excuse for dismissing me. . . .

On, as I recall, the last day of my employment at the EEOC in the summer of 1983, I did have dinner with Clarence Thomas. We went directly from work to a restaurant near the office. We talked about the work that I had done both at Education and at the EEOC. He told me that he was pleased with all of it except for an article and speech that I had done for him while we were at the Office for Civil Rights. Finally he made a comment that I will vividly remember. He said, that if I ever told anyone of his behavior that it would ruin his career. This was not an apology, nor was it an explanation. That was his last remark about the possibility of our going out, or reference to his behavior.

In July 1983, I left the Washington, DC area and have had minimal contacts with Judge Clarence Thomas since. I am, of course, aware from the press that some questions have been raised about conversations I had with Judge Clarence Thomas after I left the EEOC.

From 1983 until today I have seen Judge Thomas only twice. On one occasion I needed to get a reference from him and on another, he made a public appearance at Tulsa. On one occasion he called me at home and we had an inconsequential conversation. On one occasion he called me without reaching me and I returned the call without reaching him and nothing came of it. I have, at least on three occasions, been asked to act as a conduit to him for others. . . .

It is only after a great deal of agonizing consideration that I am able to talk of these unpleasant matters to anyone, except my closest friends as I have said before. These last few days have been very trying and very hard for me, and it hasn't just been the last few days this week. It has actually been over a month now that I have been under the strain of this issue. Telling the world is the most difficult experience of my life, but it is very close to hav[ing] to live through the experience that occasioned this meeting. I may have used poor judgment early on in my relationship with this issue. I was aware, however, that telling at any point in my career could adversely affect my future career. And I did not want, early on, to burn all the bridges to the EEOC.

As I said, I may have used poor judgment. Perhaps I should have taken angry or even militant steps, both when I was in the agency or after I had left it, but I must confess to the world that the course that I took seemed the better, as well as the easier approach.

I declined any comment to newspapers, but later when Senate staff asked me about these matters, I felt that I had a duty to report. I have no personal vendetta against Clarence Thomas. I seek only to provide the committee with information which it may regard as relevant.

It would have been more comfortable to remain silent. I took no initiative to inform anyone. But when I was asked by a representative of this committee to report my experience, I felt that I had to tell the truth. I could not keep silent.

THE CHAIRMAN: Thank you, very much. . . .

THE CHAIRMAN: Now, I must ask you to describe once again, and more fully, the behavior that you have alleged he engaged in while your boss, which you say went beyond professional conventions, and which was unwelcome to you. Now, I know these are difficult to discuss, but you must understand that we have to ask you about them. . .

Ms. HILL: Well, when the incidents occurred in the cafeteria, we were not alone. There were other people in the cafeteria, but because of the way the tables were, there were few individuals who were within the immediate area of the conversation.

THE CHAIRMAN: Of those incidents that occurred in places other than in the cafeteria, which ones occurred in his office?

Ms. HILL: Well, I recall specifically that the incident about the Coke can occurred in his office at the EEOC.

THE CHAIRMAN: And what was that incident again?

Ms. HILL: The incident with regard to the Coke can, that statement?

THE CHAIRMAN: Once again for me, please?

Ms. HILL: The incident involved his going to his desk, getting up from a work-table, going to his desk, looking at this can and saying, "Who put pubic hair on my Coke?"

THE CHAIRMAN: Was anyone else in his office at the time?

Ms. HILL: No.

THE CHAIRMAN: Was the door closed?

Ms. HILL: I don't recall.

THE CHAIRMAN: Are there any other incidents that occurred in his office?

Ms. HILL: I recall at least one instance in his office at the EEOC where he discussed some pornographic material and he brought up the substance or the content of pornographic material.

THE CHAIRMAN: Again, it is difficult, but for the record, what substance did he bring up in this instance at EEOC in his office? What was the content of what he said?

Ms. HILL: This was a reference to an individual who had a very large penis and he used the name that he had referred to in the pornographic material—

THE CHAIRMAN: Do you recall what it was?

Ms. HILL: Yes; I do. The name that was referred to was Long John Silver [Long Dong Silver]. . . .

THE CHAIRMAN: With regard to the other incidents—and my time is running down, and I will come back to them—but with regard to the other incidents that you mentioned in your opening statement, can you tell us how you felt at the time? Were you uncomfortable, were you embarrassed, did it not concern you? How did you feel about it?

Ms. HILL: The pressure to go out with him I felt embarrassed about because I had given him an explanation, that I thought it was not good for me, as an employee, working directly for him, to go out. I thought he did not take seriously my decision to say no, and that he did not respect my having said no to him.

I—the conversations about sex, I was much more embarrassed and humiliated by. The two combined really made me feel sort of helpless in a job situation because I really wanted to do the work that I was doing; I enjoyed that work. But I felt that that was being put in jeopardy by the other things that were going on in the office. And so, I was really, really very troubled by it and distressed over it.

THE CHAIRMAN: Can you tell the committee what was the most embarrassing of all the incidents that you have alleged?

MS. HILL: I think the one that was the most embarrassing was this discussion of pornography involving women with large breasts and engaged in a variety of sex with different people, or animals. That was the thing that embarrassed me the most and made me feel the most humiliated.

THE CHAIRMAN: If you can, in his words—not yours—in his words, can you tell us what, on that occasion, he said to you? You have described the essence of the conversation. In order for us to determine—well, can you tell us, in his words, what he said?

MS. HILL: I really cannot quote him verbatim. I can remember something like, you really ought to see these films that I have seen or this material that I have seen. This woman has this kind of breasts or breasts that measure this size, and they got her in there with all kinds of things, she is doing all kinds of different sex acts. And, you know, that kind of, those were the kinds of words. Where he expressed his enjoyment of it, and seemed to try to encourage me to enjoy that kind of material, as well.

THE CHAIRMAN: Did he indicate why he thought you should see this material?

MS. HILL: No.

THE CHAIRMAN: Why do you think, what was your reaction, why do you think he was saying these things to you?

MS. HILL: Well, coupled with the pressures about going out with him, I felt that implicit in this discussion about sex was the offer to have sex with him, not just to go out with him. There was never any explicit thing about going out to dinner or going to a particular concert or movie, it was, "we ought to go out" and given his other conversations I took that to mean, we ought to have sex or we ought to look at these pornographic movies together.

THE CHAIRMAN: Professor, at your press conference, one of your press conferences, you said that the issue that you raised about Judge Thomas was "an ugly issue." Is that how you viewed these conversations?

MS. HILL: Yes. They were very ugly. They were very dirty. They were disgusting.

THE CHAIRMAN: Were any one of these conversations—this will be my last question, my time is up—were any one of these conversations, other than being asked repeatedly to go out, were any one of them repeated more than once? The same conversation, the reference to—

MS. HILL: The reference to his own physical attributes was repeated more than once, yes.

THE CHAIRMAN: Now, again, for the record, did he just say I have great physical attributes or was he more graphic?

Ms. HILL: He was much more graphic.

THE CHAIRMAN: Can you tell us what he said?

Ms. HILL: Well, I can tell you that he compared his penis size, he measured his penis in terms of length, those kinds of comments.

THE CHAIRMAN: Thank you. . . .

SEN. SPECTER: We have a statement from former dean of Oral Roberts Law School who quotes you as making laudatory comments about Judge Thomas, that he "is a fine man and an excellent legal scholar." In the course of three years when Dean Tuttle knew you at the law school, that you had always praised him and had never made any derogatory comments. Is Dean Tuttle correct?

Ms. HILL: During the time that I was at Oral Roberts University I realized that Charles Kothe, who was a founding dean of that school, had very high regard for Clarence Thomas I did not risk talking in disparaging ways about Clarence Thomas at that time.

I don't recall any specific conversations about Clarence Thomas in which I said anything about his legal scholarship. I did not really know of his legal scholarship, certainly at that time.

SEN. SPECTER: Well, I can understand it if you did not say anything, but Dean Tuttle makes the specific statement. His words are, that you said, "the most laudatory comments."

Ms. HILL: I have no response to that because I do not know exactly what he is saying.

SEN. SPECTER: There is a question about Phyllis Berry who was quoted in the *New York Times* on October 7, "In an interview Ms. Barry [*sic*] suggested that the allegations," referring to your allegations, "were the result of Ms. Hill's disappointment and frustration that Mr. Thomas did not show any sexual interest in her."

You were asked about Ms. Berry at the interview on October 9 and were reported to have said, "Well, I don't know Phyllis Berry and she doesn't know me." And there are quite a few people who have come forward to say that they saw you and Ms. Berry together and that you knew each other very well.

Ms. HILL: I would disagree with that. Ms. Berry worked at the EEOC. She did attend some staff meetings at the EEOC. We were not close friends. We did not socialize together and she has no basis for making a comment about my social interests, with regard to Clarence Thomas or anyone else.

I might add, that at the time that I had an active social life and that I was involved with other people.

SEN. SPECTER: Did Ms. Anna Jenkins and Ms. J.C. Alvarez, who both have provided statements attesting to the relationship between you and Ms. Berry, a friendly one. Where Ms. Berry would have known you [*sic*], were both Ms. Jenkins and Ms. Alvarez co-workers in a position to observe your relationship with Ms. Berry?

Ms. HILL: They were both workers at the EEOC. I can only say that they were commenting on our relationship in the office. It was cordial and friendly. We were not unfriendly with each other, but we were not social acquaintances. We were professional acquaintances.

SEN. SPECTER: So that when you said, Ms. Berry doesn't know me and I don't know her, you weren't referring to just that, but some intensity of knowledge?

MS. HILL: Well, this is a specific remark about my sexual interest. And I think one has to know another person very well to make those kinds of remarks unless they are very openly expressed.

SEN. SPECTER: Well, did Ms. Berry observe you and Judge Thomas together in the EEOC office?

MS. HILL: Yes, at staff meetings where she attended and at the office, yes.

SEN. SPECTER: Let me pick up on Senator Biden's line of questioning. You referred to the "oddest episode I remember," then talked about the Coke incident. When you made your statement to the FBI, why was it that that was omitted if it were so strong in your mind and such an odd incident.

MS. HILL: I spoke to the FBI agents and I told them the nature of comments, and did not tell them more specifics. I referred to the specific comments that were in my statement.

SEN. SPECTER: Well, when you talked to the FBI agents, you did make specific allegations about specific sexual statements made by Judge Thomas.

MS. HILL: Yes.

SEN. SPECTER: So that your statement to the FBI did have specifics.

MS. HILL: Yes.

SEN. SPECTER: And my question to you, why, if this was such an odd episode, was it not included when you talked to the FBI?

MS. HILL: I do not know. . . .

SEN. SPECTER: You testified this morning, in response to Senator Biden, that the most embarrassing question involved–this is not too bad–women's large breasts. That is a word we use all the time. That was the most embarrassing aspect of what Judge Thomas had said to you?

MS. HILL: No. The most embarrassing aspect was his description of the acts of these individuals, these women, the acts that those particular people would engage in. It wasn't just the breasts; it was the continuation of his story about what happened in those films with the people with this characteristic, physical characteristic.

SEN. SPECTER: With the physical characteristic of–

MS. HILL: The large breasts.

SEN. SPECTER: Well, in your statement to the FBI you did refer to the films but there is no reference to the physical characteristic you describe. I don't want to attach too much weight to it, but I had thought you said that the aspect of large breasts was the aspect that concerned you, and that was missing from the statement to the FBI.

MS. HILL: I have been misunderstood. It wasn't the physical characteristic of having large breasts. It was the description of the acts that this person with this characteristic would do, the acts that they would engage in, group acts with animals, things of that nature involving women.

SEN. SPECTER: Professor Hill, you testified that you drew an inference that Judge Thomas might want you to look at pornographic films, but you told the FBI specifically that he never asked you to watch the films. Is that correct?

Ms. HILL: He never said, "Let's go to my apartment and watch films," or "go to my house and watch films." He did say, "You ought to see this material."

SEN. SPECTER: But when you testified that, as I wrote it down, "We ought to look at pornographic movies together," that was an expression of what was in your mind when he—

Ms. HILL: That was the inference that I drew, yes.

SEN. SPECTER: The inference, so he—

Ms. HILL: With his pressing me for social engagement, yes.

SEN. SPECTER: That that was something he might have wanted you to do, but the fact is, flatly, he never asked you to look at pornographic movies with him.

Ms. HILL: With him? No, he did not.

THE CHAIRMAN: Will the Senator yield for one moment for a point of clarification?

SEN. SPECTER: I would rather not.

THE CHAIRMAN: To determine whether or not the witness ever saw the FBI report. Does she know what was stated by the FBI about her comments?

SEN. SPECTER: Well, Mr. Chairman, I am asking her about what she said to the FBI.

THE CHAIRMAN: I understand. I am just asking that. Have you ever seen the FBI report?

Ms. HILL: No; I have not.

THE CHAIRMAN: Would you like to take a few moments and look at it now?

Ms. HILL: Yes; I would.

THE CHAIRMAN: Okay. Let's make a copy of the FBI report. I think we have to be careful. Senator Grassley asked me to make sure—maybe you could continue—it only pertains to her. We are not at liberty to give to her what the FBI said about other individuals.

SEN. SPECTER: I was asking Professor Hill about the FBI report.

Obviously because the portion I am questioning you about relates to their recording what you said, and I think it is fair, one lawyer to another, to ask about it.

THE CHAIRMAN: No, I would continue, because you are not asking her directly. I just wanted to know whether or not her responses were at all based upon her knowledge of what the FBI said she said. That is all I was asking.

SEN. SPECTER: Well, she has asked to see it, and I think it is a fair request, and I would be glad to take a moment's delay to—

THE CHAIRMAN: This is the FBI report as it references Professor Hill, only Professor Hill. . . .

SEN. SPECTER: Professor Hill, now that you have read the FBI report, you can see that it contains no reference to any mention of Judge Thomas's private parts or sexual prowess or size, et cetera. My question to you would be, on something that is as important as it is in your written testimony and in your responses to Senator Biden, why didn't you tell the FBI about that?

Ms. HILL: Senator, in paragraph two on page 2 of the report it says that he liked to discuss specific sex acts and frequency of sex. And I am not sure what all that summarizes, but his sexual prowess, his sexual preferences could have—

SEN. SPECTER: Which line are you referring to, Professor?

MS. HILL: The very last line in paragraph two of page 2.

SEN. SPECTER: Well, that says—and this is not too bad, I can read it—"Thomas liked to discuss specific sex acts and frequency of sex." Now are you saying, in response to my question as to why you didn't tell the FBI about the size of his private parts and his sexual prowess and "Long John Silver," that information was comprehended within the statement, "Thomas liked to discuss specific sex acts and frequency of sex"?

MS. HILL: I am not saying that that information was included in that. I don't know that it was. I don't believe that I even mentioned the latter information to the FBI agent, and I could only respond again that at the time of the investigation I tried to cooperate as fully as I could, to recall information to answer the questions that they asked.

SEN. SPECTER: Professor Hill, you said that you took it to mean that Judge Thomas wanted to have sex with you, but in fact he never did ask you to have sex, correct?

MS. HILL: No, he did not ask me to have sex. He did continually pressure me to go out with him, continually, and he would not accept my explanation as being valid.

SEN. SPECTER: So that when you said you took it to mean, "We ought to have sex," that that was an inference that you drew?

MS. HILL: Yes, yes. . . .

SEN. SPECTER: The testimony that you described here today depicts a circumstance where the chairman of the EEOC is blatant, as you describe it, and my question is: Understanding the fact that you are twenty-five and that you are shortly out of law school and the pressures that exist in this world—and I know about it to a fair extent. I used to be a district attorney and I know about sexual harassment and discrimination against women and I think I have some sensitivity on it—but even considering all of that, given your own expert standing and the fact that here you have the chief law enforcement officer of the country on this subject and the whole purpose of the civil rights law is being perverted right in the office of the chairman with one of his own female subordinates, what went through your mind, if anything, on whether you ought to come forward at that stage? If you had, you would have stopped this man from being head of the EEOC perhaps for another decade. What went on through your mind? I know you decided not to make a complaint, but did you give that any consideration, and, if so, how could you allow this kind of reprehensible conduct to go on right in the headquarters, without doing something about it?

MS. HILL: Well, it was a very trying and difficult decision for me not to say anything further. I can only say that when I made the decision to just withdraw from the situation and not press a claim or charge against him, that I may have shirked a duty, a responsibility that I had, and to that extent I confess that I am very sorry that I did not do something or say something, but at the time that was my best judgment. Maybe it was a poor judgment, but it wasn't dishonest and it wasn't a completely unreasonable choice that I made, given the circumstances.

SEN. LEAHY: Did they ask you if you would be willing to take a polygraph?

MS. HILL: They asked if I would be willing to take a polygraph.

SEN. LEAHY: And what did you say?

MS. HILL: I answered, "yes.". . .

SEN. SPECTER: In your statement and in your testimony here today, you have said that you were concerned that "Judge Thomas might take it out on me by downgrading me, or by not giving me important assignments. I also thought that he might find an excuse for dismissing me."

As an experienced attorney and as someone who was in the field of handling sexual harassment cases, didn't it cross your mind that if you needed to defend yourself from what you anticipated he might do that your evidentiary position would be much stronger if you had made some notes?

MS. HILL: No, it did not.

SEN. SPECTER: Well, why not?

MS. HILL: I don't know why it didn't cross my mind.

SEN. SPECTER: Well, the law of evidence is that notes are very important. You are nodding yes. Present recollection refreshed, right?

MS. HILL: Yes, indeed.

SEN. SPECTER: Prior recollection recorded, right?

MS. HILL: Yes.

SEN. SPECTER: In a controversy, if Judge Thomas took some action against you, and you had to defend yourself on the ground that he was being malicious in retaliation for your turning him down, wouldn't those notes be very influential if not determinative in enabling you to establish your legal position?

MS. HILL: I think they would be very influential, yes.

SEN. SPECTER: So, given your experience, if all this happened, since all this happened, why not make the notes?

MS. HILL: Well, it might have been a good choice to make the notes. I did not do it though.

SEN. SPECTER: All right. I am prepared to leave it at that. There is some relevancy to that continuing association questioning your credibility, but you have an explanation. I will leave it at that.

I want to ask you about one statement of Charles Kothe, Dean Kothe, because he knew you and Judge Thomas very well. I want to ask you for your comment on it. . . . And this is his concluding statement: "I find the references to the alleged sexual harassment not only unbelievable but preposterous. I am convinced that such are the product of fantasy." Would you care to comment on that?

MS. HILL: Well, I would only say that I am not given to fantasy. This is not something that I would have come forward with, if I were not absolutely sure about what it is I am saying. I weighed this very carefully, I considered it carefully, and I made a determination to come forward. I think it is unfortunate that that comment as made by a man who purports to be someone who says he knows me, and I think it is just inaccurate.

SEN. SPECTER: Well, you have added, during the course of your testimony today, two new witnesses whom you made this complaint to. When you talked to the FBI, there was one witness , and you are testifying today that you are now "recalling more," that you had "repressed a lot." And the question which I have for you is, how reliable is your testimony in October 1991 on events that occurred eight, ten years ago, when you are adding new factors, explaining them by saying you have repressed a lot? And in the context of a sexual harassment charge where the Federal law is very firm on a six-month period of limitation, how sure can you expect this committee to be on the accuracy of your statements?

MS. HILL: Well, I think if you start to look at each individual problem with this statement, then you're not going to be satisfied that it's true, but I think the statement has to be taken as a whole. There's nothing in the statement, nothing in my background, nothing in my statement, there is no motivation that would show that I would make up something like this. I guess one does have to really understand something about the nature of sexual harassment. It is very difficult for people to come forward with these things, these kinds of things. It wasn't as though I rushed forward with this information.

I can only tell you what happened to the best of my recollection, what occurred, and ask you to take that into account. Now, you have to make your own judgments about it from there on, but I do want you to take into account the whole thing. . . .

SEN. HEFLIN: Are you a zealoting civil rights believer that progress will be turned back, if Clarence Thomas goes on the Court?

MS. HILL: No, I don't—I think that—I have my opinion, but I don't think that progress will be turned back. I think that civil rights will prevail, no matter what happens with the Court.

SEN. HEFLIN: Do you have a militant attitude relative to the area of civil rights?

MS. HILL: No, I don't have a militant attitude.

SEN. HEFLIN: Do you have a martyr complex?

MS. HILL: No, I don't. [Laughter.]

SEN. HEFLIN: Well, do you see that, coming out of this, you can be a hero in the civil rights movement?

MS. HILL: I do not have that kind of complex. I don't like all of the attention that I am getting. I don't—even if I liked the attention, I would not lie to get attention.

SEN. HEFLIN: Well, the issue of fantasy has arisen. You have a degree in psychology from the University of Oklahoma State University.

MS. HILL: Yes.

SEN. HEFLIN: Have you studied in your psychology studies, the question of fantasies? Have you ever studied that from a psychology basis?

MS. HILL: To some extent, yes.

SEN. HEFLIN: What are the traits of fantasy that you studied and as you remember?

MS. HILL: As I remember, it would require some other indication of loss of touch with reality other than one instance. There is no indication that I am an individual who is not in touch with reality on a regular basis and would be subject to fantasy.

SEN. HEFLIN: The reality of where you are today is rather dramatic. Did you take, as Senator Biden asked you, all steps that you knew how to take to prevent being in the witness chair today?

MS. HILL: Yes, I did. Everything that I knew to do, I did.

SEN. HEFLIN: There may be other motivations. I just listed some that you usually look to relative to these. Are you interested in writing a book? [*Laughter.*]

MS. HILL: No, I'm not interested in writing a book. . . .

Testimony of Hon. Clarence Thomas
of Georgia, to be Associate Justice
of the U.S. Supreme Court

THE CHAIRMAN Do you have anything you would like to say?

JUDGE THOMAS: Senator, I would like to start by saying unequivocally, uncategorically that I deny each and every single allegation against me today that suggested in any way that I had conversations of a sexual nature or about pornographic material with Anita Hill, that I ever attempted to date her, that I ever had any personal sexual interest in her, or that I in any way ever harassed her.

Second, and I think a more important point, I think that this today is a travesty. I think that it is disgusting. I think that this hearing should never occur in America. This is a case in which this sleaze, this dirt, was searched for by staffers of members of this committee, was then leaked to the media, and this committee and this body validated it and displayed it in prime time over our entire nation.

How would any member on this committee or any person in this room or any person in this country would like sleaze said about him or her in this fashion or this dirt dredged up and this gossip and these lies displayed in this manner? How would any person like it?

The Supreme Court is not worth it. No job is worth it. I am not here for that. I am here for my name, my family, my life and my integrity. I think something is dreadfully wrong with this country, when any person, any person in this free country would be subjected to this. This is not a closed room.

There was an FBI investigation. This is not an opportunity to talk about difficult matters privately or in a closed environment. This is a circus. It is a national disgrace. And from my standpoint, as a black American, as far as I am concerned, it is a high-tech lynching for uppity blacks who in any way deign to think for themselves, to do for themselves, to have different ideas, and it is a message that, unless you kow-tow to an old order, this is what will happen to you, you will be lynched, destroyed, caricatured by a committee of the U.S. Senate, rather than hung from a tree. . . .

SEN. HEFLIN: Judge Thomas, in addition to Anita Hill, there have surfaced some other allegations against you. One was on a television show last evening here in Washington, Channel 7. I don't know whether you saw that or not?

JUDGE THOMAS: No.

SEN. HEFLIN: You didn't see it. It was carried somewhat in the print media today, but it involved a man by the name of Earl Harper, Jr., who allegedly was a senior trial lawyer with the EEOC at Baltimore in or around the early 1980's. Do you recall this instance pertaining to Earl Harper, Jr.?

JUDGE THOMAS: I remember the name. I can't remember the details.

SEN. HEFLIN: The allegations against Mr. Harper involved some twelve or thirteen women who claim that Mr. Harper made unwelcome sexual advances to several women on his staff, including instances in which Mr. Harper masturbated in the presence of some of the female employees. The allegations contain other aspects of sexual activity.

The information we have is that the General Counsel of the EEOC, David Slate, made a lengthy internal investigation and found that this had the effect of creating an intimidating, hostile and offensive working environment, and that on November 23, 1983, you wrote Mr. Slate a memo urging that Mr. Harper be fired. Mr. Slate eventually recommended dismissal. Then the story recites that you did not dismiss him, you allowed him to stay on for eleven months and then he retired.

Does that bring back to you any recollection of that event concerning Mr. Earl Harper, Jr.?

JUDGE THOMAS: Again, I am operating strictly on recollection. If I remember the case, if it is the one I am thinking of, Mr. Harper's supervisor recommended either suspension or some form of sanction or punishment that was less than termination.

When that proposal—the supervisor initially was not David Slate—when that proposal reached my desk, I believe my recommendation was that, for the conduct involved, he should be fired. The problem there was that if the immediate supervisor's decision is changed—and I believe Mr. Harper was a veteran—there are a number of procedural protections that he had, including a hearing and, of course, he had a lawyer and there was potential litigation, et cetera.

I do not remember all of the details, but it is not as simple as you set it out. It was as a result of my insistence that the General Counsel, as I remember, upgraded the sanction to termination.

SEN. HEFLIN: Do you know a Congressman by the name of Scott Kluge, a Republican Congressman who was defeated by Robert Kastenmeier of Wisconsin, who now serves in Congress, who back in the early 1980's, 1983 or something, was a television reporter for a channel here in Washington and that he at that time disclosed this as indicating that, after the recommendation of dismissal, that you did not move in regards to it for some eleven months and let him retire? Do you know Congressman Kluge?

JUDGE THOMAS: I do not know him. Again, remember, I am operating on recollection. There was far more to it than the facts as you set them out. His rights had much to do with the fact that he was a veteran and that we could not simply dismiss him. If we could, that was my recommendation, he would have been dismissed.

SEN. HEFLIN: There was no political influence brought to bear on you at that time to prevent his dismissal? Do you recall if any political—

JUDGE THOMAS: There was absolutely no political influence. In fact, it was my policy that no personnel decisions would in any way be changed or influenced by political pressure, one way or the other.

SEN. HEFLIN: Now, it is reported to me that Congressman Kluge, after your nomination, went to the White House and told this story and, I hear by hearsay, that the White House ignored his statement and that Congressman Kluge further came to the Senate Judiciary Committee and made it known here.

As far as I know, I attempted to check—I have not been able to find where it was in the Judiciary Committee, if it was, and I think the chairman has attempted to locate it—but the point I am asking is, in the whole process pertaining to the nomination and the preparation for it, were you ever notified that Congressman Kluge went to the White House in regards to this?

JUDGE THOMAS: I do not remember that, Senator.

SEN. HEFLIN: Nobody ever discussed that?

JUDGE THOMAS: No.

SEN. HEFLIN: Well, that is the way it has been reported to me and it is very fragmented relative to it, but I have asked that all the records of the EEOC be subpoenaed by *subpoena duces tecum* pertaining to that, in order that we might get to the bottom of it.

SEN. HATCH: Mr. Chairman, if I could interrupt Senator Heflin, I really think this is outside the scope, under the rules. I would have to object to it.

THE CHAIRMAN I would have to sustain that objection. . . .

SEN. HEFLIN: All right, sir, I will reserve an exception, as we used to say. Now, I suppose you have heard Professor Hill, Ms. Hill, Anita F. Hill testify today.

JUDGE THOMAS: No, I haven't.

SEN. HEFLIN: You didn't listen?

JUDGE THOMAS: No, I didn't. I have heard enough lies.

SEN. HEFLIN: You didn't listen to her testimony?

JUDGE THOMAS: No, I didn't.

SEN. HEFLIN: On television?

JUDGE THOMAS: No, I didn't. I've heard enough lies. Today is not a day that, in my opinion, is high among the days in our country. This is a travesty. You spent the entire day destroying what it has taken me forty-three years to build and providing a forum for that.

SEN. HEFLIN: Judge Thomas, you know we have a responsibility too, and as far as I am involved, I had nothing to do with Anita Hill coming here and testifying. We are trying to get to the bottom of this. And, if she is lying, then I think you can help us prove that she was lying.

JUDGE THOMAS: Senator, I am incapable of proving the negative that did not occur.

SEN. HEFLIN: Well, if it did not occur, I think you are in a position, with certainly your ability to testify, in effect, to try to eliminate it from people's minds.

JUDGE THOMAS: Senator, I didn't create it in people's minds. This matter was investigated by the Federal Bureau of Investigation in a confidential way. It was then leaked last weekend to the media. I did not do that. And how many members of this committee would like to have the same scurrilous, uncorroborated allegations made about him and then leaked to national newspapers and then be drawn and dragged before a national forum of this nature to discuss those allegations that should have been resolved in a confidential way?

SEN. HEFLIN: Well, I certainly appreciate your attitude towards leaks. I happen to serve on the Senate Ethics Committee and it has been a sieve.

JUDGE THOMAS: But it didn't leak on me. This leaked on me and it is drowning my life, my career and my integrity, and you can't give it back to me, and this committee can't give it back to me, and this Senate can't give it back to me. You have robbed me of something that can never be restored.

SEN. DECONCINI: I know exactly how you feel.

SEN. HEFLIN: Judge Thomas, one of the aspects of this is that she could be living in a fantasy world. I don't know. We are just trying to get to the bottom of all of these facts.

But if you didn't listen and didn't see her testify, I think you put yourself in an unusual position. You are, in effect, defending yourself, and basically some of us want to be fair to you, fair to her, but if you didn't listen to what she said today, then that puts it somewhat in a more difficult task to find out what the actual facts are relative to this matter.

JUDGE THOMAS: The facts keep changing, Senator. When the FBI visited me, the statements to this committee and the questions were one thing. The FBI's subsequent questions were another thing. And the statements today, as I received summaries of them, are another thing.

I am not—it is not my fault that the facts change. What I have said to you is categorical that any allegations that I engaged in any conduct involving sexual activity, pornographic movies, attempted to date her, any allegations, I deny. It is not true.

So the facts can change but my denial does not. Ms. Hill was treated in a way that all my special assistants were treated, cordial, professional, respectful.

SEN. HEFLIN: Judge, if you are on the bench and you approach a case where you appear to have a closed mind and that you are only right, doesn't it raise issues of judicial temperament?

JUDGE THOMAS: Senator? Senator, there is a difference between approaching a case objectively and watching yourself being lynched. There is no comparison whatsoever.

SEN. HATCH: I might add, he has personal knowledge of this as well, and personal justification for anger.

SEN. HEFLIN: Judge, I don't want to go over this stuff but, of course, there are many instances in which she has stated, but—and, in effect, since you didn't see her testify I think it is somewhat unfair to ask you specifically about it.

I would reserve my time and go ahead and let Senator Hatch ask you, and then come back.

THE CHAIRMAN: Senator Hatch?

SEN. HATCH: Judge Thomas, I have sat here and I have listened all day long, and Anita Hill was very impressive. She is an impressive law professor. She is a Yale Law graduate. And, when she met with the FBI, she said that you told her about your sexual experiences and preferences. And I hate to go into this but I want to go into it because I have to, and I know that it is something that you wish you had never heard at any time or place. But I think it is important that we go into it and let me just do it this way.

She said to the FBI that you told her about your sexual experiences and preferences, that you asked her what she liked or if she had ever done the same thing, that you discussed oral sex between men and women, that you discussed viewing films of people having sex with each other and with animals, and that you told her that she should see such films, and that you would like to discuss specific sex acts and the frequency of sex.

What about that?

JUDGE THOMAS: Senator, I would not want to, except being required to here, to dignify those allegations with a response. As I have said before, I categorically deny them. To me, I have been pilloried with scurrilous allegations of this nature. I have denied them earlier and I deny them tonight.

SEN. HATCH: Judge Thomas, today in a new statement, in addition to what she had told the FBI, which I have to agree with you is quite a bit, she made a number of other allegations and what I would like to do is—some of them most specifically were for the first time today in addition to these, which I think almost anybody would say are terrible. And I would just like to give you an opportunity, because this is your chance to address her testimony.

At any time did you say to Professor Hill that she could ruin your career if she talked about sexual comments you allegedly made to her?

JUDGE THOMAS: No.

SEN. HATCH: Did you say to her in words or substance that you could ruin her career?

JUDGE THOMAS: No.

SEN. HATCH: Should she ever have been afraid of you and any kind of vindictiveness to ruin her career?

JUDGE THOMAS: Senator, I have made it my business to help my special assistants. I recommended Ms. Hill for her position at Oral Roberts University. I have always spoken highly of her.

I had no reason prior to the FBI visiting me a little more than two weeks ago to know that she harbored any ill feelings toward me or any discomfort with me. This is all new to me.

SEN. HATCH: It is new to me too, because I read the FBI report at least ten or fifteen times. I didn't see any of these allegations I am about to go into, including that one. But she seemed to sure have a recollection here today.

Now, did you every say to Professor Hill in words or substance, and this is embarrassing for me to say in public, but it has to be done, and I am sure it is not pleasing to you.

Did you ever say in words or substance something like there is a pubic hair in my Coke?

JUDGE THOMAS: No, Senator.

SEN. HATCH: Did you ever refer to your private parts in conversation with Professor Hill?

JUDGE THOMAS: Absolutely not, Senator.

SEN. HATCH: Did you ever brag to Professor Hill about your sexual prowess?

JUDGE THOMAS: No, Senator.

SEN. HATCH: Did you ever use the term "Long Dong Silver" in conversation with Professor Hill?

JUDGE THOMAS: No, Senator.

SEN. HATCH: Did you ever have lunch with Professor Hill at which you talked about sex or pressured her to go out with you?

JUDGE THOMAS: Absolutely not—

SEN. HATCH: Did you ever tell—

JUDGE THOMAS: [continuing]—I have had no such discussions, nor have I ever pressured or asked her to go out with me beyond her work environment.

SEN. HATCH: Did you ever tell Professor Hill that she should see pornographic films?

JUDGE THOMAS: Absolutely not.

SEN. HATCH: Did you ever talk about pornography with Professor Hill?

JUDGE THOMAS: I did not discuss any pornographic material or pornographic preferences or pornographic films with Professor Hill.

SEN. HATCH: So you never even talked or described pornographic materials with her?

JUDGE THOMAS: Absolutely not.